Anchored in the Word

52 Devotional Reflections Rooted in the King James Bible for Spiritual Renewal

Gary E. Risenhoover

TABLE OF CONTENTS

Preface

In the tumultuous cadence of our modern lives, amid the ceaseless noise and the swift currents of time that rush past in an unyielding torrent, there arises a profound and pressing need: the need to be still, to be rooted, to be anchored in a steadfast truth that transcends the shifting sands of circumstance. It is this yearning, this deep spiritual hunger, that beckons us beyond the fleeting distractions and into the enduring embrace of the Divine Word , a sanctuary where the soul may find calm, where faith may be rekindled, and where hope may rise anew with every dawning day. It is with a heart imbued with this sacred longing and an earnest desire to guide and uplift that I offer to you "Anchored in the Word," a collection of 52 devotional reflections crafted with reverence, poetic grace, and a profound respect for the timeless majesty of the King James Bible.

This volume is not merely a book; it is an invitation to embark on a year-long spiritual odyssey, a pilgrimage through the luminous landscapes of Scripture woven with prayer, meditation, and personal reflection. Each of its pages is meant to serve as a harbor from the storms of life , a place where the soul may cast its anchor deep into the blessed promises of God, where the heart may find rest, and the spirit may be renewed. The reflections are thoughtfully arranged, clustered into sixteen distinct chapters, each a gem of contemplation focusing on themes essential to the believer's journey: faith that stands unwavering amid trials, the renewing balm of grace, the power and necessity of prayer, the ceaseless flow of divine love, and the abiding light of hope that never flickers even in the darkest night.

The language that sings through these devotionals is lovingly planted in the sacred soil of the King James Bible, a treasure of majestic phrasing and profound poetic cadence. I have sought to honor this revered text not merely as a source of scriptural insight but as a wellspring of spiritual poetry, each verse a tapestry of divine truth that weaves together the eternal and the intimate. Through this elevated yet accessible style, I strive to evoke a sense of reverence that is both ancient and immediate, that binds the soul to centuries of faithful seekers while speaking tenderly to the individual heart in its present need. Here, the words of old blaze with renewed fire, illuminating the pathway toward spiritual renewal, strength, and peace.

The very structure of this book reflects the rhythms of spiritual life itself, sometimes slow and profound, other times swift and stirring, varying in intensity and length, mirroring the unpredictable tides of the human experience. Some chapters linger tenderly on a handful of rich scriptural truths, inviting lingering meditation and deep infusions of grace; others spread their wings over a broader landscape, exploring multiple facets of a theme, reflecting the expansive nature of God's kingdom grace. This ebb and flow is intentional, allowing the reader a harmonious balance of depth and breadth, solemnity and encouragement, challenge and comfort. It is my hope that each reader, regardless of their spiritual background or season of life, may find within these pages a companion tailored to the unique cadence of their faith journey.

The central thread that weaves through every reflection is the irresistible call to remain anchored, to stand firm in faith as the storms of doubt and despair buffet the soul; to drink deeply from the well of divine love and grace when the heart feels parched; to lift prayers in trust and thanksgiving; to find solace and renewed strength in the promises that never fail. While grounded deeply in scriptural exposition, these devotionals also draw freely from the wells of personal encounter and practical application, inviting readers not only to know the Word but to live it moment by moment. Each passage concludes with a prayer or a meditation, a gentle hand extended to you, dear reader, to draw you into active engagement with these sacred truths, to carry these divine whispers forward into your daily walk.

As you turn these pages, you may find yourself enveloped in a peaceful sanctuary where spiritual renewal is not a distant ideal but a living reality. There will be moments of quiet reflection that beckon your soul to rest; moments of gentle challenge that stir your faith to rise; moments suffused with gratitude that liberate your heart to praise. This book endeavors to be more than a mere reading experience, it aspires to be a spiritual hearth, a wellspring of encouragement, a light unto your path across the varied seasons of your life.

I invite you now to embrace this sacred journey with an open heart and a soul ready to be anchored. Let the ancient words of the King James Bible enfold you with their eternal beauty, their passionate declarations, and their tender assurances. May you find in them a steadfast foundation upon which to build a life of unwavering faith and serene hope. May the reflections within these pages breathe new vitality into your prayer life, deepen your understanding of God's boundless grace, and fortify your spirit against the trials you face.

Above all, may this book serve as a faithful companion, steering you through the tempests, lighting your way through shadowed valleys, and celebrating with you on mountaintops of joy and peace. For it is in being anchored in the Word that we find the true hope that does not fade, the peace that surpasses all understanding, and the strength to persevere with holy confidence.

Welcome, dear reader, to this sacred voyage. May your soul find rest. May your faith be renewed. And may the everlasting Word be the anchor of your heart forever.

Foundations of Faith

The Rock of Ages

In the endless tempests of life, when the waves of uncertainty crash fiercely upon the fragile shores of our existence, there flickers the radiant assurance of a steadfast Refuge, an unyielding Rock upon which the soul may safely rest. The very thought of a foundation that never wavers summons consolation deep within the heart, a balm that quiets the tumultuous storms of doubt and fear. The King James Bible, with its majestic cadence and timeless truths, speaks to this eternal refuge in words that have echoed through centuries: "The Lord is my rock, and my fortress, and my deliverer; my God, my strength, in whom I will trust; my buckler, and the horn of my salvation, and my high tower" (Psalm 18:2). Such scripture draws us inward to a sacred sanctuary where faith is not a fragile hope but a solid certainty, carved as steadfast as the mountains that defy the erosion of time. Here, in this spiritual citadel, uncertainty dissolves, and the soul finds rest, secured not by fleeting circumstances but by the immutable nature of God himself.

To consider God as the Rock of Ages is to anchor one's faith beyond the whims of the shifting sands that mark the transitory world. The metaphor stretches beyond mere image; it is an invitation to trust in an unmovable foundation that stands firm regardless of life's upheavals. We live amid a generation marked by rapid change, unforeseen trials, and the unsettling rhythm of chaos. Yet amidst this turbulence, the psalmist's declaration is a radiant beacon, a divine anchor calling us away from the fragile refuges of fleeting comfort and into the embrace of the eternal. Our hearts are prone to tremble as the winds of adversity howl and the earth beneath us quakes with relentless uncertainty. But in acknowledging God as our Rock, we adopt a posture of unwavering confidence, a spiritual stance that proclaims neither death nor despair can triumph over the comfort bestowed by our Almighty Guardian.

Meditating deeply upon the weight of this truth invites us to reframe our understanding of stability itself. Like a mighty cliff rising defiantly above storm-tossed seas, God's presence is both shelter and stronghold. When we place our trust in Him, our footing ceases to be at the mercy of the deceptive ground beneath us and instead is secured by divine omnipotence. This is not a faith swayed by the ebbs and flows of emotion nor a hope resting upon transient human effort; it is a profound surrender to the eternal, a yielding to the incorruptible love and faithfulness of the Savior who declares, "I am the true vine, and my Father is the husbandman" (John 15:1). The Rock of Ages is a refuge not only in name but in the very essence of His being, an immovable Pillar of truth holding fast to those weary of their burdens and fearful of the morrow.

Reflecting on this image draws the mind to narratives in Scripture where faith in God's solid foundation yields victories amid trials. The Apostle Paul, imprisoned and afflicted, boldly professed that he was "not ashamed of the gospel: for it is the power of God unto salvation" (Romans 1:16), showing us that even within chains and suffering, the Rock remains immovable. The storms he endured struck neither his hope nor his peace. Similarly, Christ's own teaching in the Sermon on the Mount places undeniable emphasis on the necessity of grounding life upon this Rock. "Whosoever cometh to me, and heareth my sayings, and doeth them, I will liken him unto a wise man, which built his house upon a rock" (Matthew 7:24). This wisdom beckons us to fashion our lives and consciences, our hopes and fears, upon a foundation that transcends the fickle and the temporary. The day will come when the rains fall, and the floods rise, and the winds beat upon the house; yet, when built upon the Rock, the house shall not fall, a lesson woven with eternal implications for the life of faith.

Yet, this divine immovability challenges us beyond mere acknowledgment; it calls for an intimate trust and surrender that transcends intellectual assent. How often do our hearts cling to false securities, wealth, reputation, human approval, only to have them crumble and leave us bereft? The Rock of Ages demands from us a relinquishment of these fragile crutches, inviting a faith that ceases striving and rests fully in the assurance of God's unwavering presence. To be anchored in the Word is to recognize that in every trial, every moment of fear, and every shadow of doubt, God's steadfastness not only holds us but transforms our comprehension of strength. It is a renewing grace that replaces wavering assurance with abiding peace, that exchanges restless striving for settled rest.

Imagine standing upon a cragged precipice, the skies darkening and the storm's fury nearing. The ground beneath trembles; yet, the Rock remains unmoved. It is this image that Scripture paints for our souls, a portrait of divine constancy. The Lord Jehovah, declared by the prophet Isaiah as "the everlasting God, the Creator of the ends of the earth, fainteth not, neither is weary" (Isaiah 40:28), offers His nature as refuge. We find in Him a strength beyond our own frailty, the sustaining might that enables perseverance beyond what seems possible. He is not a distant deity but a present help in times of trouble, as the Psalmist comforts, "God is our refuge and strength, a very present help in trouble" (Psalm 46:1). Our journey toward spiritual renewal begins with this recognition: to be truly anchored is to stand upon God himself, the Rock of Ages, immovably faithful amidst every shaking circumstance.

As this truth permeates the heart, prayer naturally wells forth like a perennial spring, drawing us into deeper fellowship and trust. It is in the sacred communion of prayer that the soul whispers its vulnerabilities and hears in return the mighty reassurance of God's abiding love. We may approach Him with the fragility of our fears and the heaviness of our doubts, yet find in His presence a peace that "passeth all understanding" (Philippians 4:7). In uttering such prayers, we confess our dependence and acknowledge the futility of our own striving apart from Him. "Lord, be Thou my rock and my fortress; let me not be moved from Thy promises," echoes in the chambers of a heart seeking refuge. The prayer is more than mere supplication, it is an act of faith sealed upon the foundation of divine constancy. It is the holy moment when the soul loosens its grip on shifting sands and clasps the truth that endures forever.

In weaving this reflection into the fabric of our daily lives, we begin to notice subtle transformations within. The storms that once provoked panic are met with a quiet confidence, the uncertainties that once bred despair now invite a humble trust in divine providence. Trusting in the Rock of Ages molds our perspective, allowing the spirit to rise above immediate fears and to behold the grand tapestry of God's sovereign unfolding. Even the darkest trials become a part of a greater design, one held firmly in the hands of a faithful Creator who does not relinquish His beloved. The steadfastness we find in God nourishes patience, deepens hope, and inspires courage to face each new dawn with renewed vigor.

Thus, as we embark on the sacred journey of this devotional voyage, the Rock of Ages stands as our unshakable starting place. It is a solemn pledge whispering across the expanse of time that though "the earth be removed, and though the mountains be carried into the midst of the sea" (Psalm 46:2), those who trust in the Lord shall find a refuge that no force can overturn. To be anchored in the Word is to anchor in the person and promises of God, where faith finds shelter, hope finds strength, and love becomes the unbreakable bond that secures the heart. May this truth dwell richly within us, a living cornerstone upon which every thought, prayer, and deed may rest with perfect confidence, for in the Rock of Ages alone is our soul truly safe, unshaken, and eternally anchored.

Faith That Moves Mountains

In the quiet chambers of the heart, where doubts and fears often seek dominion, there arises a call to summon a faith beyond the mere whispers of hope, a faith that moves mountains. This faith, so powerfully extolled in the King James Bible, is not a fleeting fancy nor an idle wish; it is rather the very bedrock upon which the soul is anchored amidst the shifting sands of uncertainty and trial. To believe with such steadfastness is to grasp the promises of God with the hands of unwavering trust, confident that no obstacle is too great nor circumstance too dire for the Almighty to transform. The scripture declares, "If ye have faith as a grain of mustard seed, ye shall say unto this mountain, Remove hence to yonder place; and it shall remove; and nothing shall be impossible unto you" (Matthew 17:20). Thus, faith is not measured by the magnitude of the challenge, but by the immensity of the trust placed in the Lord's sovereign power. It is a sacred confidence which, though small in semblance, erupts with divine might when nurtured in a sincere heart and spirit.

As one embarks upon this spiritual journey, it becomes clear that faith is not an abstract concept lifted from the realm of lofty theology; it is incarnate in the fabric of daily living, woven through the countless decisions and moments where reliance on God must triumph over sight and sense. In moments when the tempest roars and shadows deepen, the call to faith is to stand immovable, to hold fast to the rock of ages, and to declare with boldness that God's word remains true, undiminished by the evanescence of circumstance. It is here, in the tension between human frailty and divine omnipotence, that true faith is forged. It is not the absence of struggle but the presence of trust in God's timing and providence that defines this holy confidence. To live by faith is to cast aside the heavy cloak of anxiety and to clothe the soul in the garments of hope and assurance, for "faith is the substance of things hoped for, the evidence of things not seen" (Hebrews 11:1).

Thus, faith acts as both a shield and a lamp, protecting against the attacks of doubt, illuminating the path forward when the night is deep.

The journey toward mounting faith requires a conscious and deliberate turning to the sacred scriptures, those timeless wells of divine wisdom and encouragement. In our meditation upon God's holy word, we discern the narrative of promises kept and miracles wrought, reminding us that the God who parted the Red Sea and called forth life from the barren womb of the earth remains unchangeable and present. By immersing the spirit in verses imbued with authority and reverence, the heart is emboldened, and a deeper root of trust is cultivated. The omnipotence of God revealed in Scripture beckons us beyond passive assent toward active belief. Faith becomes an act of will, a daily decision to believe the unbribable promises of God despite contrary appearances. This scriptural foundation renews the soul's courage to face mountain-sized challenges, to pray with expectancy, and to walk the path of steadfast conviction. The spiritual landscape is thus transformed from a place of fear to a sanctuary of bold assurance.

Yet, faith that moves mountains is not merely a vehicle for personal triumph; it is a sacred trust that intertwines intimately with the will of God and His redemptive purposes. To pray "remove this mountain" is to cast every burden upon Him who careth for us, to yield our deepest desires within the framework of divine wisdom. Faith is therefore both humble and daring, recognizing God's sovereign sovereignty even as it dares to ask for the impossible. The interplay of human petition and divine response creates a holy dance, one that calls the believer to patience, persistence, and a profound sensitivity to the Spirit's guidance. In this dance, the soul learns that not every mountain is moved in the manner or timing desired, but that always the believer is upheld by a grace surpassing understanding. Faith is the thread that weaves together hope with obedience, trust with surrender. It is a beacon blazing across the valleys of uncertainty, proclaiming that the Almighty reigns and that His promises endure forever.

As the heart contemplates these truths, it cannot help but be moved toward worship and prayer, a sacred dialogue that reinforces faith's vitality. Prayer becomes not only petition but a declaration of trust, a holy communion with the God who invites us to "believe in Me." In the sanctuary of prayer, faith is revived, nourished by the whispered assurance of God's presence and power. The supplicant learns to rest in God's sovereignty, releasing anxiety and fear to the One who holds all things in His hands. The spirit of prayer itself is animated by faith, for to enter the throne room boldly is to step forth upon the solid ground of divine promise. Here, one learns the artistry of waiting with expectation, the patience of hope, and the joy of trust. Every prayer distance the soul from despair and draws it into the embrace of God's perfect peace.

Moreover, living by faith in daily life requires the believer to foster a continuous awareness of God's handiwork and providence. The mundane and the monumental alike become arenas wherein faith manifests by recognizing and trusting God's sovereignty. At times, faith calls for courageous endurance when the mountain looms large and immovable; at other times, it reveals itself in quiet moments of obedience and trust. This faith is nurtured in the heart that pauses to reflect upon God's faithfulness in past trials, remembering that He who helped before will never forsake. Such remembrance is a balm for the weary spirit, anchoring the soul amid storms and tempests that life inevitably brings. The believer thus finds strength not in self, but in the consistent and unchanging character of the Lord. In this anchoring, one discovers that faith is neither passive resignation nor empty wish, but a living and active trust that renews every morning. "The Lord is my strength and my shield; my heart trusted in him, and I am helped" (Psalm 28:7) becomes a resonant anthem for the weary pilgrim.

To embrace this faith fully is also to embrace the paradox of weakness and strength intertwined. The apostle Paul, conscious of his own frailty, declared, "For when I am weak, then am I strong" (2 Corinthians 12:10), revealing the divine mystery that faith is made perfect not in human might but in divine power. It is in moments when human effort fails that the sufficiency of God's grace shines brightest, and mountains are moved not by human hand but by the omnipotent Spirit. This humbling acknowledgment sweetly dissolves pride and fosters a humble confidence, one that leans not on understanding but on the steadfast promises of God. Such faith is a shelter in the time of storm, a refuge that withstands the fiercest winds and floods. It is a bold declaration that no circumstance shall sever the soul's union with the living God, the One who upholds the universe with a word.

As this reflection draws toward its prayerful close, let this be the daily meditation: Lord, grant me a faith that moves mountains, that in the shadows of doubt and fear I may yet proclaim Thy promises with unwavering assurance. Let me trust not in worldly strength but in Thy unchanging grace, resting assured that Thou art ever faithful to fulfill Thy word. May my heart be fortified to stand firm amid trials, persistent in prayer, and joyful in hope, knowing that Thou art the God of all power and love. Root my soul deeply in Thy word, that like the mustard seed, my faith may grow beyond measure, removing every obstacle in my path. Teach me to embody this faith in my daily walk, that my life may bear witness to Thy glory and power. In Jesus' name, Amen.

Thus anchored in the word, behold how faith awakens even the smallest mustard seed into a mighty force, capable of moving the tallest mountain. May this truth ignite within us an enduring spirit of trust and confidence, that our souls may remain steadfast, our vision clear, and our hearts ever anchored in His boundless love and unyielding promises. This is the faith that sustains the pilgrim through every season, the luminous light that guides through every shadow, and the eternal assurance that all things are indeed possible with God.

Trust Without Sight

In the quiet recesses of the soul, where doubt and fear often seek to take root, there lies a profound invitation to entrust oneself wholly to the unseen hand of God, a hand that guides even when the path is shrouded in darkness, and the journey's end remains veiled beyond mortal sight. Trust without sight is no mere act of hopeful wishing; it is a sacred act of surrender wherein the believer contracts heart and spirit in harmonious accord with the divine will, embracing a hope that breathes life amidst uncertainty. As the Apostle Paul exhorts the Hebrews, "faith is the substance of things hoped for, the evidence of things not seen" (Hebrews 11:1). This declaration serves not only as a theological axiom but as a mighty fortress in moments when the eyes falter before the inscrutable mysteries of providence. Indeed, to trust without sight is to anchor oneself in the eternal promises of God's Word, to set one's feet upon the rock of His unchanging nature while the shifting sands of circumstance murmur their false alarms.

When the tempest roars and the soul's vision blurs, it is the memory of God's faithfulness throughout the ages that sustains the believer. Scriptures abound with testimony to this truth: from the patient obedience of Abraham, who ventured without knowing the exact land to which he was called, to the quiet endurance of Job, whose afflictions veiled God's providence for a season; all these herald a tapestry woven of trust strung delicately with patience and hope. It is not the absence of uncertainty, but the courage to embrace uncertainty armed with the conviction that God's purposes are good and His timing perfect, that illumines the way. The Word beckons with the tender assurance, "Commit thy way unto the LORD; trust also in him; and he shall bring it to pass" (Psalm 37:5), reminding us that trust is both a command and a promise: a divine entreaty to lean not on our own understanding but to repose in the wisdom of the Almighty, whose eyes perceive the end before the beginning unfolds.

Yet, the struggle to trust without sight is as human as it is holy. The natural tendency to demand visible proof, to have the shimmer of certainty before the taking of a step, arises from a place of fear and frailty. How easily the shadows lengthen and the heart falters when the expected signposts of assurance remain concealed! Nonetheless, herein lies a paradox; the true and abiding trust called for by God's Word transcends visible evidence and dwells in a realm where sight yields to faith. It is the still, small voice within that whispers steadfastly amidst chaos, echoing the prophet Isaiah's words, "Thou wilt keep him in perfect peace, whose mind is stayed on thee: because he trusteth in thee" (Isaiah 26:3). To have the mind stayed upon the Lord is to fix one's gaze not on the wavering waves of present circumstance, but on the firm foundation of His unwavering character. This steadfast focus cultivates an inner peace that defies external tumult, a peace that flows from the wellspring of trust even when the future appears as a cloaked mystery.

The reflections upon trust without sight are not merely theoretical musings but deeply personal journeys of the heart's pilgrimage toward spiritual maturity. The believer is invited to reckon daily with the tension between what is seen and what is promised, to practice a trust that, by its very nature, must engage the will and the heart as much as the mind. It is no passive resignation but an active commitment to believe in the goodness and sovereignty of God, especially when tangible evidence seems scarce. In this space of waiting and hoping in the unseen, the soul learns to be sculpted by grace and perseverance. The divine pattern unfolds repeatedly throughout Scripture: God calls His children into seasons of obscurity before revealing the fullness of His plan. Thus, the believer is drawn into a spiritual rhythm, waiting patiently, trusting fully, and watching expectantly, not for the appearance of certainty, but for the quiet unfolding of His perfect will.

Prayer becomes a vital lifeline in cultivating trust without sight. It is in the intimate dialogue with God, where doubts may be laid bare and fears confessed, that the believer finds renewed strength to say, "Lord, I believe; help thou mine unbelief" (Mark 9:24). Prayer does not demand defenses or masks; rather, it acknowledges the frailty of the human heart while appealing to the infinite faithfulness of God. It is in this sacred conversation that trust is knitted deeper, as the soul leans upon the assurance that God is near, that He hears every whisper of the heart, and that He carries us in His everlasting arms. The psalmist's cry, "Lead me in thy truth, and teach me: for thou art the God of my salvation" (Psalm 25:5), illustrates this yearning for divine guidance amidst the unknown, an unceasing plea that equips the soul to persevere in faith until the dawn breaks upon the horizon.

Moreover, the imagery of the anchor resonates profoundly with the theme of trust without sight. The apostle's metaphor of faith as "an anchor of the soul, both sure and stedfast" (Hebrews 6:19) captures the essence of trust that holds firm amidst life's tempests. Though the way before us may be engulfed in darkness, the soul anchored in God's promises remains immovable, steadfast against the tides of doubt and fear. The anchor, unseen beneath the waves, provides security not by sight but by its firm hold. In similar fashion, the believer's confidence rests not on visible assurances but on the unshakable truth of God's covenant love. The knowledge that the divine anchor is sunk deep into the immutable reality of God's Word brings peace to the heart troubled by uncertainty and calms the mind tormented by anxious forebodings.

Contemplation of God's attributes further bolsters trust without sight. The omniscience of God assures us that every detail, every path, every step in our journey is known and overseen by a sovereign hand that never errs nor slumbers. The omnipotence of God provides the power to bring to fruition every promise, even when appearances suggest delay or denial. His unchanging faithfulness guarantees that

His vows endure forever and that His love for His children neither falters nor fades. These eternal qualities inspire a confidence that surpasses reason, inviting the believer to let go of control and embrace the mystery of divine providence. In doing so, a spiritual maturity blossoms, wherein trust becomes a living testimony to God's glory and grace, a witness that shines brightly amid the obscurity of life's valleys.

At times, trust without sight demands a courageous surrender of personal desires and timelines. The believer learns to relinquish the urge to control and to submit wholeheartedly to God's perfect will, recognizing that the divine plan transcends human understanding and temporal measurement. This surrender is not weakness but profound strength, an act of faith that declares, "Not my will, but thine be done" (Luke 22:42). In this yielding, the soul discovers freedom: freedom from the bondage of anxiety, from the relentless pursuit of answers, and from the tyranny of fear. Instead, a peaceful confidence blooms, rooted in the assurance that God's ways are higher and His intentions always perfect. The quiet assurance that God orders all things for good imbues the soul with tranquility even in seasons of waiting and uncertainty.

In the breadth of life's challenges, trust without sight becomes the language of the heart when human wisdom fails and circumstances disorient. It is the song of the believer whose eyes are fixed beyond the trials of today to the glory that is to come. This trust is a lifeline thrown across the chasms of despair, a lamp shining in the darkness, a balm soothing the wounded spirit. Each step taken in faith writes a testament of hope upon the tapestry of one's spiritual journey, weaving a story of perseverance that will echo in eternity. The devotional life nurtures this trust daily, through meditation upon the Word, through prayerful surrender, through the fellowship of believers who encourage one another in the journey. Together, these spiritual disciplines fortify the believer's soul to persist with an anchored heart, steadfast and unwavering.

Let the reader then be encouraged, dear soul, to embrace this divine invitation to trust without sight, not as a burden, but as a blessed grace that refines and strengthens. Allow the sacred Scriptures to infuse the heart with their eternal promises, those golden threads of hope and assurance which run through every page of the King James Bible. Contemplate the words of Jeremiah, "For I know the thoughts that I think toward you, saith the LORD, thoughts of peace, and not of evil, to give you an expected end" (Jeremiah 29:11), and find in them a fortress against the storms of doubt. Let them be a melody that soothes and a light that guides when the way is obscure. In the sacred stillness of contemplation and the fervent breath of prayer, may the soul grow courageous to step forward into the unseen, anchored firmly in the unshakable Word of God.

Thus, trusting without sight becomes not merely a test but a triumph of faith, a blessed journey into the depths of God's mystery where the soul is refined, and love revealed. The sovereign God who commands the stars and numbers the hairs on our head invites us into an eternal fellowship of trust, whereby we rest assured that our feet may walk even where eyes cannot see. In every shadowed valley, in every unknown tomorrow, His covenant-keeping presence remains our unfailing guide. May this truth enfold the heart in tranquility, inspire hope beyond the horizon, and kindle an ever-deepening trust that carries the believer onward, undaunted, unwavering, and forever anchored in the Word.

Prayer as the Foundation

In the quiet stillness of the soul's awakening, before the stirrings of doubt and despair can take hold, there lies a sacred space where prayer emerges as the cornerstone of all spiritual dwelling. This blessed communion with the Almighty is not a mere habit or occasional utterance; it is the very foundation upon which the edifice of faith is built, secured by the enduring promises found within the Holy

Scriptures. To approach prayer as the bedrock of our spiritual life is to acknowledge that faith, much like a mighty oak anchored deep within the earth, draws its strength and nourishment from a source unseen yet ever present, God Himself. King David, that harpist of Israel, with divine inspiration did declare, "I will call upon the Lord, who is worthy to be praised: so shall I be saved from mine enemies" (Psalm 18:3). This profound declaration is not simply a poetic flourish, but a spiritual truth that guides the believer into the sacred retreat of prayer, where trust is forged in the crucible of divine encounter.

When we draw near to God in prayer, we thereby affirm our absolute dependence upon Him, recognizing that faith is not a solitary venture nor a self-generated force but a relational tether to the everlasting God. To pray is to humble our will, to silence the clamor of human striving, and to enter that holy dialogue wherein the soul is anchored and fortified. As the Psalmist so beautifully voices, "Commit thy way unto the Lord; trust also in him; and he shall bring it to pass" (Psalm 37:5). Prayer is the act of laying our burdens and our hopes at His feet, declaring a trust that transcends circumstance and reason, and embracing a divine will that is both sovereign and benevolent. In this sacred space, the believer's heart is refined, shaped by the Spirit's gentle whispers and God's unerring guidance.

The Apostle Paul, in his wisdom, exhorts the faithful to "pray without ceasing" (1 Thessalonians 5:17), a charge that underlines the necessity of continual, steadfast prayer as the heartbeat of a living faith. Such prayer is not to be confined to solemn moments alone but is to permeate the daily walk, becoming the sustaining breath of the spirit. It is through this unbroken communion that the believer is both grounded and lifted, riveted to God's unshakable promises even amid the tempests of life. For it is written, "Be careful for nothing; but in every thing by prayer and supplication with thanksgiving let your requests be made known unto God" (Philippians 4:6). The act of prayer invites peace to take up residence within the heart, fostering a spirit of thanksgiving that springs forth not from abundance alone but from a deep-rooted trust in God's faithful provision.

Thus, prayer is not solely a cry of need but a profound declaration of faith and trust. When Moses lifted his hands in intercession before the Lord, it was an act of surrender and dependence, pleading for Israel's deliverance yet affirming the certainty of God's power and mercy. Likewise, our prayers serve as both a reaching forth and an anchoring back, a reaching forth to lay hold of the divine grace that strengthens, and anchoring back into the truth that God's Word is sure and steadfast. To pray with the words of Scripture woven into our supplications is to possess a wellspring of hope and assurance, for the Word of God is described as being "a lamp unto my feet, and a light unto my path" (Psalm 119:105), illuminating the way and dispelling the shadows of doubt.

God invites us into this sacred dialogue, beckoning us to "call upon me in the day of trouble: I will deliver thee, and thou shalt glorify me" (Psalm 50:15). Herein lies the beauty of prayer as the foundation of faith: it is the divine invitation to abide, to trust, to cling without wavering to a God who hears and answers. It is in this dialogue that faith finds its roots sunk deep into the fertile soil of God's unconditional love and covenantal grace. Prayer becomes the place where we witness the interplay of divine sovereignty and human trust, where our trembling hearts, trembling even over the smallest uncertainty, find steadfast courage and renewed strength.

To neglect prayer is to loosen the beads of a rosary, allowing the chain of faith to unravel. Without prayer, faith becomes an abstraction, a fragile hope easily swayed by the winds of circumstance. But with prayer, faith is tempered as steel, forged in the heat of consistent communion and the continual remembrance of God's promises. When Daniel knelt in prayer thrice daily, even before the threat of the lions' den, he exemplified a faith that was no fleeting sentiment but an unyielding covenantal relationship anchored in steadfast prayer. Such faith did not arise spontaneously but was cultivated through intentional practice, a ceaseless turning of the heart toward God.

Moreover, prayer shapes our perception of God's sovereign will, casting light upon the path that often eludes the weary eye and granting clarity in seasons of confusion. It reorients the soul, transforming the gaze from burdensome present trials to the eternal perspective established by God's eternal Word. "Trust in the Lord with all thine heart; and lean not unto thine own understanding" (Proverbs 3:5) is not merely a biblical dictum but a living reality birthed in the fertile ground of prayer. Through persistent seeking and heartfelt conversation with God, the believer surrenders personal understanding and embraces divine wisdom, finding solace and direction.

Prayer then, in its highest form, is not a one-sided entreaty but a sacred dialogue, a dance between the soul and the Divine where faith is both expressed and deepened. It nurtures a resilience that stabilizes amidst spiritual storms, cultivating patience when answers tarry and fortitude when the night grows long. Even when silence seems to answer, the commitment to prayer sustains, reminding us of the truth found in Jesus' words: "Men ought always to pray, and not to faint" (Luke 18:1). To faint here means to lose heart or to give up hope; prayer is the mighty anchor preventing such spiritual collapse.

In the daily practice of prayer, we are invited to rediscover the simple yet profound act of entrusting our whole being to God's care. We bring our fears, our joys, our confusions, and our gratitude, laying them upon the altar of divine attentiveness. We declare in the stillness, in the words shaped by centuries past, that we believe God is able, that His promises hold true, and that His love is unfailing. The sacred script of the King James Bible, with its majestic cadence and holy rigor, powerfully fortifies this declaration, embedding it within the heart's deepest chambers.

As we embark upon this spiritual journey, let us remember that prayer is the sacred threshold that leads us into the embrace of God's presence. It is the wellspring from which the living water of faith flows copiously, irrigating the parched lands of doubt and fear. Through prayer, the believer is yoked to the divine strength that enables endurance and the courage that kindles hope. May our hearts be ever inclined to this holy conversation, allowing prayer to anchor us firmly within the protective shadow of God's wings, ever mindful of the promise, "The Lord is my shepherd; I shall not want" (Psalm 23:1).

And so, beloved reader, as you take up this journey of faith rooted in these sacred pages, may your prayers ascend like incense, fragrant and pleasing unto the Lord, securing your soul in the unchanging truth of His Word. May you hold fast to prayer as to a lifeline, a firm foundation whose stones are the very promises of God, and whose corners are established in His eternal love. In the stillness and in the storm, may prayer be your constant refuge, your shield from the fleeting shadows, and the sacred channel through which the Spirit breathes new life into your weary heart. Thus, every whispered prayer becomes a declaration of faith, each moment spent in sacred talk transforming the soul into a sanctuary anchored immovably in the Word of God.

Grace and Mercy

Unmerited Favor

In the sanctuary of the soul, where light gently falls upon the heart's tender chambers, there lies a truth so profound that it eludes human comprehension yet beckons with irresistible allure, the unmerited favor of God. Grace stands as a pillar of divine generosity, a blessing bestowed without pretense or condition, an overflowing fountain that springs forth not from the worthiness of man but from the boundless love and mercy of the Creator. We dwell in a world that defines value by achievement, merit, and reward, yet the grace revealed in the sacred pages of the King James Bible shatters this human paradigm. It is a gift freely given, anointed with compassion, suffused with forgiveness, and offered to the humble and the proud alike. This grace whispers to the weary heart, "Thy sins be forgiven," not because of penance performed or righteousness earned, but because the Almighty's love cannot be contained by any formula of deeds. The Apostle Paul, in his epistle to the Ephesians, proclaims this wondrous truth with fervent clarity: "By grace are ye saved through faith; and that not of yourselves: it is the gift of God." Herein lies the very heart of the Gospel, that salvation, the restoration of the soul, the renewal of spirit, is not a fruit wrought by human hands but the divine inheritance poured forth from heaven's treasure house.

Contemplating such unmerited favor invites the soul to a sacred stillness, where the mind relinquishes its striving and the heart surrenders to awe. It is here in the quietude that one begins to grasp the immensity of divine generosity, a love that met us while we yet trod paths of folly and sin, that embraced us while we were far off and wandering. The prodigal son, wandering in the wastelands of self-destruction, found no condemnation upon his return but was met with open arms, a robe of mercy, and a feast of reconciliation. This parable is not merely an ancient tale but a living testament that grace never waits for perfection or achievement. It is not parceled out to reward the deserving but lavished upon the undeserving, for God's nature is rich in mercy and abounding in steadfast love. To truly comprehend grace is to perceive that it is a divine mystery, surpassing knowledge, transcending justice, and overwhelming any sense of personal entitlement.

Yet, the reception of grace must engage the heart with humility, for it is not a cloak to justify rebellion nor a license to continue in waywardness. Rather, grace calls forth transformation, beckoning the soul to cast aside pride and embrace the gentle yoke of discipleship. The knowledge that forgiveness is extended not by works but by God's undeserved favor inspires a profound gratitude that ignites the desire for holiness. The psalmist, touching the essence of this grace, cries out, "Blessed is the man unto whom the Lord imputeth not iniquity, and in whose spirit there is no guile." This blessing is not the fruit of human effort but the wondrous effect of divine pardon. When the soul beholds the infinite mercy that covers transgressions like a flood of purifying waters, it finds the courage to forsake old paths and to walk anew in righteousness. Grace, therefore, is not passive but a dynamic force that molds and shapes, gently yet irresistibly drawing the believer into the likeness of Christ, who Himself is the embodiment of unmerited favor.

In the natural world, human affection often hinges on reciprocity and merit; yet divine grace shatters these scales. It reaches out to the outcast, uplifts the brokenhearted, and renews the contrite soul. To embrace grace is to encounter the heart of God who declares, "For I will be merciful to their unrighteousness, and their sins and their iniquities will I remember no more." Such mercy dissolves condemnation, liberating the spirit from the shackles of guilt and despair. The weight of sin, once a crushing burden, is lifted by this gracious hand, unveiling a path toward peace and restoration. This divine favor does not merely cover sin but redeems the very space where sin reigned, transforming grief into joy and death into life. It is the anchor for the soul amid life's tempests, a wondrous assurance that no failure or frailty can separate the beloved from God's care.

As recipients of such grace, the believer is called also to a life marked by compassion and forgiveness toward others. The beauty of divine favor is not meant to be hoarded but reflected in the mirror of human relationships. When we grasp the magnitude of God's mercy extended to us, undeserved and unearned, we are moved to extend similar grace to those who trespass against us. Herein lies a challenge and a blessing, for grace compels us to forgive seventy times seven, to love our enemies, and to pray for those who persecute us. The King James Bible unerringly impresses upon the soul the imperative of mercy: "Be ye therefore merciful, as your Father also is merciful." To embody grace is to become a conduit of God's love, a vessel through which the fragrance of forgiveness and kindness is poured out upon a thirsty world. It is a sacred responsibility awakened by the profound realization that we ourselves stand in need of pardon and habilitation. In extending grace, we reflect the divine image, illuminating the world with the light of Christ.

Moreover, the journey toward understanding and embracing unmerited favor is neither swift nor effortless; it is a pilgrimage of the spirit. There are moments when the heart wrestles with feelings of unworthiness or the hardness of forgiveness toward others. Yet it is precisely in these trials that grace manifests its power most strikingly. The believer learns that grace is sufficient even in weakness, that God's strength is made perfect in human frailty. The Apostle Paul's testimony is the vibrant echo of this truth: "My grace is sufficient for thee: for my strength is made perfect in weakness." Each failure, each moment of brokenness, is met with a steadying hand that lifts the soul and whispers hope. The unmerited favor of God becomes the believer's fortress and shield, a sanctuary where doubt bows and trust takes root.

Prayer becomes the sacred conduit through which one communes with this grace, inviting its transformative presence to permeate every corner of life. In humility and reverence, the soul petitions the Almighty to enkindle a deeper understanding and a livelier experience of grace. The poetic cadences of Scripture serve as both guide and balm, drawing the believer into a posture of awe and thanksgiving. Prayerful reflection reveals that grace is not confined to moments of spiritual ecstasy but walks with us through the ordinary and the mundane, infusing daily existence with holy meaning. It softens the heart, liberates from bitterness, and kindles the fire of love that fuels perseverance and faith. In such communion, the soul discovers that grace sustains beyond comprehension, nurtures beyond measure, and restores without limit.

Finally, to rest wholly in unmerited favor is to anchor the spirit in the eternal foundation of God's unwavering promise. It is to stand on the rock of divine mercy when the floods of life rise and threaten to overwhelm. This grace assures the believer that no condemnation waits for those in Christ Jesus and that the eternal hope of salvation is not contingent upon human effort but secured by the blood of the Lamb. It is this assurance that grants peace amid uncertainty, joy amid sorrow, and courage amid trial. The believer's heart, thus anchored firmly in the vast ocean of God's grace, can navigate every storm with unshaken trust. Time and again, the scriptures summon us to dwell in this sanctuary of grace: "Let us therefore come boldly unto the throne of grace, that we may obtain mercy, and find grace to help in time of need." What a sublime invitation this is, to approach with confidence, knowing that grace awaits to embrace, uphold, and transform.

In embracing the rich tapestry of unmerited favor, the soul finds renewal and strength, an unshakable peace woven from the eternal love of God. It is a mystery to be cherished, a gift to be treasured, and a power to be lived. Let us then, with grateful hearts, receive this grace, permit it to soften and illumine our lives, and extend it generously to others, becoming living testaments of the mercy and love that flow inexhaustibly from the hand of God. As we meditate on this divine favor, may our spirits rise in joyful praise, our lives echo with compassion, and our faith deepen into a steadfast trust anchored forever in the immutable Word.

Mercy That Redeems

In the quiet stillness of the soul, where shadows of past transgressions linger, and the weight of shortcomings presses heavily upon the heart, there resides a divine whisper, one of mercy that redeems beyond measure. It is a mercy not born of human understanding, but of the boundless and unfathomable nature of God, whose compassions fail not and whose love endures forever. "The LORD is merciful and gracious, slow to anger, and plenteous in mercy" (Psalm 103:8) declares the sacred text, and herein lies the foundation of our hope and the wellspring of our restoration. To contemplate God's mercy is to gaze upon a light that pierces the darkest nights of despair, offering solace where guilt might otherwise confound, and release where bondage to sorrow might seek to hold fast. It is this mercy, so rich and abundant, that not only pardons but profoundly transforms, drawing the soul from death unto life, from alienation to intimacy with the Divine.

The merciful nature of God reveals itself most vividly in the narrative of redemption, where mankind's fallibility met the unyielding grace of heaven's embrace. The apostle Paul, steeped in the traditions of his faith, yet humbled before the saving power of grace, wrote to the Corinthians, "And such were some of you: but ye are washed, but ye are sanctified, but ye are justified in the name of the Lord Jesus, and by the Spirit of our God" (1 Corinthians 6:11). This profound truth embodies mercy's power, it reaches into the deepest mire of human frailty and rescues, not because of deserving, but solely by the loving kindness of God's initiative. To be washed is to be drawn into a cleansing that purifies the heart from the taint of sin, sanctified to be set apart for holy purpose, and justified, a legal declaration of righteousness bestowed upon the unworthy. This act cannot be earned, for mercy is the gift that overturns the scales that would otherwise condemn. It invites every repentant heart into a renewed covenant, secured not by works but by the unshakeable promise of divine compassion.

In our mortal journey, we often wrestle with the concept of mercy, not only as recipients but as conduits called to mirror God's grace to others. The King James Bible, with its majestic and poetic cadence, speaks clearly to the transformative power of extending mercy, "Be ye therefore merciful, as your Father also is merciful" (Luke 6:36). Here lies a sacred charge, not merely to bask in the mercy bestowed upon us but to become vessels of that mercy in a world yearning for kindness amidst its brokenness. The believer who embraces this calling embarks on a pathway where forgiveness flows freely, and where compassion softens the edges of conflict and harboring resentment. To forgive is to enact the very nature of God's mercy, a surrender that heals wounds both borne and inflicted, creating ripples of peace that surpass understanding. Mercy given becomes mercy multiplied, reflecting God's image in human hearts and communities alike.

Delving deeper into the heart of mercy reveals its remarkable ability to bridge the chasms of despair and reestablish hope where none seems to dwell. An ancient psalmist cries out, "Have mercy upon me, O God, according to thy lovingkindness: according unto the multitude of thy tender mercies blot out my transgressions" (Psalm 51:1). This prayer encapsulates a divine longing intrinsic to all humankind: the yearning for cleansing and restoration. Mercy here is not a mere notion or abstract concept; it is a tangible, powerful force that blotts out transgressions, erases the stains of sin, and breathes new life into souls bowed beneath the weight of regret. For the believer, such mercy is a daily renewal, an ever-present balm for the aching spirit, assuring that no fault or failure can separate one irreparably from God's love. Thus, mercy becomes the foundation of hope itself, a living promise that no darkness is too deep, and no night is too long for the dawn of forgiveness to break forth.

The richness of this mercy is unveiled also in its patient endurance, a mercy that holds back wrath, grants time for repentance, and invites the wandering back to the fold. This patience speaks volumes of God's character, for mercy does not act rashly nor dismiss the seriousness of sin but rather moves with a gentle pacing that allows hearts to be softened and transformed. "For I will be merciful to their unrighteousness, and their sins and their iniquities will I remember no more" (Hebrews 8:12) declares the promise of the new covenant, signaling a merciful forgetfulness, a divine pardon that blots sins from the ledger of blame. Such mercy is freedom from the chains of guilt, enabling believers not only to reconcile with God but also to walk in newness of life, liberated from the past and empowered for the future. Herein lies a tender mercy that not only addresses the consequences of sin but heals the roots of its despair by opening the gates to joy and peace.

Yet, to grasp this mercy fully is also to encounter the mystery of its cost, mercy that redeems was purchased on Calvary's cross, where the Son of God bore the burden of human sin in an act of ultimate love. The echo of mercy resounds through the words of Christ, "Come unto me, all ye that labour and are heavy laden, and I will give you rest" (Matthew 11:28). The merciful invitation extends beyond mere pardon; it offers rest to the weary, strength to the weak, and restoration to the broken. This rest is a profound peace that fills the soul with assurance and quietness, transcending the turmoil of life's trials and anchoring the believer firmly in God's steadfastness. Mercy, therefore, is not only a retrospective forgiveness but a present help and a future hope, anchoring us in the unchanging love of God, assuring that our lives are held secure beneath the shadow of His wings.

In the light of such mercy, the believer is called to respond with a heart softened and lives transformed. It is an invitation to let mercy govern thoughts, words, and deeds, enabling a faith that does not merely profess belief but actively embodies love. The merciful are blessed, for they reflect the character of their Heavenly Father and partake in the blessings of divine favor. This truth encourages introspection and challenges the soul to relinquish pride and judgment, embracing humility and grace. As God's mercy has reached us, so we are empowered to reach out to others, becoming agents of healing where bitterness seeks to take root and witnesses of hope where despair threatens to prevail. This sacred reciprocation fosters a community knit together by compassion, where mercy is both the bond and the blessing.

Prayer beckons here as the conduit through which mercy is both received and extended. In sincere conversation with God, the heart can lay bare its frailties and seek the renewing touch of mercy. A heartfelt prayer might rise in the spirit, "O Lord, pour out Thy mercy upon me, that I may be cleansed and made whole. Teach me to mirror Thy compassion in my dealings with my brethren, that through me Thy love may flow forth as a river of grace. Grant me the courage to forgive as I have been forgiven, and the strength to endure as Thou art patient with me." Such prayers are not mere supplications but declarations of faith, affirmations that mercy is the sustenance of the soul and the beacon that guides the believer onward.

Thus, as one meditates upon the merciful nature of God, a profound transformation begins within, a surrendering to the truth that, in mercy, God's heart beats in unison with ours. This mercy redeems the past, sanctifies the present, and certifies the future. It frees from condemnation, fills with hope, and beckons us to a higher calling. In embracing God's mercy, the believer discovers a refuge and a strength, a profound peace that neither time nor trial can diminish. Resting in this mercy, the soul is anchored securely, able to face life's tempests with unwavering trust, assured that the same mercy that saved shall continue to sustain and renew, now and forevermore.

Forgiveness Frees

In the vast tapestry of spiritual renewal, the thread of forgiveness is woven with a strength and beauty that surpasseth all human understanding. It is a divine act that liberateth the soul from the bondage of bitterness and the heavy chains of resentment, delivering the weary heart unto a place of peace and restoration. As the Psalmist declareth, "Blessed is the man unto whom the LORD imputeth not iniquity, and in whose spirit there is no guile" (Psalm 32:2). Herein lies the surpassing grace of God, which inviteth us to receive forgiveness as a wellspring of renewal and to extend it as a beacon of mercy to others. Forgiveness is not merely a token word or shallow gesture; it is a transformative journey, one that calleth us to lay aside our pride, relinquish the desire for vengeance, and embrace the gentle love that Christ hath manifested for us upon the cross.

Consider the profound insight given in the Epistle to the Ephesians, "And be ye kind one to another, tenderhearted, forgiving one another, even as God for Christ's sake hath forgiven you" (Ephesians 4:32). Here the Apostle Paul exhorteth the faithful not only to accept God's boundless forgiveness but to become conduits of that same grace toward our brethren. This sacred reciprocity embodyeth the heart of divine love, wherein each act of forgiveness draweth us nearer to the likeness of Christ and deepeneth our communion with the Holy Spirit. To forgive is to unshackle the soul from the prisons of wrath and grievance, setting it free to dwell in the liberty wherewith Christ hath made us free (Galatians 5:1). The written word portrayeth forgiveness as a divine attribute, God is merciful and gracious, slow to anger, and plenteous in mercy (Exodus 34:6), and we, as His children, are called to imitate this holiness by walking in gracious pathways.

Yet, the path of forgiveness is oftentimes rugged and steep, fraught with the valleys of pain and the shadows of wounded pride. It doth not come naturally to the carnal heart, for our flesh resisteth the surrender required to forgive those who have wronged us deeply. It is at this crossroad that we must look unto Jesus, the Author and Finisher of our faith, who in His agony on the cross prayed, "Father, forgive them; for they know not what they do" (Luke 23:34). In that moment of excruciating suffering, He exemplified the sublime power of forgiveness, offering mercy even to those who had crucified Him. Through His sacrifice, the fountain of forgiveness was opened wide, inviting all who come longing for peace and reconciliation. In meditating upon this divine forgiveness, our own souls find solace and strength to release the burdens of grudges and hatred that so easily entangle us. Indeed, through forgiveness, we partake in the life-giving grace that reneweth our hearts and restoreth the image of God within us.

When forgiveness is withheld, the spirit becometh ensnared in bitterness, a poison that corrodeth the very essence of joy and peace. The Apostle James warneth us, "For he that will love life, and see good days, let him refrain his tongue from evil, and his lips that they speak no guile: Let him eschew evil, and do good; let him seek peace, and ensue it" (James 1:12-13). To seek peace, therefore, is to embrace forgiveness; to pursue it with fervency, as though our souls' well-being doth depend thereupon, for indeed it doth. Forgiveness is a divine instrument of healing, capable of mending the broken spirit and restoring wholeness where division and strife had taken root. It breaketh down walls of hostility and openeth the door to reconciliation, not only between men but between man and God. The release of forgiveness is a sacred act that reflecteth the new creation we are in Christ, past sins swallowed up eternally in the mercy of God's covenant of grace.

Moreover, the practice of forgiveness is not confined solely to others; it extendeth equally to the self. The soul that hath been ensnared by guilt and shame must also reach out to God's grace, acknowledging the need for His cleansing mercy. The King James Bible proclaimeth, "If we confess our sins, he is faithful and just to forgive us our sins, and to cleanse us from all unrighteousness" (1 John 1:9), a sweet assurance that Christ's forgiveness embraceth even our own fallibility. To forgive one's self is to step into the light of God's redeeming love, confident that no sin is too great to be washed away by the blood of the Lamb. This inward forgiveness beareth as much significance as forgiveness toward others, for the kingdom of God is built upon the foundation of restored hearts, renewed minds, and spirits made whole. Without it, the soul is weighed down by condemnation, unable to fully partake in the freedom and joy promised by the gospel.

The heart of forgiveness also beateth in the rhythm of prayer, that sacred dialogue wherein we open ourselves fully unto God's working in us. In our prayers, we seek not only pardon but also the grace to forgive, an act that requireth humility and surrender. As we bow before the Lord, confessing our own need for mercy, we are softened and prepared to extend the same mercy to those who have trespassed against us. Prayer nurtureth a spirit of compassion, teaching us to see others through God's eyes, where even those who harm us are known and loved by Him. In this sacramental space, forgiveness is birthed anew, and the soul findeth refuge from the tempest of resentment. It is here, in the quiet communion with God, that the wounds of offense begin to heal, replaced by the fragrant scent of grace and reconciliation.

Furthermore, forgiveness doth not negate justice, nor doth it render the sins of others inconsequential; instead, it transcendeth human judgment and inviteth us into the divine economy of grace. It riseth above the clamor for retribution, offering peace that passeth understanding, even in the face of grave injustice. Christ's teaching remindeth us that forgiveness is to be lavished without measure, "for if ye forgive men their trespasses, your heavenly Father will also forgive you" (Matthew 6:14). This noble command calls forth a generosity of spirit that reflecteth heaven's own boundless mercy, a mercy that covereth a multitude of sins, and through which the soul is renewed and fortified. In embracing forgiveness, we are delivered from the victimhood of our offenses and empowered to walk forward in restoration and hope, no longer captive to the darkness of unforgiveness.

The transformative power of forgiveness extendeth beyond individual renewal, rippling outward into the fabric of relationships, communities, and the church itself. When congregations embody forgiveness, they become sanctuaries of grace where brokenness is met with healing rather than condemnation. Forgiveness cultivateth humility, patience, and love, virtues that not only heal wounds but build bridges of unity and fellowship. Each act of forgiveness within the body of Christ strengthens the bonds of brotherhood and exemplifieth the living presence of God among His people. The collective embrace of forgiveness is a testament to the resurrection power at work in hearts, breaking the cycle of hurt and retaliatory strife, and paving the way for lasting peace and spiritual flourishing.

Let us, therefore, be ever mindful of the treasure we hold in forgiveness, a divine gift that kindleth light in the darkest corners of the soul. May we carry it with reverence and zeal, recognizing that to forgive is to be freed, freed from the chains of anger, freed from the burdens of pain, freed to walk in the fullness of God's grace. May our hearts be softened to release every offense and to receive the healing balm of God's mercy, that we might be renewed and restored in spirit, reflecting His glory in a world longing for peace. And as we journey through this year of reflection, may forgiveness be both the lamp unto our feet and the anchor of our souls, holding us steadfast through every trial and triumph, bound in the eternal love of Christ Jesus. Amen.

Extending Grace

As we journey through the unsearchable depths of God's mercy, there emerges a call most gentle and profound, to extend grace to others as we ourselves have been graciously showered with divine favour. The Lord, in His boundless compassion, hath drawn nigh to us, bearing our infirmities and ignominies, not sparing even His own beloved Son to provide the price for our transgressions. Thus, grace is no mere abstraction nor idle sentiment; it is the very living water from the fount of heaven, coursing through the veins of our existence, quickening the soul and sanctifying the heart. To receive such grace is an ineffable blessing, yet it equally becomes a sacred injunction, a mandate planted deep within our spirits to mirror that mercy in our relationships. How often do we falter in extending this grace, ensnared as we are by the barbs of bitterness and the constrictions of pride, forgetting the magnitude of forgiveness bestowed upon us freely without merit? It is a profound mystery and a holy task to walk in grace, walking not as conduits of condemnation, but rather as vessels rich with patience, kindness, and tenderness toward those who stumble along life's rugged path.

Consider the radiance of grace as portrayed in the scriptures , "For by grace are ye saved through faith; and that not of yourselves: it is the gift of God: Not of works, lest any man should boast." These solemn words from the epistle to the Ephesians kindle within us a sacred understanding: grace is unmerited, a sovereign act of divine benevolence that elevates the lowly and redeems the fallen. It challenges our human inclination to weigh, measure, and withhold. Therein lies the beauty and the burden of the Christian life, a calling not only to receive mercy but to offer it, abundant like dew upon the grass, an ever-renewing grace that cleanses wounds and bridges divides. To extend grace is to relinquish the ledger of offenses, to unclench the fist of resentment, to embrace the broken with a tenderhearted compassion that mirrors the heart of Christ himself. It is in these moments of grace extended that divine love is most vividly made manifest; the love that seeks restoration over retribution, healing over hurt, and peace over pride.

Reflect, dear reader, upon the times thou hast erred and found succor in God's forgiving embrace. Whether in ignorance or frailty, thou hast known the sweet balm poured from the chalice of grace. Such mercy was not earned but gifted, a testimony to the great patience of the Almighty. Now, in the sanctified exchange of human fellowship, thou art beckoned to dispense this grace liberally, even when the recipient is unworthy or slow to repent. For it is not in our sanctity or righteousness that we extend grace, but in our remembrance of the greater grace given unto us, an everlasting fountain that replenishes the soul and empowers us to forgive as we have been forgiven. Amidst frail humanity's tumults and trials, grace becomes the adhesive that binds hearts together, a divine balm for relationships bruised by misunderstanding, hurt, and neglect. Extending grace to others does not come without challenge; oft it requires a crucifixion of self-will, a dying to the urge for vindication, and a rising to the call of love incarnate.

In the fabric of daily relationships, grace transforms conflict and tension into opportunities for divine encounter. When a harsh word is spoken or a deed done in error, grace bids us pause, to look beyond the immediate sting and see the person wounded and struggling beneath. It infuses our spirit with empathy, enabling us to respond not with retaliation but with gentle correction and wholesome forgiveness.

The grace we extend is a living testament to the power of love to transcend failure, a beacon of hope illuminating the darkest corners of human frailty. Such grace reflects the heart of our Savior, who, hanging upon the cross, entreated, "Father, forgive them; for they know not what they do." In those words, the very essence of grace is distilled, an unyielding love that forgives even in the face of cruelty and ignorance, that chooses restoration over judgment, that redeems suffering with mercy.

Yet, let us not mistake grace for weakness or laxity; it is no license to tolerate sin but rather the bold and holy power to overcome evil with good. The one who extends grace does so with the strength born of spiritual maturity, wielding compassion as a sword to cut through misunderstanding and bitterness. Grace restores dignity to the fallen and encourages growth in the redeemed. It creates a sacred space where wounds may be healed and trust rebuilt. This is a high calling, for to extend grace requires humility and courage, a willingness to suffer wrong silently and respond with love profoundly, just as Christ hath shown us the way. When we extend grace, we participate in the divine economy of redemption, weaving threads of mercy into the tapestry of human fellowship, and in so doing, we reflect the very character of God, whose nature is love perfected.

In homes, within communities, and amid the marketplace of life, grace stands as the sentinel of peace, restraining the tongue from bitterness and the heart from judgment. It compels us to hear with patience, to forgive without bitterness, and to love without condition. This is the grace that transforms relationships, turning estrangement into reconciliation, fear into trust, and sorrow into joy. How often do we fail to realize that every encounter is an opportunity ordained by God to extend grace, to soften a hardened heart, to repair a broken bond, to pour sunshine where shadows lurk? The ministry of grace is not merely for the saint or the scholar but for every believer who desires to walk in the footsteps of Christ. It is the currency of the kingdom, the language of heaven spoken in humble acts of kindness, mercy, and forgiveness.

Moreover, extending grace equips the soul for spiritual renewal and strengthens resilience amidst trials. When we extend grace, we release ourselves from the bondage of bitterness and resentment, which otherwise weigh heavily upon the spirit. Forgiveness is not a singular act but a continual posture, an ongoing surrender to the divine will that promises peace beyond understanding. It renews the heart by dismantling the strongholds of anger and pride, inviting us into deeper communion with God, who alone sustains and heals. Through this sacred practice, our faith is fortified; we learn to trust in the justice and timing of God rather than our mortal impulses. The grace we extend becomes a mirror through which we behold God's unfailing mercy, increasing our capacity to love and endure.

Let us then approach each relationship with a heart attuned to grace, recognizing that all are but frail vessels bearing the image of the Divine, marred but not forsaken. When we stumble upon offenses great or small, let grace rise within us as a wellspring of divine compassion. Pray that God would soften your heart to forgive as you have been forgiven, to act with tenderness even when wounded, and to speak words of healing rather than harm. Ask for the wisdom to discern when to confront in love and when to bear patiently in silence, remembering always that the true victor is the one who overcomes evil with good. In extending grace, we lay hold upon the promise that God's love is made perfect in weakness, that the humble shall be exalted, and that peace shall spring forth like a river in the hearts of those who abide in His mercy.

O Lord, whose grace is an ocean vast and deep beyond measure, grant us the heart to embody Thy mercy. Teach us to forgive as we have been forgiven, to love without condition, and to extend compassion to those who trespass against us. May Thy Spirit move within us to sanctify our relationships, healing every breach and binding every wound with cords of love unbreakable. Let the grace we give be a reflection of Thy own, that in our weakness Thy strength may be glorified. Sustain us day by day to walk humbly and tenderly, that our lives may bear witness to Thy endless mercy and the transforming power of Thy grace. Amen.

The Power of Prayer

Prayer in the Storm

When the tempest rages, and the heavens appear as brass, when life's trials beat upon the soul like the unrelenting waves upon the shore, there is a refuge deeper than the mountains and firmer than the ancient rocks; it is the sacred practice of prayer. In the midst of darkness and disquiet, when the heart is fraught with fear and the world seems to close in with shadows, prayer stands as the channel through which the weary spirit may reach forth and grasp the hand of the Almighty. The King James Bible illuminates this truth with a majesty of language that reverberates through the ages, when the Psalmist cries, "Call upon me in the day of trouble: I will deliver thee, and thou shalt glorify me" (Psalm 50:15), we are beckoned to lean into the very presence of God as our fortress and shield. Prayer is not merely a ritual or a fleeting word before the storm, but rather the tether that anchors the soul, the quiet breath that steadies the trembling heart amid the fiercest gales.

In those moments when the night grows thick and silent, and the cares of this world seek to suffocate hope, prayer invites us to lift our eyes unto the hills, from whence cometh our help. This sacred discipline is a conversation, not confined by formalities but birthed in the intimacy of a heart laid bare before the Creator. As David found solace in the stillness, pouring out lament and praise alike, so too does the believer in the storm find that prayer transforms the harrowing turmoil into a sacred dialogue with the divine. It is here that the soul is drawn out of its prison of despair and into the spaciousness of God's grace. For prayer is the breath of the spirit, the whisper of trust when all human certainties fail, echoing the words of the Savior: "Come unto me, all ye that labour and are heavy laden, and I will give you rest"

(Matthew 11:28). In prayer, the storm loses its frightful mastery, not necessarily through the quieting of external circumstance, but by the peace which surpasseth all understanding that God imparts.

The Apostle Paul, imprisoned and beleaguered, revealed the power of ceaseless prayer, exhorting believers to "pray without ceasing" (1 Thessalonians 5:17). Such a mandate carries the profound implication that prayer is not confined to particular hours or seasons but serves as a continual lifeline sustaining the soul's communion with God. When the tempest threatens to consume all joy, it is prayer that recalibrates the heart's compass, redirecting attention from the storm unto the steadfast hand of the Almighty. This divine dialogue shifts the believer's focus from the roaring winds to the eternal promises, reminding that "the Lord is my shepherd; I shall not want" (Psalm 23:1). Prayer, then, functions as both shield and sword, not to fend the storm's existence but to enable the heart to endure, to trust, and to emerge sanctified through trial.

Different forms of prayer unfold within the sacred pages of Scripture, each revealing dimensions of the soul's approach to God in times of calamity. There is the prayer of petition, where the soul boldly lays its needs before the throne of grace, inviting God's intervention and mercy. Yet this is balanced by prayers of confession, in which believers acknowledge their frailty and sinfulness, restoring fellowship and cleansing their consciences. The Psalmist's many cries oscillate between heartfelt confession and impassioned supplication, illustrating the complexity and depth of communion with God in the storm. Prayer also manifests as adoration, where the heart, recognizing God's holiness and power, bows in worship despite circumstances. This act of praise amidst affliction testifies to a faith unshaken by the fiercest gales, echoing the triumphant melody that "the righteous shall sing and rejoice before God" (Psalm 68:3). Thus, prayer in the storm is not a monolithic act but a multifaceted communion that nurtures and sustains in myriad ways.

In Jesus Christ, the perfect exemplar of prayer in the tempest, we discern the model for our own petitioning in trials. On the night preceding His passion, He withdrew to solitary prayer, seeking the Father's will amid the weight of the cross. His anguished cries in Gethsemane reveal an honest, vulnerable engagement with God, capturing the essence of prayer as both surrender and appeal: "O my Father, if it be possible, let this cup pass from me: nevertheless not as I will, but as thou wilt" (Matthew 26:39). This prayer teaches us that in the storm, yielding our will to God's higher purpose lies at the heart of spiritual resilience. Prayer is thus both a refuge and a refining fire, shaping the soul into conformity with the divine image and will. It carries the paradox of human weakness and divine strength, where trembling hearts find boldness and trembling lips find confidence in the unchanging God.

It is worth considering that prayer, while intimate and personal, is also profoundly communal. The early Church gathered in unified supplication, their cries piercing the veil of the heavenly realms, resulting in miraculous deliverances and renewed boldness. In the context of the storm, communal prayer fashions a sacred net of support, buoying the isolated spirit with shared faith and witness. The words of James remind believers that "the effectual fervent prayer of a righteous man availeth much" (James 5:16), underscoring the potent efficacy of intercessory prayer when hearts join in holy concord. In the solitude of difficulty, this shared spiritual practice invites the believer not to despair, but to stand emboldened by the prayers of the saints surrounding them, friends, family, and all the faithful past and present.

Moreover, the discipline of prayer in the storm pulses with paradoxical peace: while the turmoil of circumstance may remain unaltered, the believer's soul is mercifully quieted. The King James text beautifully describes this peace as a "peace of God, which passeth all understanding" (Philippians 4:7), that guardeth the heart and mind in Christ Jesus. Prayer invites the soul into this divine peace, a sanctuary untouched by temporal distress, where one can lay down burdens and receive solace. It is a stillness fashioned not by absence of conflict but by the presence of the Almighty. As the writer of Hebrews exhorts, "Let us hold fast the profession of our faith without wavering; (for he is faithful that promised;)" (Hebrews 10:23), the act of prayer seals this reassurance in the believer's heart, nurturing a faith that does not flicker but burns steadfast and bright.

To engage in prayer during the storm is to engage in a holy labor of spiritual endurance. It requires a deliberate turning away from the cacophony of fear and doubt and a turning towards God's enduring promises. It is, as the psalmist declares, "a strong tower: the righteous runneth into it, and is safe" (Proverbs 18:10). The soul finds strength not in the silencing of trials but in the transcendent assurance that God's presence is ever near. The act of lifting one's voice upward, even when the heart falters, embodies a radical trust and hope that transcends sight, a hope springing eternal from the promised word, "I will never leave thee, nor forsake thee" (Hebrews 13:5). Such prayer becomes the anchor that holds fast in the fiercest storm, the unshaken faith that defies the tempests of life.

In closing our reflection upon prayer in the storm, let us remember it is not the storm's absence we pray for, but the God who calms the storm within. It is not a guarantee of ease, but a divine invitation to inhabit peace amid trials. To pray is to step onto the sacred ground where heaven and earth meet, where the eternal touches the temporal, and where the soul, though tempest-tossed, finds repose. May this practice become a refuge deeper than despair, a light more radiant than the darkest night, and a steadfast anchor in the boundless ocean of God's faithful love. In the storm, may the believer's heart continually rise in trust and adoration, to dwell evermore in the tranquil haven of the Divine presence through the sacred gift of prayer.

Listening in Prayer

In the sacred realm of prayer, amidst the fervent entreaties and the whispered supplications that ascend like incense before the throne of God, there lies a discipline oft neglected yet profoundly vital, the art of listening. To listen in prayer is to enter a tranquility beyond the clamor of our desires and beseechments, penetrating into the quiet recesses of the soul where God's still, small voice may be discerned. Herein is a truth as profound as it is simple: prayer is not solely the outpouring of words, but the receiving of divine whisperings. It is in the silence, the surrender, that the spirit is most richly nourished and the heart attuned to the mysteries of the Almighty. The King James Bible, with its majestic cadence, invites the believer not merely to speak but to hearken; for it is written, "Be still, and know that I am God" (Psalm 46:10), a summons to cease striving and embrace a sacred quietude.

The discipline of listening in prayer demands a spiritual posture of humility and receptivity, a readiness to set aside one's own agenda and to incline the ear toward heavenly counsel. It is a practice that fortifies faith, for in the absence of immediate answers or visible change, the soul learns to trust the unseen hand that guides all things according to divine wisdom and mercy. The patriarchs of old exemplified this sacred stillness. Abraham, when called to sacrifice, lingered in the silence of trust, and Isaac, upon the altar, heard the bounding ram in the thicket, a token of salvation. Elijah, fleeing despair, found God not in the tempest, fire, or earthquake, but in a gentle whisper that calmed his anxious heart (1 Kings 19). Such biblical narratives remind us that God's voice is often a soft murmur beneath the roar of worldly noise.

As we yield ourselves to this quiet discipline, may we recognize that prayer is less a torrent and more a steady stream, a communion of souls wherein the deepest dialogues unfold in silence. The ceaseless busyness of our hearts and minds tends to drown out these sacred murmurs; yet, as one who dips a vessel into a still pool finds a clear reflection, so too does the soul that abides in quietness beheld the shining face of God. To listen in prayer is to cultivate an interior sanctuary where doubt is stilled, fear is assuaged, and the promise of divine guidance illuminates each step. It is a grace that leads to transformation, as the Word that dwells within grows alive, shaping thoughts, softening wills, and inspiring acts of love that echo eternity.

This practice also teaches patience, for the answers we seek do not always come with the swiftness our human nature craves. The psalmist, in his many laments and praises, exhibits this trust in the delayed but certain providence of God. "Wait on the Lord: be of good courage, and he shall strengthen thine heart: wait, I say, on the Lord" (Psalm 27:14), is not merely counsel but a keystone of spiritual endurance. Such waiting, active and expectant, is not idleness; it is a sacred readiness, a fertile soil into which the seeds of divine wisdom may be sown and fruitfully harvested. As we listen in prayer, we become co-laborers with the Spirit, partners in the unfolding of God's eternal purposes.

Repeatedly, the Scripture illustrates that prayer entwined with listening creates a fertile ground for peace to flourish. The apostle Paul exhorts believers to "pray without ceasing," a command that suggests a prayerful openness to the Spirit's ongoing work within the heart (1 Thessalonians 5:17). Yet, this prayer without ceasing encompasses not endless vocalizing but an abiding consciousness of God's presence, a still mind attentive to the Spirit's promptings. It is within this sacred attentiveness that the restless soul is calmed, and the tumult of life finds a haven. The psalmist's declaration of God as a refuge and fortress (Psalm 91) is realized in those who practice the art of listening, discovering a sanctuary where faith is renewed, and the spirit is fortified against despair.

In practical realms, to cultivate the habit of listening in prayer may begin with intentional silence, a few moments each day set apart to hush the outward noise and quiet the inner turmoil. In these intervals, we open our hearts not only to speak but to receive, acknowledging that God communicates through Scripture, through the whisperings of conscience, through the gentle stirrings of the Holy Spirit. This attentive silence requires a diverted gaze from the distractions of the world, a turning inward to commune with the divine, much like Mary, who "kept all these things, and pondered them in her heart" (Luke 2:19), exemplifying contemplative receptivity. Here, prayer transcends petition and becomes a sacred dialogue, a dance of grace wherein the soul is progressively conformed to the image of Christ.

Moreover, listening in prayer enriches the believer's capacity to discern God's will amid life's manifold perplexities. When anguish, uncertainty, or decision presses heavily upon us, it is the silence of listening that often reveals the pathway illuminated by divine wisdom. It is within this quiet that the scriptures come alive; words that may have seemed distant suddenly burst forth with relevance and clarity, guiding the steps of the weary pilgrim. The Psalmist declares, "Thy word is a lamp unto my feet, and a light unto my path" (Psalm 119:105), a promise fulfilled not only through reading but through the meditative reception that prayerful listening nurtures.

Yet, this sacred art is not without its struggles. The soul accustomed to rushing and the habitually distracted mind must be disciplined to enter into this holy stillness. Temptations to fill every pause with thought or speech, to demand immediate answers, and to neglect the gentle nudges of the Spirit must be consciously resisted. The faithful pilgrim, nevertheless, presses onward, trusting that in due season the desire to listen will blossom into an intimate knowledge of God's heart. Such perseverance echoes the Apostle's own declarations of suffering and patience, as he embraced affliction with a spirit unbroken, knowing that "weeping may endure for a night, but joy cometh in the morning" (Psalm 30:5). The discipline of listening stands as a sentinel, guarding the soul through the darkest hours until dawn's first light of reassurance breaks.

Ultimately, to listen in prayer is to embrace a profound paradox: silence is not emptiness but fullness; stillness is not resignation but vibrant expectancy. Each prayerful pause beckons the believer into a deeper communion, where God's presence is palpably near, cradling the heart in divine love and peace. The soul learns that divine answers may come in the absence of spoken words, through peace that surpasses understanding, through the renewing of the mind, through the inexplicable assurance that God's purposes stand firm. This holy listening anchors the spirit amid life's storms, enabling the believer to stand unshaken, "rooted and built up in him, and stablished in the faith" (Colossians 2:7).

May the reader be encouraged, then, to slow the hurried pace, to hush the restless mind, and to enter at last into the sacred stillness where God awaits. In this sanctuary of silence, the whispered secrets of heaven become audible; grace descends as promised rain; hope is rekindled; and the soul is anchored in the eternal word. As you embark daily upon this journey of listening in prayer, may you find therein a wellspring of peace, the revival of faith, and the abiding presence of the God who speaks lovingly to all who will but stop and hear. Thus, prayer becomes not merely the lifting of words, but the ceaseless offering of the heart, attentive and open, to the divine voice that ever calls, comforts, and commands with unfailing love.

Prayers of Thanksgiving

In the quiet sanctuary of the soul, where the heart communes with the Eternal, there blossoms a sacred practice, a divine communion known as prayer. Among its many expressions, prayers of thanksgiving hold a place of profound significance, for they do more than merely utter gratitude; they cultivate a spirit attuned to the bounty of God's grace and mercy. To pray with thanksgiving is to lift one's eyes beyond the immediacy of circumstance and to behold the vast tapestry of divine providence that enfolds every moment of existence. It is a practice that transforms the heart, rendering it a wellspring of peace and joy, even amid the trials and tempests of life. In the majestic cadence of the King James Bible, we find this truth enshrined: "In every thing give thanks: for this is the will of God in Christ Jesus concerning you" (1 Thessalonians 5:18). These words invite us not only to a posture of gratitude but to the very will of God, an obedience that anchors the soul and sustains faith when shadows gather thick.

As we embark upon the journey of cultivating thanksgiving through prayerful reflection, consider how such prayers arise from an intimate recognition of God's innumerable blessings. This recognition is no mere list of favors received, but a deep, abiding awareness of the divine hand that guides creation and the individual believer alike. The psalmist, whose poetic meditations sing forth with reverence and praise, declares with earnest fervor, "O give thanks unto the LORD; for he is good: for his mercy endureth for ever" (Psalm 107:1). Here, thanksgiving is inseparable from the acknowledgment of God's unchanging goodness and enduring mercy. It is this constancy that invites our hearts to respond with thanksgiving, a response that, when made through prayer, becomes a sanctified exchange, a dialogue where human gratitude mingles with divine benevolence.

The act of thanking God in prayer transforms our gaze, shifting it from scarcity to abundance, from complaint to blessing. It pierces the veil of daily struggle, revealing treasures that might otherwise remain unseen. Even the simplest breath is a gift; every sunrise speaks of hope reborn; the presence of loved ones whispers the assurance of grace. When prayers of thanksgiving spring forth from such realizations, they weave a tapestry of spiritual vitality that bolsters faith and nurtures resilience. This phenomenon is not merely psychological but intrinsically theological, for in acknowledging God's wondrous works, we participate in the life of the Spirit, "Enter into his gates with thanksgiving, and into his courts with praise: be thankful unto him, and bless his name" (Psalm 100:4). Through our thanksgiving, we bear witness to the divine glory and invite God's sanctifying presence to dwell richly within our hearts.

It is essential to understand that prayers of thanksgiving are not rehearsed rituals but living conversations, expressions of a heart awakened to the sacred. The Apostle Paul's epistles exhibit this vitality as he frequently commends prayers of thanksgiving, exemplifying how gratitude forms the backbone of a vibrant spiritual life. In Philippians 4:6, he exhorts believers to "be careful for nothing; but in every thing by prayer and supplication with thanksgiving let your requests be made known unto God." Here, thanksgiving accompanies supplication, suggesting that gratitude does not preclude honest petitions but enriches them, framing our needs within the greater context of God's providential care. In this dynamic interplay, our prayers transcend mere asking; they become acts of trust, acknowledgments of God's sovereignty and grace even as we seek aid.

From the earliest chapters of Scripture, the motif of thanksgiving resonates as an enduring theme. The patriarchs and prophets, imperfect as they were, frequently lifted up their voices in grateful acknowledgment of God's faithfulness. Consider the Exodus narrative, where after deliverance from Egypt, Israel raised a song of thanksgiving: "I will sing unto the LORD, for he hath triumphed gloriously" (Exodus 15:1). This historic moment of praise reveals that thanksgiving is integrally linked to remembrance, the conscious recalling of God's saving acts. When we pray with thanksgiving, we too are invited into this sacred remembrance, allowing the truth of God's mercy to anchor our souls firmly against the shifting tides of circumstance.

Moreover, thanksgiving in prayer acts as a balm to the restless spirit. It cultivates contentment and peace that the world cannot give nor take away. As we recognize all good things as gifts, from the breath in our lungs to the love extended by a friend, our hearts are softened and renewed. The weight of burdens is eased, and the soul finds rest in the assurance that the God who has given so richly will continue to uphold us. This assurance is eloquently echoed in the words of the psalmist: "Thou hast put gladness in my heart, more than in the season that their corn and their wine increased" (Psalm 4:7). The gladness borne of thanksgiving is not contingent upon external abundance but springs from the inner well of divine grace.

Practically speaking, to cultivate prayers of thanksgiving, one might begin by setting apart moments in the day to reflect on God's blessings, large and small. This spiritual discipline involves a mindful attention to the presence and gifts of God, inviting the believer to articulate gratitude not as a fleeting sentiment but as a steadfast habit. This mindful thanksgiving engages the faculties of memory and imagination, reconstructing the day with eyes lifted toward heaven. Such prayerful reflection may be accompanied by scripture reading, allowing the sacred words to shape and expand the heart's gratitude. As the Psalmist exhorts, "My heart shall rejoice in thy salvation" (Psalm 13:5), so too may we learn to rejoice continually, even amid trials, knowing that thanksgiving is the altar where faith offers up its most fragrant sacrifice.

In addition, it is fruitful to recognize the communal dimension of thanksgiving. Though prayer is a personal encounter with the Divine, Thanksgiving prayers often find fuller expression within the gathered body of believers. The early Church practiced this in unity, offering "the sacrifice of praise to God continually" (Hebrews 13:15), thereby reinforcing bonds of faith through shared recognition of God's goodness. In this communal spirit, believers encourage one another to see beyond present adversity, to testify of God's faithfulness, and to rejoice together in hope. In our contemporary practices, whether in quiet solitude or in fellowship, prayers of thanksgiving remain a vital means of deepening faith and cultivating mutual encouragement.

The transformative power of thanksgiving in prayer cannot be overstated. It is not merely a duty or a formality, but a profound exchange in which our souls are anchored to the divine truth amidst the flux of life. To cultivate such prayers is to participate in a spiritual renewal that reorients the heart toward God, fostering resilience, peace, and joy. As the Apostle Paul attests, thanksgiving births contentment and wards off the corrosive influences of worry and despair. It is, in essence, the soul's hymn of trust and praise, a melody that lingers long after the moment of prayer has passed. Through this devotion, we come to understand that thankfulness is not the conclusion of the spiritual journey but its vital pulse, the rhythm that sustains and enlivens the faith within us.

Therefore, dear reader, let us embrace the prayers of thanksgiving as an indispensable discipline, a sacred habit that draws us ever closer to the heart of God. Let every breath be a note of grateful praise; every experience, a testament to His boundless mercy. In thanksgiving, the soul finds anchorage; in gratitude, we behold the face of the Eternal. May these reflections inspire you to infuse your prayers with heartfelt thanks, that your spirit may be renewed and your faith made steadfast, as you journey onward, anchored ever in the Word.

Intercessory Prayer

In the sacred art of intercessory prayer, we find ourselves drawn into a divine dialogue that transcends the mere utterance of words and becomes a profound ministry of the heart. This prayer, offered on behalf of others, is a tender expression of godly compassion, a spiritual act that bridges the abyss between human frailty and the boundless grace of the Almighty. When we lift our voices in fervent petition for another, we participate in a holy covenant, exercising faith not only in God's power but in His infinite mercy, which moves with special tenderness toward those for whom we plead. Intercession thus becomes both a gift and a solemn responsibility, an outpouring of love that seeks to entwine the hopes and burdens of others with the unfailing promises found within the hallowed pages of the King James Bible.

As the Psalmist declares, "The effectual fervent prayer of a righteous man availeth much" (James 5:16), so too does the intercessor discover that their prayers carry a potency that reaches far beyond their understanding. This efficacy is not born of eloquence or human might, but from a deep communion with God's will and a humble surrender to His sovereign will. It is in these moments of earnest entreaty that hearts are softened, lives are renewed, and the invisible hand of God moves to bring peace amid tumult. We must therefore approach intercessory prayer as a sacred trust, recognizing that it is not simply a ritual or duty, but a living outflow of God's love through us to others, a channel through which divine grace flows toward healing, justice, and restoration.

In the pages of Scripture, we are beckoned to behold the powerful examples of intercession. The patriarch Abraham, standing before the Lord, pleads for Sodom, imploring God's mercy for the sake of the righteous found within that doomed city. His words echo through the ages: "Wilt thou also destroy the righteous with the wicked?" (Genesis 18:23). Abraham's prayer reveals the intercessor's heart, a heart that stands in the breach, wrestling with God for mercy on behalf of the undeserving. Then we behold Moses, who, after the great sin of the Israelites with the golden calf, falls upon his face before the Lord, pleading not for his own sake but for the people he shepherds. His intercession is a moving testament of love and responsibility, for he stands between a holy God and a rebellious people, seeking God's forgiveness with fervent passion. Moses' prayers remind us that intercession is not casual but costly, a humble offering of self on behalf of others.

These scriptural giants teach us that intercessory prayer requires more than superficial petitions; it demands a heart deeply engaged and a spirit aligned fully with God's purposes. When we pray in this manner, we are not merely speaking into the void but entering a sacred conversation where divine justice, mercy, and grace are stirred to action. The Apostle Paul calls us to "make supplication, prayers, intercession, and giving of thanks for all men" (1 Timothy 2:1), underscoring the breadth of our calling to envelop the world in prayer. This call reaches into the little corners of our daily lives where named individuals, family members wrestling with trials, friends beset by uncertainty, communities enduring hardship, become the objects of our holy advocacy. Just as the Good Shepherd seeks after the lost, we too are invited to seek the welfare of the souls entrusted to our care through persistent, loving intercession.

The discipline of intercessory prayer cultivates spiritual empathy and nurtures the soul's capacity to bear witness to another's suffering and hopes. It is in this sacred labor that we learn what it means to "weep with those that weep" and to "rejoice with those that do rejoice" (Romans 12:15). Our prayers do not merely catalogue needs or transcribe a litany of requests; rather, they immerse our spirits in the sacred mystery of bearing one another's burdens. This deep sharing reshapes our hearts, softening pride, igniting compassion, and expanding our vision beyond self to encompass the collective body of Christ. In praying for others, we are drawn closer into the divine embrace, discovering that the heart that intercedes is itself transformed by grace and made more like the heart of God.

Moreover, intercessory prayer is a means by which faith is both exercised and strengthened. As we wrestle in prayer on behalf of another, uncertainty and hope entwine, offering a spiritual discipline that refines our trust in God's timing and sovereignty. The tranquility of faith is forged when we relinquish control, submitting our loved ones into the hands of the Everlasting. This surrender is no sign of weakness but a courageous act of dependence, acknowledging that while we cannot control outcomes, we can lift the needs of others before the throne of grace with persistence and humility. In this sacred exchange, we learn the beauty of waiting on the Lord, trusting that He who hears the cries of the humble will answer in His perfect wisdom and boundless love.

Intercession also serves as a balm for the petitioner's own soul, an oasis of peace amid the storms of life's complexities. When the heart is burdened by the pain and strife witnessed in the lives of others, prayer becomes a refuge, a sacred place where anxiety is exchanged for divine peace. The Apostle Paul's repeated prayers for the early churches illustrate how intercession is bound up with gratitude and hope, weaving worship into petition and fostering a devotional rhythm that sustains both giver and recipient. Through intercessory prayer, we participate in a divine economy in which grace begets grace and love is multiplied through our faithful words of entreaty.

To embrace the discipline of intercessory prayer, one must cultivate quietude and attentiveness to the Spirit's prompting. It demands that we slow the relentless pace of our lives and enter moments of stillness where we can truly hear the groaning of the Spirit within us and the call to advocate for others. This spiritual posture invites reflection on the vastness of God's mercy and the profound truth that no soul is forgotten in His sight. Our prayers, fueled by compassion, become luminous threads woven into the tapestry of redemption, connecting hearts across time and space in a harmonious chorus of supplication and praise.

In praying for others, we also align ourselves with the intercession of Christ Himself, the eternal High Priest who "always liveth to make intercession for us" (Hebrews 7:25). This divine intercession supplies both assurance and inspiration as we recognize that our petitions are carried before God by the perfect love and righteousness of Jesus. His presence encourages us to persist in prayer, knowing that He advocates continually on our behalf, bends the ear of Heaven toward our cries, and dispenses grace beyond measure. We are therefore invited to embody this sacred ministry on earth, standing as representatives of God's mercy and expressing His love in active communion with those in need.

As the spiritual guide for this journey, I encourage the reader to enter into this holy practice with a heart wide open, filled with compassion and grounded in sacred Scripture. Let each intercession be saturated with the words of the King James Bible, drawing strength from its majesty and timeless wisdom. Meditate upon the narrative arcs of those who prayed with earnestness and power, allowing their passion and perseverance to inform your own dialogue with God. Prayer, in this mode, is no further than the breath we take and as intimate as the deepest cries of our soul. It is in the stillness of such prayers that the world is irrevocably altered and the hearts of men and women are transformed by the unfathomable power of divine love.

Therefore, as we conclude this reflection on intercessory prayer, let us be mindful that each petition is an act of sacred service, a bridge between human need and heavenly provision. With humility and faith, let us lift the burdens of others, confident that our prayers are heard and that God's hand moves wondrously to heal, guide, and sustain. May our intercessions flow continuously like a river of grace, refreshing souls and bearing witness to the endless compassion of our Heavenly Father, whose love never fails and whose mercy endures forever. Amen.

Persistent Prayer

In the sacred discipline of prayer, there resides a profound and enduring power that transcends the fleeting distractions of this world. To persist in prayer is to anchor oneself securely in the eternal presence of God, even when the heavens seem silent, and the soul feels barren of comfort. The scripture exhorts us to "continue instant in prayer," urging a steadfastness that neither waneth nor fainteth, but endureth with the certainty of divine attentiveness. Truly, it is in the persistent, unyielding act of communing with our Heavenly Father that our hearts are transformed, our faith refined as gold in the fire, and our weary spirits restored to a place of tranquility and hope. Prayer, then, is not simply an utterance of words or a momentary petition; it is a continual abiding with God, a spiritual lifeline that nourisheth the soul amidst trials, and an unfailing channel through which grace is poured upon us in abundance.

Consider the examples writ large upon the tapestry of biblical narrative, men and women of God who exemplified the fruit of persistent prayer. The prophet Elijah, for instance, knelt upon Carmel's mount and called upon the Lord with fervent supplication, refusing to yield until fire descended from heaven and revealed God's power unto all the people. His persistence was met not by weariness, but by the Almighty's unmistakable presence. Likewise, the widow in Luke's gospel showed the power of relentless petition; she came before an unjust judge time and again, unwavering until justice was secured. Through such stories, the sacred Word reveals to us that perseverance in prayer is not a mere exercise of persistence unto human ends, but a holy invitation to participate in the unfolding of divine will. When our prayers are prolonged in devotion and faith, they shape not only our circumstances but our very souls, aligning our desires with the heart of God.

Yet, the path of persistent prayer is not without its seasons of challenge. The heart may grow faint, the eyes weary with tears, and the silence of heaven may stir questions within the depths of our being. It is in these moments of seeming deafness that the discipline of steadfast prayer is tested and proven most precious. Remember the exhortation given to the disciples by our Lord: "Men ought always to pray, and not to faint." The encouragement here is not for weariness to claim us, but for endurance to be the melody of our spirits. Prayer, when practiced as an unwavering habit, becomes the balm that soothes doubts, the fire that renews courage, and the anchor that holds firm against the tempestuous seas of anxiety and despair. Our persistence reflects the confidence that God's timing is perfect, His wisdom surpassing our understanding, and His love unceasing.

Moreover, within the embrace of persistent prayer lies the mystery of transformation. It is not always our prayers that are changed, but our hearts that are softened and made receptive to God's answers, sometimes in unexpected forms. The Lord's response may be a gentle whisper in the quiet stillness, a profound peace that surpasseth all understanding, or a divine redirection that unfolds with gracious clarity over time. In continuing to pray, we cultivate a sacred space where trust flourishes, a trust that, though we tarry long, God remains sovereign and ever faithful. This endurance in prayer is a testimony to the intimate fellowship between the believer and the Almighty, a fellowship built not on instant gratification but on patient, committed dialogue with the Eternal One.

The variety and richness of prayer life also invite us into a deeper appreciation of its persistent nature. There is the prayer of adoration, which steadfastly magnifies God's name and exalts His majesty throughout the changing seasons of life. This prayer, sustained over time, anchors the soul in reverence and awe, preventing us from succumbing to the distractions of the world. There is the prayer of confession, which persistently brings our frail humanity before the

Holy One, illuminating the path toward repentance and renewal. Through continual confession, the heart is cleansed and restored. Then, there is the prayer of thanksgiving, a sacred habit that seizes upon every blessing, no matter how small, and offers grateful praise day after day. Such thanksgiving, when practised with persistence, cultivates a heart resilient against despair. Lastly, intercessory prayer, lifting others continually before God's throne, is itself a powerful exercise in persistent love and compassion, reflecting the boundless grace of the Divine.

As you journey through this sacred practice, remember that persistent prayer is not measured in the eloquence of words, but in the sincerity of the heart and the constancy of seeking presence with God. It is not a test of strength but a humble submission to the one who giveth mercy and grace. In the quiet moments when words fail, faith alone can carry the burden of prayer, holding fast to the promise that "the effectual fervent prayer of a righteous man availeth much." This enduring prayer becomes the spiritual heartbeat that pulses through the believer's life, maintaining connection with the source of all hope and strength.

May this truth inspire the soul to embrace persistent prayer as a sacred discipline, a refuge in times of trouble, and a joyous communion in every season. Let these reflections draw you into the sacred rhythm of continual supplication, where the spirit may find its rest, and the soul may rise renewed with steadfast trust. As you persist in prayer, may the peace of God, which passeth all understanding, keep thy heart and mind through Christ Jesus. In persevering prayer, find the sacred invitation to dwell in the light of divine presence, ever anchored in the unchanging Word.

Hope in Trials

Light in the Darkness

Amid the shadows that often cloak the pathway of life, there shines a steadfast beacon, a light undimmed by the tempest that howls and the night that presses ever so heavily upon the heart. It is the light of God's presence, a divine illumination summoned forth from the everlasting Word, piercing the gloom of affliction and despair. In the midst of our trials, when the fabric of our resolve seems threadbare and the weight of sorrow bends the soul low, the sacred promise that God is our guide and strength stands as an unshakable refuge. The psalmist declares, "Thy word is a lamp unto my feet, and a light unto my path" (Psalm 119:105), a truth that resonates through the ages, whispering peace into the tempest's roar. This divine light does not merely flicker in the distance; it envelops us, dispelling doubt and anxiety, and beckons the weary to press forward with a hope that transcends understanding.

In the palpable darkness of hardship, when human sight falters and earthly wisdom fails to provide clarity, the faithful soul finds solace in the radiant guidance of God. It is here, within the valleys shadowed by affliction, that the luminous Word fortifies the spirit and kindles an invincible courage. To trust in this heavenly illumination is to embrace a paradox, that in acknowledging our weakness and helplessness, the power of God is made perfect, and thus the light shines brightest where darkness once prevailed. Life's storms rage fierce and unrelenting, yet the Good Shepherd, whose countenance glows with mercy and grace, leads His flock beside still waters and restores the soul. The believer, anchored firm in this truth, fears not the darkness, for in the divine light there is no cause for dread but a deepening assurance that no night lasts forever, and the dawn is certain to follow.

How beautiful is the ordaining of divine providence, whereby the trials designed to test and refine find their resolution in the illumination of heavenly wisdom! When the heart is sorely tried by loss, loneliness, or uncertainty, the Spirit breathes life into weary limbs anew and fainting courage. It is as though a lantern is lifted high over the chasm of despair, throwing golden beams on the promises contained within the sacred text. "Yea, though I walk through the valley of the shadow of death, I will fear no evil: for thou art with me" (Psalm 23:4), assures the eternal Shepherd, whose rod and staff comfort amidst the deepest gloom. This pastoral care transcends temporal suffering, inviting the soul into a communion of peace that the world neither understands nor confers. The divine light becomes not only a guide through physical danger but a balm for the spirit, searing away the wounds of doubt and kindling a flame of eternal hope.

In such moments, the devotional heart rests upon the sacred anchor of God's steadfast promises, the very foundation upon which one's faith securely stands. Darkness may arise from various sources; the loss of a loved one, the sting of betrayal, the fog of illness, or the weight of personal failure. Yet, within these shadows, the light of Scripture emerges as a steadfast companion. Consider the words of Isaiah: "When thou passest through the waters, I will be with thee; and through the rivers, they shall not overflow thee: when thou walkest through the fire, thou shalt not be burned; neither shall the flame kindle upon thee" (Isaiah 43:2). This assurance is not mere comfort but an active promise of divine presence in every trial. The God who commands the sun to rise and the stars to sing their silent hymns is also intricately attentive to the trembling footsteps of the suffering. In the darkest glooms, His illumination shines unceasingly, a beacon of hope and a promise of deliverance for those who cling to His word.

To dwell within this holy light is to experience a transformation of spirit, wherein despair is transmuted into strength and fear into faith.

The believer is invited to lift eyes upward, to behold the brightness that dispels the night, trusting that "the light shineth in darkness; and the darkness comprehended it not" (John 1:5). In this divine radiance, the soul finds clarity, it is a clarity born not of human reason alone but of spiritual revelation, where God's purposes outstrip the fleeting comprehension of mortal minds. The trials endured are refined through the lens of eternal hope, and within the crucible of suffering, the faithful emerge renewed, their faith not only preserved but deepened. Every step taken in the grace-filled light strengthens the spirit's resolve to persevere, to continue walking in trust even when the path lies obscured by the mists of uncertainty.

Moreover, this light is not static or distant but dynamically alive within the communion of prayer and worship, where the believer communes with the Source of all hope. Prayer becomes the sacred channel through which the soul draws near to this guiding illumination, and worship the joyful proclamation of trust in God's providence. It is through the sacred dialogue with the Almighty that the believer finds the courage to endure, the peace that surpasseth understanding, and the joy hidden deep amid tribulation. A heart anchored in prayer is fortified against the corrosive forces of despair, drawing strength from the throne of grace where mercy flows abundantly. This communion also nurtures resilience, allowing the soul to bloom amid adversity and to rise each day with renewed vigor, confident that the light of God's Word will guide every step in righteousness.

Indeed, the enduring power of this divine illumination lies in its ability to shape one's perspective, to grant a vista beyond the immediate affliction toward the eternal horizon. While shadows here on earth may be thick and the night long, the believer's gaze is lifted to the promise of morning and the unending light of God's kingdom. The apostle Paul exhorts us to fix our eyes not on temporal trials but on the unseen everlasting glory, encouraging a perseverance that outlasts and outshines all earthly sorrow. It is this spiritual vantage point, rooted steadfastly in the Word, that sustains the soul during hardship, granting the fortitude to rise each day with hope and trust anew. Through this divine lens, what once appeared as insurmountable darkness becomes but a fleeting shadow, a foil to the brilliant light of God's mercy and faithfulness shining eternally.

Thus, the journey through difficulty is transformed by the sacred illumination that the King James Bible so eloquently reveals. It is in this light that the weary find rest, the fainthearted find courage, and the wandering soul finds direction. May this be a balm to your spirit amidst trials, a guiding beacon that banishes all despair and renews your faith with each dawn. As the Psalmist entreats, may your heart ever rejoice in the light of God's Word, confident that He "will never leave thee, nor forsake thee" (Hebrews 13:5). Let this divine illumination be the anchor that holds firm your soul, the gentle fire that warms your night, and the steady lamp that guides your feet. Embrace this light, dear reader, and walk forth in hope, assured that no darkness can overcome the brilliance of God's everlasting love.

Joy Comes in the Morning

In the quiet moments before dawn, when the world still lies in shadow, and the heart wrestles with weariness, there blooms an ancient truth that carries the soul beyond despair: joy comes in the morning. This profound declaration, echoing from the sacred verses of the King James Bible, offers hope that is not fleeting or fragile, but steadfast and enduring, a hope anchored in the promises of the Almighty. Life, in its relentless unfolding, often casts long shadows of hardship, sorrow, and uncertainty. The burdens borne by the heart can weigh heavily, threatening to snuff out the light of joy and peace that once kindled within. Yet it is precisely in these moments of darkness and despair that hope, rooted in divine assurance, emerges as a sustaining flame, tender though it may be, calling the soul to persevere and to trust in the God who ordains the dawn.

There is a sacred rhythm to our existence, a divine cadence set by the Creator who declares the morning will come, no matter how long the night prevails. This is not merely poetic consolation but a promise etched into the fabric of heaven and earth. When the Psalmist intones, "Weeping may endure for a night, but joy cometh in the morning," he proclaims not only a temporal truth but a spiritual principle: hardships and sufferings, as real and piercing as they are, are transient shadows that cannot withstand the rising light of God's deliverance. It is this hope that summons the believer to hold fast, to tarry in faith when the present moment is filled with grief or trial. For morning, both literal and metaphorical, is emblematic of renewal, restoration, and the unyielding faithfulness of God's mercies made new each day.

To embrace this hope is a courageous act, a conscious choice to trust beyond the immediate pain and confusion. It requires a steadfast heart that refuses to be subdued by despair, a spirit willing to look beyond the veil of suffering to the dawn's radiant promise. Consider the seasons of your life when storms raged fiercely; the night may have felt unceasing, the burdens relentless, yet if you paused and listened, the whisper of hope gently stirred within, urging you to endure. Such hope is not idle wishfulness, but the confident expectation rooted in the character of God, who is unchanging, who promises to never leave nor forsake His children. This divine hope is a fortress in times of trouble, an anchor when the waves of life threaten to uproot your peace.

Prayer, too, becomes a vital channel through which hope sustains the weary soul, connecting us to the eternal source of strength and comfort. In the sacred space of communion with God, burdens are cast upon His shoulders, and grace is replenished as a wellspring of joy springs from the depths of the spirit. Through prayerful reflection on Scripture, the soul is reminded that God's promises shine like stars in the dark vault of night, steadfast and unwavering. It is here, in the trembling yet faithful utterances of the heart, that the believer finds solace and the fortitude to rise again with renewed vigor. The morning does not come solely as a passing of time but as a spiritual awakening, a moment when the soul discerns the presence of God's sustaining love breaking forth like the dawn.

Moreover, this hope is transformative; it is not merely about awaiting a brighter day but about cultivating a joy that transcends circumstances. It nurtures resilience, that sacred strength which allows one to face each trial with courage and grace. Such joy is woven with threads of gratitude, faith, and trust, qualities born from dwelling in God's Word and resting in His promises. When the heart fixes its gaze upon the eternal rather than the temporal, the soul discovers a well of peace that remains unshaken even amidst the fiercest storms. The vision of joy coming in the morning becomes a beacon that guides the believer, illuminating the path through darkness with the knowledge that suffering and sorrow are but brief interludes in the grand symphony of God's redemption.

As the first rays of sunlight pierce the horizon, so too does hope break through the despair within. It is the divine assurance that no matter how dense the night or how unrelenting the trial, God's faithfulness prevails, and joy is restored in due season. This awakening joy is a testament to the resurrection power that undergirds the believer's journey, a proof that the soul, though tested, is never forsaken. It is an invitation to embrace each new day with a heart brimming with expectation, allowing the light of God's presence to dispel fear and foster a serene confidence in His sovereign plan.

In this, the believer is called to actively participate in hope's renewal, standing resolute amid adversity and holding onto the eternal promises as an anchor for the soul. It is a hope that deepens with time, fortified by prayer, Scripture, and the communion of saints, drawing strength from the collective witness of those who have persevered before. The morning's joy is thus both a gift and a discipline, cultivated in the fertile soil of faith and watered by tears of trust. It instructs the soul that while night may bring shadows, morning invariably brings new mercies and fresh opportunities for rejoicing in the goodness of God.

So let the heart, though troubled and wearied, not despair but await the dawn with unwavering faith. For joy that cometh in the morning is not a distant dream but a present reality to be embraced in hope. It is the solemn promise that every sorrow will yield to gladness, every tear to laughter, and every affliction to victory. Anchored in this truth, the soul finds strength to persevere, courage to endure, and peace that surpasses all understanding. In the fullness of time, the morning breaks to illuminate the path ahead, revealing the constancy of God's love and the everlasting sanctuary found only in Him.

Strength Renewed

In the tumult of our earthly sojourn, when shadows lengthen, and the heart feels faint beneath the weight of affliction, there rings forth a clarion call from the sacred text, an invitation to gird the loins of the soul and to find strength anew in the immutable promises of the Almighty. The prophetic voice of Isaiah resounds as a beacon through the dusk of despair: "But they that wait upon the LORD shall renew their strength; they shall mount up with wings as eagles; they shall run, and not be weary; and they shall walk, and not faint." Herein lies a timeless truth, an assurance whispered down through the ages, that amidst the shifting sands of our mortal trials, there abides a refuge unshaken, waiting upon the Lord, a deliberate posture of patient faith, becomes the wellspring from which fresh vigor flows. To wait, in this sacred sense, is not mere idleness nor passive endurance, but an active, expectant hope fortified by steadfast trust. It is to place one's reliance not on the frailty of human effort but on the eternal character of God, whose boundless grace reneweth the weary spirit and replenisheth the parched soul.

The soul that embraces this divine promise is not exempt from the tempests of life, yet it is endowed with an inner might, a resilient stoutness born not of outward circumstance but of inward divine companionship. The Apostle Paul, though beset by trials manifold, affirms this profound reality in his epistle to the Corinthians: "When I am weak, then am I strong." How paradoxical and yet how true, that in the very crucible of weakness and affliction, the spirit may be refined and empowered by the strength imparted of God. Such strength transcends mere physical vigor or intellectual resolve; it is a mysterious sustenance that steadies the heart when hope flickers and courage falters, enabling the believer to press forward through the wilderness of desolation.

To persist in faith amid hardship demands a steadfast anchoring in the divine word, a continual returning to Scripture where God's promises stand as pillars of light amidst the darkness. As the psalmist so beautifully expresses, "Thy word is a lamp unto my feet, and a light unto my path." The scriptures are not mere stories of ancient days but living waters that nourish the thirsty soul and awaken courage where despair lurked. Each sacred passage breathed by the Spirit serves as a fortress, a sanctuary where weariness is soothed and the faltering spirit is uplifted. Meditating upon the steadfast love of the Lord, the believer is invited to mirror the patience of Job, who in his profound suffering exclaimed, "Though he slay me, yet will I trust in him," thereby demonstrating a profound resilience that transcends understanding. Such faith is not naive or blind but is anchored deeply in the experience and testimony of God's unwavering faithfulness.

In the journey of endurance, the believer often finds strength not only in scripture but in the quiet, abiding presence of God, which imparts a peace surpassing all understanding. This peace is not the absence of struggle but an interior stillness that calms the tumultuous waters of the soul. It is the hand of God upon the shoulder of the anxious, the silent whisper that steals into the night song of the weary heart, assuring that the trials of the present are but momentary afflictions working out a far more exceeding and eternal weight of glory. The psalmist affirms this when he declares, "This God is our God for ever and ever: he will be our guide even unto death." The knowledge of such steadfast companionship kindles a fire of hope that cannot be quenched by circumstance, for it rests not on shifting sands but on the eternal rock of divine fidelity.

Moreover, spiritual resilience is nurtured within the fellowship of the faithful, where burden-bearing is shared, and prayers ascend like incense to heaven. In the communion of saints, the weary are uplifted by the encouragement of others who have traversed similar valleys and emerged clothed not in their own strength but in the power of Christ. The epistle to the Hebrews exhorts believers to "consider one another to provoke unto love and to good works, not forsaking the assembling of ourselves together," reminding us that strength is often renewed through the mutual support and shared faith of a community bound by the spirit of Christ's love. The intertwining of hearts in prayer and encouragement forms an enduring bond that fortifies the individual and kindles a collective hope that burns brightly even in the coldest winters of the soul.

Prayer, too, is the secret wellspring of renewed strength, a sacred dialogue where the soul unburdens itself before the Lord and is filled with divine comfort and courage. The words of the Psalmist become a melody of assurance: "Cast thy burden upon the LORD, and he shall sustain thee: he shall never suffer the righteous to be moved." This heavenly exchange transforms weakness into strength and fear into faith, inviting the believer to lay down every care, every anxiety, and to arise, strengthened and emboldened by the gentle whisper of God's presence. Prayer becomes a lifeline stretched across the tumultuous sea of trial, drawing the weary to the shore of peace where the spirit can breathe deeply once more.

Yet, this renewal of strength is not a one-time occurrence but a continual process, a daily grace that beckons the believer to rise each morning with eyes fixed upon the cross, where Christ's own suffering and victory proclaim the ultimate triumph over every adversary. The Apostle Paul, in his letter to the Philippians, exhorts, "I can do all things through Christ which strengtheneth me." This declaration embodies the essence of spiritual perseverance: the acknowledgement that human frailty is met and overcome through divine empowerment. The renewing of strength, therefore, is not reliant on human resolve but is an ongoing infusion of grace that flows from communion with Christ, enabling the believer to run, and not be weary; to walk, and not faint.

In the quiet reflection of these truths, the soul is invited to a profound rest, an acceptance that strength renewed is a gift, not earned by might but received through faith. It is the balm that soothes the bruised spirit, the light that dispels the encroaching gloom, the unshakable foundation upon which one may stand firm amid the fiercest storms. Here, in the sanctuary of God's promises, the weary find rest and the faint-hearted are lifted, for the Lord Himself is their refuge and strength, an ever-present help in trouble. Let the heart, therefore, be kindled with hope, embracing the eternal assurance that those who wait upon the Lord shall indeed renew their strength, mount up with wings as eagles, and soar beyond the limitations of earthly trial into the boundless skies of divine grace and peace. Amen.

Peace Beyond Understanding

Amid the swirling tempests and the unrelenting storms that buffet the soul, there abides a peace that surpasseth all understanding, a peace not fashioned by the fleeting comforts of the world, nor wrought by the hands of men, but a divine serenity bestowed from the very throne of God. This peace, as the Apostle exhorts in his epistle to the Philippians, "passeth all understanding," guarding the hearts and minds of all who tether their spirits to its infinite source. To embrace this peace amid trials is not merely to endure adversity, but to lay hold of a supernatural quietude that transcends reason, rising like a fragrant incense above the din of despair. It is a gentle yet unmovable anchor entrenched deep within the soul, set firm by the sure promises of Him who maketh all things work together for good to them that love Him.

In the midst of tribulation, when the shadows lengthen and the night seems without end, the believer is summoned to a higher vantage, a sacred refuge where sorrow acquiesces to hope, and fear is stilled by trust. The King James Bible, in its majestic cadence, proclaims that the peace of God shall keep your hearts and minds through Christ Jesus. This is the peace that does not require the absence of conflict or trial, but rather thrives amidst them, shining brightest when the world around seems cloaked in uncertainty. It is not a fragile truce against the chaos, but a mighty fortress in which the soul finds solace, fortified by the omnipotent hand of the Almighty. To surrender to such peace is to rise above the tumult of the moment, to clasp the eternal rather than the transient, and to see with eyes enlightened by faith the tapestry God weaveth from the threads of suffering and grace.

Yet, this divine peace is no cheap gift, nor is it granted to the idle or the faithless. It is a prize wrought from the furnace of affliction, a treasure revealed when the self is laid bare and pride yields to the sovereign will of God. The believer, faced with trials that threaten to overwhelm, must cultivate patience and perseverance as companions upon this journey inward, a pilgrimage toward the heart of divine calm. Like David, who found in God a refuge when enemies encompassed him, so must we seek our sanctuary not in the shifting sands of circumstance, but in the immovable rock of God's truth. Herein lies the paradox of peace: it is born not of ease but of surrender, not of control but of trust, and not of understanding but of faith. To know this peace is to enter into a sacred silence where the tumult of questions and doubts are stilled by the quiet assurance of God's presence.

How often, in the throes of suffering, do we seek understanding where none is given, striving to unravel the mysteries of pain with finite minds that grasp but a shadow of divine purpose? The peace that passeth understanding guards against such restless searching. It consoles the heart that cannot comprehend, and comforts the soul that cannot discern. This tranquil state arises when the believer lays down the burden of explanation, releasing control and resting wholly in the hands of a loving and sovereign God who worketh all things after the counsel of His own will. It is here, in this relinquishment, that the soul is freed from the tyranny of fear and anxiety, and sheltered beneath the wings of everlasting love. We are invited, then, to be still and know that He is God, not to fret or flurry, but to anchor ourselves in the sure and steadfast promise that He who holds the universe also holds our trembling hearts.

Embracing this sacred peace transforms the trials themselves; hardship ceases to be merely a burden and is transfigured into a refining flame. The soul that rests in God's peace is not untouched by sorrow, yet it is sheltered from despair. Like the quiet night that follows the fiercest storm, this peace brings rejuvenation and clarity, enabling the believer to press onward with renewed strength. The words of the Psalmist echo the enduring truth that those who trust in the Lord shall not be moved, their steadfastness founded upon the rock of divine faithfulness. The peace of God becomes a balm in the night watches, a lamp unto the feet, a shield in the battle. It is both refuge and fortress, a hidden strength in weakness, a wellspring of hope that flows unceasingly despite the trials that rage without.

To grasp this peace fully is to embark upon a daily surrender, a continuous choosing to align one's heart with the voice of God rather than the tumult of the world. In moments of prayer and meditation upon His word, the believer invites this peace to dwell richly, cultivating a spirit attuned to the presence of the Holy One who quieteth all storms. The devotional journey through Scripture reveals how the saints of old, from Job's patient endurance to Paul's triumphant declaration of joy in tribulation, found their anchor in this very peace. Their lives become a testimony that God's peace is no fleeting feeling but a powerful reality accessible to all who draw near in faith. This peace nurtures the soul, enabling love to flourish even in adversity and hope to kindle anew when all seems lost.

Finally, the embrace of peace beyond understanding is inseparable from a heart fortified by prayer. Through prayer, the believer enters into communion with God, casting every care upon Him and finding rest in His presence. Prayer is the channel through which the still waters of peace flow into a restless soul, uniting mind and spirit in harmonious trust. It is through such holy conversation that the turbulent waves of worry are calmed, and the mind, once occupied with anxious musings, is renewed with tranquil confidence. In this sacred dialogue, the believer learns to see beyond the immediacy of suffering and fix their gaze upon the eternal glory that awaits those who endure. Thus, prayer is both the gateway and the nourishment of peace, drawing the soul ever closer to the heart of God.

May we, therefore, embrace this precious peace in the midst of our trials, allowing it to anchor our weary hearts and quiet our troubled minds. Let us rest not upon our own understanding, but upon the unshakeable promises of our God, who is the Author and Finisher of our faith. Though the storms of life may rage and the night may grow long, the peace of God standeth eternal as a beacon of hope and refuge, guiding us safely home. With hearts attuned to this divine quietude, may we persevere with joy, trusting that this peace which passeth all understanding shall keep us, now and forevermore.

Gary E. Risenhoover

Walking in Love

Love is Patient

Love, in its purest and most enduring form, reveals itself through patience. To say that love is patient is not merely to suggest a quiet endurance of time or circumstance, but rather to portray a divine disposition that flows with grace and tempered strength amidst the trials and imperfections of human existence. The apostle's august words, "love is patient," echo through the corridors of Scripture with a solemn majesty, inviting the reader into the profound reality that patience is not a reluctant bearing of burdens but an active, tender choice that nurtures and sustains the beloved. It is through this patience that love manifests its full glory, allowing for growth, healing, and transformation, not only in the lives of others but within ourselves.

Patience, when viewed through the lens of divine love, takes on a sacred character. It is not a passive wait or a stoic withholding of emotions; instead, it is a holy waiting, a fertile pause that embraces the imperfections and frailties of those we cherish. In a world rife with hastiness, where instant gratification often undermines depth and understanding, to love patiently is to defy the current of impatience that flows so strongly through human hearts. It requires a steadfastness that mirrors the eternal constancy of God's love, which abides unwavering through all seasons. This steadfast love is patient with our faults and hesitations, our faults and slow progression, and teaches us that to truly love another person is to give them the sacred space of time, to grow, to change, and to be fully known without condemnation.

The transformative power of this patient love is seen most clearly in its capacity to foster spiritual growth. Just as the farmer waits patiently for the tender shoots to rise from the earth, so does the patient lover wait for the unfolding of the soul in others. This waiting is imbued not with frustration but with hope and expectation, planted deep in the knowledge that love's labor is never in vain. Faith, hope, and love intertwine here beautifully, for patient love trusts in God's timing rather than its own desire for immediate reward or recognition. It speaks, therefore, to the deepest of spiritual truths: that growth is a journey, not a race; that mercy is more powerful than judgment; and that kindness flourishes not by force but by gentle and enduring presence.

The patience borne from love also transforms our daily interactions, coloring the way we move through the bustling, often unpredictable landscape of community and relationships. Each encounter becomes an opportunity to practice this divine love, to embody for others the forbearance we ourselves hope to receive. How often do misunderstandings, differing opinions, or petty irritations test the limits of our forbearance? How frequently does the glow of love falter in the face of inconvenience or fatigue? It is through patient love that these moments become touchstones for grace rather than triggers for discord. When we pause, breathe, and choose love's patience over the rush to amend or blame, we cultivate an environment where hearts are safe to reveal their true selves, where friendships deepen, and where the bonds of community are strengthened.

Moreover, patient love in action is a balm to the weary soul, both for the giver and the receiver. In moments of trial, when anxiety and sorrow press heavily upon the spirit, to be met with patient love is to be wrapped in a cloak of divine reassurance. This gentle endurance suggests a sacred solidarity that whispers, "I am here with you; I will not rush past your pain or overlook your struggles." The patience that love grants does not waiver at hardship but steadies the heart to endure alongside the sufferer, offering hope that dawn will break and healing will come in due season. Such love mirrors the great mercy of Christ, who bore our infirmities and carried our sorrows with an unyielding patience that restores and redeems.

Yet patient love also demands a peculiar courage, not the brash valor of the world, but a quiet, sustained fortitude that persistently chooses kindness over bitterness, understanding over judgment. In loving patiently, one often subsumes the desire to control or correct, embracing instead the mystery of another's journey. This humility resonates deeply with the recognition that we ourselves are not perfect and that we, too require the patient love of God and others. It is this mutual dependence on patient love that knits the fabric of genuine community, where each person can be seen and loved as they are, not as we wish them to be. The willingness to wait, to forgive, and to hope despite obstacles becomes a living testimony to the power of divine love shaping human hearts.

Furthermore, the poetic cadence of "love is patient" invites a meditation on the rhythm of grace that governs the heart of Christian life. Patient love stands at the intersection of time and eternity, inviting believers to slow their hurried pace and dwell in the sacred now, where God's kingdom is both present and promised. In this divine temporality, patience is an act of worship, a surrender of self to the will of God, who orchestrates all things for good according to His perfect plan. Through patience, love aligns itself not with the fleeting desires of the moment but with the eternal purposes of justice, mercy, and peace. To embody patient love, then, is to walk daily in the footsteps of Christ, who, for the joy set before Him, endured the cross, despising the shame, and patiently bore the weight of the world's sin so that all might be reconciled.

The practice of love's patience also opens a sacred space for forgiveness and reconciliation, where lingering wounds may be tenderly healed over time. It invites the heart to resist the urge to despair or to sever ties in frustration, instead holding fast to hope that brokenness may be mended. This patience is not passive submission to wrong but an active, enduring resolve to seek restoration and peace. It is the slow turning of the heart toward compassion even when hurt lingers, the continued extending of grace even when forgiveness is difficult. Through this process, love's patient hand becomes a force of renewal, polishing the rough edges of human frailty into the smooth brightness of sanctified relationship.

In reflecting upon patience as an expression of love, we come to see it as a gift both received and given, a sacred channel through which the endless love of God flows into and through us. To love patiently is to mirror the heavenly love that never hastens, never falters, and never fails. It is a transformative power that reshapes our souls and the souls of those around us, creating communities of grace where each person feels valued and upheld. The patience that love insists upon may seem small or even burdensome at times, yet it bears within it the seeds of resurrection and new life. Patience teaches us to trust not only in others but in the very goodness and sovereignty of God, whose love patiently sustains the cosmos and each fragile heart within it.

As we meditate upon the truth that love is patient, let us invite this divine truth to permeate our relationships and our daily walk. Let us ask for the grace to embody this love in moments of frustration and conflict, recognizing that in patience we bear witness to God's enduring mercy. May our hearts be softened, our spirits calmed, and our faith deepened as we embrace the slow, steady, unshakable love that waits, endures, and nurtures. In doing so, we not only participate in the sacred dance of divine love but also become vessels of that love, bringing warmth, healing, and hope to a world in desperate need of patient hearts.

Love is Kind

In the boundless expanse of divine love, kindness emerges as the gentle expression that breathes life into the heart of every believer. The Apostle Paul, in his timeless epistle to the Corinthians, reminds us that love "suffereth long, and is kind." This kindness is not a mere sentiment or fleeting emotion; it is a steadfast, deliberate soul-choice that reflects the very nature of God's tender compassion toward humanity. As vessels fashioned by the Maker's hand, we are called to mirror this heaven-born kindness, that our lives might become radiant reflections of His grace, fostering bonds that transcend the ephemeral and ground us in the eternal. To understand love as kind is to grasp a cornerstone of Christian living, for it beckons us beyond mere tolerance, to a proactive benevolence that seeks the good of others with a heart unfeigned and spirit willing.

The divine kindness we are enjoined to embody is woven richly throughout the sacred text, portrayed vividly in parables, prophetic exhortations, and the compassionate deeds of Christ Himself. When the Savior approached the outcast, the leper, the woman with the issue of blood, or even the tax collector Zacchaeus, His kindness was unmistakable, tender, restoring, and luminous. This kindness bore no record of wrongs but extended the hand of restoration and love, breaking the chains of societal rejection and elevating the soul to a place of dignity. Such kindness, dear reader, is transformative. It is not a weakness, but a power that breaks down barriers and builds up hope within the weary and the brokenhearted. It turns the cold hearth of judgment into a warm fire of mercy, offering light to the shadows of despair.

To live in this kindness is to cultivate an attitude that prizes patience and forgives readily, that offers solace where there is pain, and comfort where there is sorrow. This is the kindness that moves beyond the superficial exchanges of civility to the depths of self-emptying sacrifice, as exemplified by Christ's own passion for mankind. In daily life, such kindness might manifest in the gentle word to a hurried stranger, the helping hand extended to one in need, the quiet act of forgiveness where resentment longed to take root, or the listening ear offered without judgment or haste. Each act, though small in the eyes of the world, echoes the grand narrative of God's redemptive love and re-weaves the fabric of community into a tapestry rich with grace. This love is kind, indeed, and its fruitfulness is seen in relationships that heal rather than harm, in communities that nurture rather than neglect.

Consider also the Apostle Paul's stirring exhortation in the letter to the Ephesians, where kindness is listed among the fruits of the Spirit, a hallmark of the transformed life. To be kind, then, is a divine calling to embody God's own nature, adopting His tenderness as the lens through which we view others. It is to be sensitive to the struggles of the soul, to rejoice with those who rejoice, and to weep with those who weep. Such kindness refuses to tally grievances or retaliate in anger, but rather embraces humility and gentleness, remembering how great a debt we ourselves have been freely forgiven. In this way, kindness becomes a sacred currency within the kingdom of heaven, a means by which we dispense grace upon grace, imitating the Lord whose mercy endures forever.

Yet, the call to kindness is not without its challenges. The world often rewards the harsh and the hurried; cruelty masquerades as strength, and weakness is mistaken for kindness. But the believer anchored in the Word knows otherwise, true strength is born of gentleness, and the greatest victories are won with the weapons of patience and love. To choose kindness, particularly in trying circumstances, is an act of courage that draws upon the sustaining power of the Holy Spirit. It requires us to rise above natural inclinations toward bitterness or retribution, to embrace instead a posture of peace and restoration. Herein lies the secret: kindness is not merely a natural virtue but a supernatural fruit, cultivated through prayer, reflection, and reliance on the divine. As we bow before God's throne with hearts open to His guidance, we receive a fresh enabling to be kind, to love not in word alone but in deed and truth.

Imagine a community where kindness reigns supreme, where the weary find encouragement and the lonely find companionship. Such a community mirrors the heavenly city, the New Jerusalem, where love and kindness flow like a river, and no heart is left untouched by divine mercy. Every act of kindness, however small, becomes a sacred offering, a fragrant incense rising to heaven in honor of the God who is love. It fosters unity amid diversity, peace amid conflict, and healing amid brokenness. In the quiet moments of reflection, one recognizes that kindness is a bridge, connecting the gulf between estranged souls, reconciling differences, and building lasting friendships rooted in the heart of God.

As we meditate upon the sacred scriptures, let us not overlook the practical outworking of kindness in our own lives. It behoves us to ask: Are our words seasoned with kindness, or do they cut like a sword? Do our hands serve willingly, or do they close in selfishness? Is our spirit quick to forgive, or slow and burdened by offense? The gentle admonitions of Scripture invite us to cultivate kindness as a daily discipline, shaping our character and molding our witness. We are reminded that in doing kindness, we serve Christ Himself, for as He declared, "inasmuch as ye have done it unto one of the least of these my brethren, ye have done it unto me." In kindness to others, we honor the Lord, and our lives become living testimonies to the transforming power of His love.

Finally, let us close this reflection with a prayerful heart: O Lord, Author of all goodness and mercy, instill within us a love that is gentle and kind, a heart that seeks to bless and not to harm. May our tongues speak words that heal, our hands do works that nurture, and our souls overflow with the kindness that mirrors Thy divine nature. Teach us to bear one another's burdens with grace and patience, reflecting the kindness which first reached out to us when we were lost. Strengthen us to respond to injuries with forgiveness, to meet hostility with love, and to cultivate a spirit of humility that esteems others above ourselves. May our lives be anchored in Thy Word, that kindness may flow freely from us as rivers of living water, bringing refreshment and renewal to all whom we encounter. Through Jesus Christ, our kind and loving Redeemer, we pray. Amen.

Forgiveness and Reconciliation

To embrace forgiveness and reconciliation is, indeed, to step upon the sacred pathway where the soul is tenderly mended by the very hand of divine love. The King James Bible presents forgiveness not merely as an act, but as a profound expression of the heart's transformation, a relinquishing of bitterness and a bold release into the realm of grace. In the epistle to the Ephesians, we are exhorted to "forgive one another, even as God for Christ's sake hath forgiven you." This sacred exhortation unfurls the eternal truth that forgiveness is not merely a favor we grant others, but a reflection of God's own mercy extended towards us. Within this holy framework, reconciliation unfolds as the natural fruit borne of forgiveness, a healing balm that restores fractured relationships and reknits the torn fabric of human communion. It is through this divine love, reflected in our willingness to forgive, that walls of resentment and discord crumble, yielding space for peace and restoration to reign.

When we meditate upon forgiveness, we perceive it first as an inward renewal, a gentle yet resolute turning away from the allure of wrath and retaliation. The scriptures remind us that the heart, though often wounded by transgression, possesses the capacity to be renewed and cleansed by the Spirit's tender working. "Be ye kind one to another, tenderhearted, forgiving one another, even as God for Christ's sake hath forgiven you," the apostle implores, weaving kindness and tenderheartedness into the very fabric of forgiveness. Such forgiveness is not borne of weakness nor feebleness but springs from the well of divine strength that enables us to extend compassion where hurt once dwelled. It transforms the receiver and the giver alike, lifting both into a higher plane of spiritual maturity.

Moreover, forgiveness is an active choice that demands courage and humility, a surrender of pride so that love may flourish unimpeded by the shadows of offense. It calls us to remember the mercy we have received, awakening a responsiveness that mirrors God's own heart. In the Gospel of Matthew, our Lord teaches that if we hold grudges, our own prayers may be hindered; thus, forgiveness becomes not only a gift to others but a key that unlocks divine communion and peace within ourselves. By forgiving, we release ourselves from the captivity of anger and bitterness, stepping instead into a freedom generated by grace, the very freedom Christ suffered and died to bestow upon us. This liberty deepens our trust in God's sovereign justice, allowing us to relinquish the desire for vengeance and embrace reconciliation as a sacred mission.

Reconciliation, then, is the beautiful unfolding of forgiveness into restoration, a divine art that heals rifts and knits souls together in love's embrace. It does not overlook the pain or deny the reality of brokenness but invites us to ascend beyond hurt through the power of love's renewal. The story of Joseph in the Old Testament offers a poignant testimony to this truth. Betrayed by his brethren, cast into the pit of betrayal and slavery, Joseph's journey culminates not in bitterness but in the gracious restoration of relationship, revealing how God's providence weaves reconciliation from the threads of human failing. Through Joseph's example, we see the transcendent grace that flows when forgiveness births reconciliation, transforming betrayal into blessing, enmity into unity.

Furthermore, this divine love extends far beyond individual relationships and touches the very heart of community and church life. Forgiveness and reconciliation are the cornerstone of the body of Christ, the spiritual community called to embody God's kingdom on earth. Within this sacred assembly, love serves as the binding force that holds us together, enabling us to bear one another's burdens and to "endeavour to keep the unity of the Spirit in the bond of peace." Such unity is not a shallow harmony but a deep accord grounded in the recognition of our shared fallibility and shared redemption. It demands a daily surrender to love, an openness to forgive and to seek forgiveness, and the cultivation of a kingdom culture where grace is spontaneous and abundant. This continuous cycle of forgiveness fosters a witness that cannot be silenced, for it speaks to the power of God's love to heal even the most grievous wounds and restore hope where despair once reigned.

As we reflect upon the role of forgiveness in spiritual growth, it becomes evident that these acts of mercy are not mere duties but paths to profound transformation. Each time we choose to forgive, the heart is enlarged, and the spirit emboldened to love more deeply, extending beyond what is comfortable or convenient. It mirrors the patient endurance and boundless mercy of the Savior, teaching us to walk in His footsteps of humility and compassion. Forgiveness draws us ever nearer to the heart of God, unveiling a depth of grace that sustains us amid trials and imperfections. It nurtures a spirit of peace within, guarding the soul from the corrosive effects of bitterness and resentment, and freeing us to pursue holiness and joy.

Moreover, forgiveness and reconciliation invite us into a daily renewal of relational love, love that is active, sacrificial, and steadfast. It prompts us to perform daily acts of kindness, gentle words of encouragement, and deeds of selfless service, all borne out of a heart yielded to divine love. In the quiet moments of prayer, we are invited to seek God's strength to forgive those who have wronged us, and likewise, to request the grace to ask forgiveness from those we have wounded. This reciprocal journey of humility and grace knits us more closely to one another and to the Lord, shaping communities that mirror heaven's peace. Our relationships become living testimonies to the divine love that redeems and restores, flourishing as spaces where the presence of God is palpably felt.

Ultimately, to be anchored in the Word's teaching on forgiveness and reconciliation is to embrace a holy freedom, a liberation from the chains of offense and a deliberate walk in the light of Christ's love. It is to recognize that through forgiveness, we mirror the heart of God, who "is slow to anger, and of great mercy." It is to open our souls to the transformative power of grace that heals wounds, rebuilds trust, and breathes life into relationships made whole. Within this spiritual embrace, we find the courage to love beyond our fears, to heal beyond our hurts, and to renew relationships not by our strength alone but by the infinite love poured forth through the Savior's sacrifice. Thus, forgiveness and reconciliation stand as living testaments to the triumph of divine love over human brokenness, inviting us all into a deeper experience of peace, restoration, and unshakable hope. In this sacred space, the soul finds rest, the heart finds healing, and love's holy work is revealed in all its radiant glory, anchored eternally in the Word.

Love in Action

To walk in the footsteps of divine love is to embrace a calling that transcends mere sentiment and blossoms into tangible expression, permeating every fiber of our daily existence. The King James Bible speaks with luminous clarity about love, not as a fleeting emotion, but as a steadfast force that binds the soul to God and to one another in sacred unity. "Charity suffereth long, and is kind; charity envieth not; charity vaunteth not itself, is not puffed up" (1 Corinthians 13:4). Herein lies a divine blueprint for love's manifestation, one that beckons us beyond the confines of self-centeredness toward a life of selfless giving. When love is put into action, it becomes a river of mercy flowing outward, nurturing the weary and sowing seeds of grace in the barren stretches of human hearts. It is this river we are invited to enter daily, quenching the thirst of those around us not only with kind words but with deeds that embody the very essence of Christ's compassion.

How then do we, frail vessels though we are, embody such love each day? Firstly, the gospel of love impels us to cultivate an active attentiveness to the needs of our neighbors, those often unseen or unheard, whose burdens may be heavy and silent. Small gestures, seemingly insignificant in the rush of the world, become vessels of divine grace when carried out with a heart attuned to God's mercy. Offering a listening ear to a troubled friend, sharing a meal with the hungry, or extending forgiveness to one who has wronged us are not mere acts of charity, but sacred rituals of love that mirror the Almighty's boundless mercy. Like the Good Samaritan who crossed the road to bind wounds and bear another's pain, so too must our love be incarnate, stepping boldly into the messiness of human need, unafraid to become the balm of healing in a fractured world.

Moreover, embodying love demands humility, that quiet surrender of pride which allows God's gentle hand to move us into places of service and sacrifice. It strips away the veils of self-importance and reveals a heart eager to serve rather than to be served. The King James Bible's call to "love thy neighbour as thyself" (Matthew 22:39) resounds not merely as an ethical commandment, but as an invitation to reorder our affections, placing the well-being of others alongside our own in harmonious balance. In practical terms, this might mean setting aside our preoccupations, our deadlines, our discomforts, our desires, in order to be present fully to someone who needs encouragement, tenderness, or restoration. It may mean greeting the stranger with a smile glowing with genuine warmth, or offering patience in moments of frustration rather than haste or indifference.

Each such act, though it may pass unnoticed by the world, is a sacred step upon the path of love incarnate, a testimony to the enduring power of God's presence alive in us.

Yet love in action is not limited to interactions alone; it reaches deeply into the fabric of how we live, the ways we use our time, energy, and resources. To love as God loves is to steward all that has been entrusted to us with care and generosity. This includes the oft-overlooked gifts of our talents and abilities, which, when employed in service to others, become instruments of grace and growth. Think of a teacher who pours patience and wisdom into nurturing young minds, or a volunteer who gives countless hours to those suffering hardship, their efforts singing a chorus of divine love through deeds. Our worldly possessions, too, can become conduits of love when shared freely rather than hoarded in selfishness. The practice of generosity transforms the mundane into the sacred, sewing threads of hope into the tapestry of community life. Thus, love is no mere abstraction but a living force that breathes through the choices we make each moment, inviting us to be co-creators with God in building a world marked by kindness and mercy.

In the journey of embodying divine love, we are also called to confront the shadows of resentment, bitterness, and judgment that can harden the heart and block the flow of grace. The King James Bible encourages us to "forgive one another, even as God for Christ's sake hath forgiven you" (Ephesians 4:32), reminding us that love and forgiveness are inextricably linked; without the courage to forgive, love remains incomplete. Whether the wounds we carry are fresh or long buried, the act of releasing another into God's hand is a radical expression of love, freeing both the giver and receiver from the chains of past hurt. This forgiveness is not denial of pain, but a courageous acceptance of God's healing hand, a surrender that allows love's pure light to shine through even the darkest valleys. In this way, love is a transformative force, dismantling barriers erected by pride and pain and paving the way for renewal.

In practice, love's manifestation can be woven into the cadence of everyday life through simple yet intentional habits of kindness and service. Consider the power of greeting each morning with a prayerful commitment to love deliberately: to seek opportunities to uplift, to act with compassion, to bear burdens gently alongside those in distress. The smallest acts, holding open a door, offering an encouraging word, writing a note of gratitude, or simply lending one's presence in attentive silence, become expressions of divine love when they flow from a redeemed heart. These focus our spirits on the eternal rather than the trivial and remind us that love's work is never finished. In cultivating such daily disciplines, the believer's life gradually becomes a living epistle, a proclamation of God's goodness and faithfulness to a watching world.

As we extend love in action, our relationships are transformed. Love becomes the mortar holding together the fragile walls of human connection, enabling communities to withstand trials and flourish amid diversity and difficulty. The patient tenderness of love soothes discord and nurtures unity, revealing a foretaste of the heavenly fellowship to which we are called. Each act of love in the ordinary sphere contributes to the sacred architecture of the Church, a living sanctuary where God's presence dwells richly. It reminds us that our spiritual renewal is inseparable from our outward expressions of grace; to love truly is to be renewed in the likeness of Christ, whose own life was the perfect embodiment of sacrificial love.

Finally, the wellspring of our love in action springs forth from constant communion with God, the source of all love. As we anchor ourselves daily in His word, we are filled with a love that knows no bounds, a love that empowers and sustains us even amidst weakness. Through prayer and meditation upon Scripture, our hearts are softened and stirred, our vision cleared to see others through God's eyes of mercy. It is in this sacred exchange, from God's heart to ours, then from ours to the world, that love's fire is fanned into a flame that never dies. Thus, love in action becomes not a burden but a joy, a divine dance in which we partner with the Spirit to reflect heaven's glory here on earth.

May this reflection stir within you a holy yearning to embody love daily, not out of obligation but as a grateful response to the magnificent love first poured into your soul. Let your hands and feet become instruments of kindness, your words bridges of hope, and your heart a sanctuary where God's love dwells without ceasing. In doing so, you partake in a sacred legacy, anchoring your life firmly in the eternal truth that "God is love," and those who abide in love abide in God, and God in them (1 John 4:16). Such love, expressed and lived, transforms not only others but your very self, crafting a life both blessed and a blessing.

God's Everlasting Love

In the quiet recesses of the soul, where the tumult of the world's clamour fades into a distant murmur, there lies a truth as steadfast as the stars, a love immutable and eternal, the divine embrace that neither time nor tempest can diminish. This love, revealed in the sacred scriptures of the King James Bible, captures the heart with a majesty that transcends mortal understanding. It is not a fleeting affection wrought by circumstance, nor a tender feeling conditioned by reciprocity; rather, it is the unchanging, all-encompassing love of God, an everlasting covenant that holds fast even when human frailty falters. To meditate upon God's everlasting love is to enter into a sanctuary of spiritual renewal, where the soul is anchored and fortified against the shifting sands of life's uncertainties. The Apostle Paul, in his epistles, extols this divine love as the very bond of perfection, the great tether by which God draws His children into union with Himself, unwavering and eternal. Thus, the believer is called to ponder this sublime truth, allowing it to transform not only their own heart but also to overflow in acts of kindness and compassion that mirror the radiance of God's love to a world hungering for hope and restoration.

As we contemplate the nature of this divine affection, we find it woven into the fabric of creation and the very breath of our existence. "For God so loved the world, that he gave his only begotten Son," the sacred text declares, a testament to the profound depth of God's mercy and grace. This love is not abstract nor distant; it is incarnate, manifest in the sacrifice and the promise of redemption, demonstrating that love's true power lies in surrender and self-giving. In this, we witness a perfect example of love's transforming power, that through divine love, even the broken, the weary, and the lost find restoration and purpose. There is a tenderness here, a gentle yet unyielding force that shapes the believer's journey, calling them to lay aside burdens of fear and doubt and to rest fully in the assurance of God's unwavering care. The heart, which at times may feel isolated or abandoned, is invited into the warmth of an embrace that never loosens, a sanctuary where the soul may find peace amidst the storm.

Moreover, the constancy of God's love serves as a mirror reflecting how His children ought to relate to one another and the world around them. Divine love is not a passive sentiment but an active choice, a commitment to embody mercy, forgiveness, and generosity in daily life. Just as God's love is enduring, so too must the love we cultivate be steadfast, resisting the erosive powers of resentment, bitterness, and selfishness. In the words of the Psalmist, "The Lord is good, a strong hold in the day of trouble; and he knoweth them that trust in him." This intimate knowledge of God's goodness inspires believers to extend grace in their relationships, fostering communities bound not by convenience but by the holy cords of love that reflect God's own heart. Such love bears all things, believes all things, hopes all things, endures all things, and in doing so, it becomes a wellspring of spiritual vitality, nourishing both the giver and receiver in a sacred exchange that honors the divine image in all people.

The transformative power of God's love is perhaps most vividly seen in its capacity to heal wounds, both hidden and apparent, that life inevitably inflicts. When embraced with full trust, this love dissolves the chains of guilt, shame, and loneliness, replacing them with a renewed sense of worth and belonging. It is a balm for the soul, a light in darkness that restores vision and renews purpose. Believers, invited to dwell within this embrace, are likewise called to become conduits of healing in the world, reflections of God's compassion extended through acts of kindness, patience, and understanding. Each gesture of love, no matter how small, echoes the eternal covenant and contributes to a communal holiness that speaks loudly amidst a culture often marked by division and despair. Indeed, to love as God loves is to participate in a redemptive work, a sacred vocation that cultivates not only personal sanctity but also heartfelt unity within the body of Christ and beyond.

In our daily walk, the reality of God's everlasting love challenges us to surrender pride and self-reliance, inviting instead a humble dependence upon divine grace. It urges a reevaluation of our motives and actions, probing whether our love is rooted in the fleeting and often fickle sentiments of the world, or firmly anchored in the sacrificial and eternal love of our Maker. This reflection fosters spiritual growth, as the believer's heart is gradually transformed to mirror the likeness of Christ, who exemplified perfect love through unwavering obedience and mercy. The journey toward such love is neither swift nor easy, yet it is marked by the ever-present assurance that God's love will never cease, will never falter, and will always guide the weary traveler home. Through prayer and meditation on scripture, one cultivates a living relationship with this divine love, nurturing it as a flame that dispels the chill of despair and kindles a holy fire of hope, faith, and endurance.

Furthermore, the richness of God's love encompasses countless dimensions that invite continual discovery and awe. It is steadfast beyond measure, extending "from everlasting to everlasting," encompassing all creation without partiality. It is patient, not insisting upon its own way, and rejoicing in the truth, unshaken by the tides of human sinfulness or doubt. This love is also just, holding accountable yet forgiving abundantly, a holy paradox that confounds worldly wisdom but embodies divine perfection. To touch the hem of this love is to be drawn into a life marked not by fear of judgment but by a deep and abiding confidence in God's faithful presence. Such confidence nurtures courage, enabling believers to face trials and tribulations with a faith anchored not in circumstances but in the unmovable foundation of God's promises.

As the reflections draw to a close, the reader is beckoned to receive this love anew, allowing it to penetrate the hidden chambers of the heart, where true renewal takes root. It is a love that whispers reassurance in moments of solitude, that sustains when the night is dark and the path uncertain. It is the love that calls forth the best within us, inspiring acts of selfless compassion that ripple outward, touching the lives of many. In embracing this divine love, the believer finds a wellspring of peace that transcends mortal understanding, an anchor sure and steadfast amid life's ceaseless waves. May each meditation upon God's everlasting love awaken within the soul a fresh yearning to abide in this holy embrace, that through it, life itself may be transformed into a living testimony of grace, mercy, and unending hope.

Love That Sacrifices

In the quiet dawn of our contemplation, when the soul turns inward seeking a glimpse of divine mystery, we are irresistibly drawn to the greatest demonstration of love ever shown, the love of Christ, a love that sacrifices all for the sake of the beloved. This love, etched in the sacred ink of the King James Bible, stands as an eternal beacon, illuminating the darkest valleys of human experience with the purest light of grace. Such love is not merely a gentle affection or a fleeting sentiment; it is a profound, unwavering commitment that entails surrender, agony, and triumph intertwined. It is the love that, beholding the multitude fraught with sin and frailty, lays down its life as a ransom for many, exemplifying the very essence of divine charity and mercy. To behold this love is to witness the boundless depths of God's heart, reaching beyond measure to embrace the unworthy and restore the broken.

The Apostle Paul, in his epistle to the Corinthians, reveals this sacrificial love in words that resound through the corridors of time: "Charity suffereth long, and is kind; charity envieth not; charity vaunteth not itself, is not puffed up... endureth all things, believeth all things, hopeth all things, endureth all things." Here, charity, agape love, is painted with strokes of enduring patience and humble strength, qualities born of selfless sacrifice rather than mere human desire. This passage beckons us to a love that does not flinch in the face of hardship or insult but rather perseveres, choosing the well-being of the other above one's own comfort and pride. In the crucible of such love, selfishness is dissolved like morning mist before the rising sun, and a new nature emerges, shaped by the merciful and redemptive hand of God.

The narrative of Christ's passion reveals a love so potent it shatters the cruelest chains of sin and despair. Upon the cross, suspended between heaven and earth, hung the incarnate Word, who bore the weight of every sorrow, every transgression, and every thorn that marred the human condition. This was love made manifest not through soft words or gentle deeds alone, but through the ultimate sacrifice of self, embracing suffering and death to secure life for others. Such a love is transformative, for it does not merely inspire admiration from afar but invites participation and imitation. As we gaze upon the lamb slain from the foundation of the world, we are called to lay down our own lives, our pride, our bitterness, our indifference, to follow in His footsteps, loving as He loved, giving as He gave.

Yet, the miracle of sacrificial love extends far beyond the cross. It moves in the quiet acts of kindness that punctuate everyday life, the patient listening to a troubled heart, the forgiveness offered where resentment might have taken root, the compassion shown to the outcast or the stranger. Each act, though seemingly small, reflects the vast ocean of God's love made tangible in human form. Such love heals invisible wounds, bridges chasms of misunderstanding, and builds communities knit together by grace rather than mere social contract. It is through these simple but profound exchanges that the Kingdom of God advances; for where love that sacrifices reigns, there is peace, there is joy, there is fellowship hidden even amidst life's storms.

Contemplating this sacrificial love challenges us to examine the motivations of our own hearts. Are we willing to endure hardship for the sake of another? Can we relinquish our desires and expectations, embracing humility and compassion as Christ did? This spiritual inquiry is not an abstract exercise but a living dialogue with the Spirit, urging us from comfort to courage, from isolation to solidarity. True love, rooted in the divine, is never self-seeking; it sacrifices not out of obligation alone, but because it knows the surpassing joy that only comes when we give freely and fully. In the Apostle's words, it "rejoiceth not in iniquity, but rejoiceth in the truth," bearing all burdens and remaining unshaken amidst trials.

Moreover, sacrificial love acts as a furnace refining our faith, purging the dross of selfishness and pride that often cloak the soul. Each act of giving, be it time, resources, forgiveness, or presence, tests and strengthens the roots of our spiritual vine. It is in these moments of surrender that our connection to God deepens, for we align ourselves with the heart of the Father who gave His only begotten Son. This alignment nurtures resilience, teaching us that true strength lies not in dominance or accumulation but in vulnerability and selflessness. Thus, love that sacrifices becomes both a lamp to our path and a balm to our spirits, guiding us steadily toward holiness.

In a world weary with division, where the clamor of self-interest often drowns the gentle voice of mercy, the call to sacrificial love is all the more urgent. It stands as a redemptive force capable of bridging ethnic, social, and ideological divides; it invites us into a fellowship that transcends circumstance and creed. When we love with a heart willing to sacrifice, we mirror the divine love that knows no bounds, becoming agents of transformation in our families, churches, workplaces, and neighborhoods. The ripple effect of a single act of sacrificial love can set in motion waves of grace that affect generations, revealing the invisible but powerful hand of God at work in human history.

Yet, embracing such love requires more than noble intentions; it demands a continual turning toward God in prayer and dependence. In the silent chambers of devotion, we learn to receive the strength to love as Christ loved, to forgive as He forgave, and to bear burdens as He bore them. Prayer becomes the wellspring from which sacrificial love flows, a sacred exchange in which we offer our wills and receive afresh the Spirit's grace. This communion transforms not only how we love others but how we perceive ourselves, not as isolated individuals but as beloved children of God called into a holy community united by sacrificial affection.

As we meditate upon the love that sacrifices, let our hearts be stirred to action and surrender. Let us pray that the same divine flame kindled on Calvary might burn within us, driving out selfishness and igniting a passion for mercy that does not waver. May we find comfort in the knowledge that this love, though it requires cost, is the path to true freedom and joy, a joy that surpasseth all understanding, rooted in the eternal embrace of God's unwavering grace. In reflecting on this love, may our spirits be anchored firmly in the Word, strengthened to face life's trials, and inspired to live a testimony of grace in a world thirsty for authentic, transformative love.

Love as a Witness

The sacred tapestry of love, as woven throughout the Scriptures, bears a testimony far deeper than mere words can express; it is in the doing of love that faith finds its truest witness before the eyes of the world. When the Apostle John declared, "Hereby perceive we the love of God, because he laid down his life for us," he spoke not only of a divine act but of a living example that beckons the believer to embody that same love in daily existence. It is through acts of kindness, humility, and mercy that the invisible grace of God takes visible form, becoming a lamp unto the feet of wandering souls who hunger not merely for doctrine, but for the tangible fragrance of Christ's compassion. This is the love which never faileth, a love not confined to the sacred pages but spilling over into quiet deeds, be it in the offering of a gentle word to the weary, the patient bearing of another's burdens, or the silent prayers whispered on behalf of enemies. Such love becomes a mirror reflecting the divine, a reservoir of light that cannot be hidden but shines forth irresistibly in community and kinship.

In the crucible of daily life, love manifests as the sacred language which transcends barriers of race, station, and creed, fostering unity where discord might otherwise reign. It is the gentle hand extended in forgiveness, the heart that chooses reconciliation over rancor, and the spirit that resists the temptation to judge, all bearing witness to a love that is rooted not in human effort alone, but in the unchanging grace of God. To love as Christ loved is to testify silently yet powerfully that faith is alive and active, for "faith without works is dead," and the works of love are its most eloquent proclamation. This love acts as a balm to the broken-hearted and a beacon to the lost, drawing others into the embrace of spiritual renewal. It is a love that offers no reproach, no boastfulness, but is clothed with humility and kindness, enduring all things and believing all things, thus reflecting the steadfastness of God's own covenant with His people.

To share one's faith through loving behavior is to participate in the sacred dance of divine grace meeting human need, where every favor shown and every kindness bestowed becomes an incarnate sermon, more compelling than spoken argument or written text. Such love calls us beyond the confines of our comfort, inviting us to live not for ourselves but for the edification of others, thereby advancing the kingdom of God in tangible ways. When the love of Christ dwells richly within, it transforms the believer into a living epistle, read of all men, whose daily walk honors the commandment to "love one another as I have loved you." Thus, love stands not as a passive sentiment but as a dynamic witness, breaking down the strongholds of fear and prejudice and sowing seeds of hope and peace. In this sacred labor, the believer becomes both recipient and dispenser of grace, a channel through which God's unyielding love flows freely to renew, restore, and reconcile a weary world.

The Fruit of the Spirit

Love and Joy

In the sacred text of the King James Bible, the fruits of the Spirit are presented not as fleeting or superficial traits, but as the very essence of a transformed life, a life anchored in divine love and the joy that only God can bestow. Among these heavenly virtues, love and joy stand as foundational pillars, deeply intertwined and inseparable from the soul's true renewal. To love, as the Scriptures teach, is not merely an emotion or a gentle inclination; it is the commandment etched upon the heart by the Almighty, a call to embody the divine nature itself. "Charity suffereth long, and is kind; charity envieth not; charity vaunteth not itself, is not puffed up," the Apostle Paul declares in his epistle to the Corinthians, elevating love as the enduring force that conquers all. This love is patient and selfless, a mirror of God's own unwavering affection toward humanity. It beckons believers not only to receive but to radiate this love outward, transforming relationships and nurturing a community built upon grace and truth.

Joy, then, flows naturally from a heart anchored in such love. It is a deep and abiding gladness that transcends the changing tides of circumstance. Unlike the mere happiness of the world, which is often tethered to fleeting pleasures and temporal successes, biblical joy roots itself in the eternal promises of God. Psalm 16:11 proclaims, "Thou wilt show me the path of life: in thy presence is fulness of joy; at thy right hand there are pleasures for evermore." Here, joy is not capricious but a sacred wellspring, springing forth from the believer's communion with the divine. It is the melody of the soul rejoicing even amidst trials, a steadfast confidence that God's presence imbues life with meaning and hope. This joy nurtures resilience and peace, anchoring the spirit when storms arise, and teaching a profound contentment that no worldly affliction can mar.

To cultivate love and joy within one's spiritual journey calls for an intentional turning toward God's word and presence. The ancient texts invite us to dwell continually upon the character of God, whose love "endureth forever" (Psalm 136:1), and whose joy is made perfect in those who trust Him. It is through prayerful meditation, sincere worship, and humble surrender that the heart opens itself to these blessings. The reader is gently urged to consider the practical outworking of this love, for it manifests in acts of kindness, in forgiveness extended beyond measure, and in a generous spirit that mirrors Christ's sacrifice. As we love others earnestly and selflessly, we begin to embody the very nature of God, thus nourishing the soul's deepest longings and cultivating a joy that defies circumstance.

Yet, love and joy do not thrive in isolation; they are fruits nurtured by the broader garden of spiritual disciplines and the abiding Spirit's work within. They are kindled alongside peace that surpasses understanding, patience that waits with hope, gentleness that comforts, and self-control that restrains the passions of the flesh. These virtues form a holy tapestry that sustains the believer, weaving resilience into the fabric of daily living. To foster love and joy is to embrace a sacred dance with the Spirit, yielding to His guidance, and allowing Him to prune away those things that would choke or impede growth. This spiritual cultivation requires vigilance and grace, an ongoing surrender to God's renewing power. With every moment spent in Scripture and prayer, love deepens and joy magnifies, revealing the fruitful harvest of a heart truly anchored in the Word.

In reflecting upon these truths, the believer is invited to examine the soil of their own heart, to ask candidly if love reigns supreme or if it has been overshadowed by impatience, neglect, or worldliness. Likewise, joy challenges us to identify what holds dominion over our spirits, are we ensnared by the cares and troubles of this ephemeral life, or do we rest securely in the unchanging grace of God? Through such meditation, we come to understand that love and joy are not passive states bestowed without effort, but living, breathing realities cultivated through faith, obedience, and intentionality. They are the radiant evidence of God's transformational work within, the testimony by which the world sees the light of Christ reflected in His followers.

May this meditation on love and joy awaken within the reader a renewed desire to nurture these divine fruits. May each day present new opportunities to love more deeply and to rejoice more fully in the Lord's presence, even when shadows lengthen and trials press heavily. For the hope secured in God's promises is steadfast; His love never faileth, and His joy is the strength of the soul. As we walk this journey with hearts tender to the Spirit's leading, may we be ever anchored in the words of Scripture, allowing love and joy to flourish and bear much fruit in our lives, to His eternal glory.

Peace and Patience

In the quiet moments when the storm clouds gather thick upon the horizon of our lives, and the winds of tribulation buffet the soul with unrelenting force, there is a sacred call to embrace peace and patience, those serene virtues bestowed from above. The oft-repeated yet deeply profound exhortation in the King James Bible beckons us to "be still, and know that I am God" (Psalm 46:10), inviting the heart to cease its fretful striving and to rest in the sovereign assurance of divine providence. This stillness is not merely the absence of disturbance but a purposeful keeping of the soul in tranquility, rooted firmly in unwavering trust. To endure trials with calmness and perseverance is to walk a difficult path graced by the fruit of the Spirit, peace and patience, as companions who steady our steps when the journey grows arduous. These twin pillars uphold the soul, allowing the believer to navigate affliction not with despair but with a quiet confidence that all things work together for good to them that love God (Romans 8:28).

Peace, as described in scripture, transcends the fleeting cease of external disorder; it encompasses an inner calm that the world cannot give nor take away. Our Lord Jesus Christ declared himself the giver of peace "not as the world giveth" (John 14:27), a peace which quells the tempests within and settles the restless passions into sublime harmony with God's divine will. This peace is a tranquil river flowing beneath the storms of circumstance, a living stream nurtured by the waters of prayer, faith, and surrender. It is a gift precious and rare, yet accessible to the soul that seeks refuge in the Word and in communion with the Holy Spirit. To possess such peace is to stand unmoved like a cedar planted by the waters (Psalm 1:3), deeply rooted even as the winds howl fiercely and the rains descend in torrents. It is not passive resignation but an active stance of confidence, borne out of the knowledge that God's hand directs the course of events and that His promises withstand every challenge.

Patience, its kindred virtue, is the steadfast endurance that remains firm despite delay, hardship, or provocation. It is the spiritual fortitude which allows the believer not only to suffer but to suffer well, without bitterness, without fainting, and without the corrosive destruction of anger or despair. The Scriptures exhort us repeatedly to "run with patience the race that is set before us" (Hebrews 12:1), a metaphor that calls for perseverance like a long-distance runner steady in pace, eyes fixed on the eternal prize. This form of patience is rooted not in human willpower alone, but in divine grace that sustains the soul from within. To be patient is to trust the timing of God, to wait with hope when deliverance tarries, and to endure contradiction without losing the spirit of meekness and humility. It is a sacred waiting, a holy restraint exercised not out of mere obligation but out of love that believes in God's faithfulness beyond the immediate moment.

When peace and patience are cultivated together, they form a spiritual peace that anchors the soul amid the uncertainty and pain that daily life often delivers. Without patience, peace can prove fragile, easily shattered by delay or disappointment; without peace, patience may become a weary burden rather than a grace-filled act of trust. It is the harmonious interplay of these virtues that allows the believer to face adversity with a heart that does not stagger nor faint. The Apostle Paul, in his epistle to the Romans, praises the beauty of a spirit that rejoices in hope, is patient in tribulation, and rests in prayer (Romans 12:12), portraying a triad of qualities indispensable for the faithful journey. Endurance, therefore, is not stoic endurance alone, there is a supple vitality in waiting and receiving, a divine energy birthed through communion with God, that transforms suffering into sanctification.

We find the most resplendent example of peace and patience embodied in the life of our Lord Jesus Christ, who, in the face of betrayal, rejection, and the agony of the cross, exhibited profound calmness and unwavering perseverance. Isaiah foretold of Him, "He is brought as a lamb to the slaughter... he opened not his mouth" (Isaiah 53:7), revealing the quiet strength of a spirit anchored not in earthly power but in heavenly obedience. His patience was a patience that bore the sins of mankind, His peace a peace that surpassed human understanding and that He imparted to His disciples as an everlasting token. To walk in His footsteps is to embrace a way of life marked by this same peaceful perseverance, a life that does not defensively resist trials in anger, but rather embraces them as instruments in the divine crafting of character and faith.

The cultivation of peace and patience requires deliberate spiritual practices that nourish the soul and enable it to abide in God's presence even amid suffering. Daily meditation upon the promises of Scripture, heartfelt prayer seeking God's sustaining grace, and intentional acts of surrender when temptation beckons, all serve as means to foster this inner tranquility. The psalmist's words ring true still: "Thou wilt keep him in perfect peace, whose mind is stayed on thee" (Isaiah 26:3). To stay one's mind upon the Lord is a discipline of the heart, a surrender of anxious dwelling and restless imagining. It is to fix faith like a steadfast anchor upon the immutability of God's love and the certainty of His covenant. In practicing patience, the believer learns to wait not as one waiting aimlessly, but as one who watches eagerly for the fruition of God's promises, confident that His timing is perfect and that each trial sharpens the soul's resolve.

In the modern age, when instant gratification and rapid solutions are highly prized, the virtues of peace and patience may seem countercultural or difficult to attain. Yet it is precisely in this moment of haste and clamor that the call to a quieter, more enduring faith becomes all the more urgent. The faithful are invited, therefore, to cultivate a spirit of peace that defies the frantic pace of the world and a patience that perseveres amidst delay and hardship, knowing that these fruits are not borne by might or power, but by the Spirit of God dwelling within. Such a disposition sustains the believer through the valleys of despair and over the mountains of opposition, allowing the soul to emerge transformed, a serene light shining amidst darkness.

Prayer becomes a vital companion on this path, a sacred dialogue that both expresses the heart's needs and receives God's reassurance. A prayer born of peace and patience is itself a balm, calming the spirit and strengthening resolve. It is the language of the humble outstretched hand and the receptive heart, petitioning for grace to endure and for faith to rest secure. In such prayer, the believer finds not only solace but empowerment, a renewed courage to meet each day's challenges with dignity and hope. The words of Scripture are oftentimes our prayers: "Grant unto me, O Lord, a steadfast spirit, that I may endure according to Thy will, and rest in Thy peace, though the night be dark and long."

Thus, to endure trials with calmness and perseverance is to traverse life's vicissitudes anchored firmly in the twin graces of peace and patience. These are not mere passive states but vibrant qualities that shape the believer's soul into a haven of trust and tranquility amidst the fiercest tempests. They affirm that in the deepest places of hardship, God's presence remains, and His promises stand sure. When the heart is anchored in His word, patience blossoms and peace flows forth, bearing testimony to a faith that neither waveth nor fainteth, but abideth forever.

Kindness and Goodness

In the quiet stillness of the soul's yearning, there lies a sacred invitation to mirror the divine image through acts of kindness and goodness, those twin virtues that echo the very nature of God Himself. As we traverse the sacred pages of the King James Bible, we are beckoned to embrace these holy attributes, not as distant ideals, but as living expressions of faith, palpable and tender in the rhythms of our daily walk. Kindness, a gentle force born out of a heart softened by grace, and goodness, the steadfast light of righteous deeds, together weave a tapestry of divine love that transforms the mundane into sacred encounters. To reflect God's nature through these actions is to become a vessel of His mercy, a beacon amidst darkness, and a balm to the broken spirit. This inward transformation is neither fleeting nor superficial; it is a deep spiritual renewal cultivated by the Spirit, nurtured in prayer, and manifested in the sacred dance of relationship, with God and with neighbor.

Consider the profound declaration in Galatians 5:22-23, wherein the Apostle Paul unfolds the fruits of the Spirit: "But the fruit of the Spirit is love, joy, peace, longsuffering, gentleness, goodness, faith, meekness, temperance." Embedded within this sacred listing lies a call to embody kindness and goodness as fruits directly borne of the Spirit's indwelling presence. Kindness, or gentleness as the original Greek intimates, carries a softness that is neither weakness nor passivity, but a robust tenderness that chooses to heal rather than harm, to uplift rather than tear down. It is a mercy extended without calculation, a sweetness pouring forth from a heart made whole by Christ's redeeming love. Goodness, in its fullness, is active righteousness; it manifests as a moral excellence that is generous, courageous, and unwavering. Together, these fruits bespeak a life anchored not in mere obligation, but in the grace that compels joyful obedience.

To cultivate kindness and goodness within our own hearts is to embark on a sacred pilgrimage, one that begins with the recognition of divine kindness bestowed upon us. The Psalmist proclaims, "O give thanks unto the LORD; for he is good: for his mercy endureth for ever" (Psalm 107:1). Here, goodness is not merely a virtue to strive for, but the very character of God Himself, an eternal mercy that shapes every moment of our existence. When our hearts are rooted deeply in this truth, kindness flows naturally, for we are responding to the infinite kindness lavished upon us. It is through meditating on the steadfast love and constancy of God that we find our own actions transformed from mechanical duty to heartfelt expressions of grace. In this sacred exchange, the humble servant who offers a simple act of kindness is as much a recipient as the grateful one who receives it.

The Scriptures further illuminate the active reciprocity of kindness and goodness through the example of our Lord Jesus Christ, who in His earthly ministry embodied these virtues in their fullest measure. The Gospels overbrim with moments where Jesus extended compassion to the weary, healed the brokenhearted, and fed the hungry with tender generosity. He taught that true goodness surpasses ritual, flowing from a heart cleansed by love and a spirit surrendered to divine will. "Blessed are the merciful: for they shall obtain mercy" (Matthew 5:7), He promises, entwining kindness and goodness with the blessedness of reciprocity that flows from God's throne. To walk in the footsteps of Christ is to inherit this mantle, to become living epistles that preach through deeds what words alone cannot express.

Yet, the path of kindness and goodness is not without its challenges. In a world marred by selfishness, indifference, and strife, it requires profound courage and steadfast patience to persist in gentle acts that often go unnoticed or are met with resistance. The admonition in Romans 12:21, "Be not overcome of evil, but overcome evil with good," serves as a clarion call to resilience. To respond to cruelty or apathy with kindness is to enact a quiet but potent victory, one that reveals the transformative power of God's love at work within us. Herein lies the paradox of Christian virtue: in yielding tenderness, we find strength; in sowing goodness, we reap peace; in embracing humility through kindness, we conquer pride and division. This divine alchemy renews the soul and reshapes the community, knitting together disparate lives with threads of compassion and righteousness.

Furthermore, kindness and goodness are intimately woven with other facets of the spiritual life, such as joy and peace. When one's heart is anchored in joy, borne not of circumstance but an abiding trust in God's promises, kindness flows more freely, unhindered by bitterness or weariness. Peace, that sovereign calm that surpasseth all understanding, guards the heart and mind, creating space for goodness to flourish amid turmoil. These qualities mutually invigorate one another, cultivating a spirit that is both steadfast and compassionate. To nurture this inner harmony, believers are invited to dwell daily in prayerful meditation upon God's word, allowing its poetic majesty and profound truths to saturate every thought and intention. The Scriptures thus become both the fertile soil and the living water that sustain this growth.

In practice, reflecting God's nature through kindness and goodness becomes an intentional posture accessible to all who seek it. It might manifest in the simplest gestures, offering a listening ear, extending forgiveness where resentment lingers, sharing resources with those in need, or speaking words that heal rather than wound. These acts, though small in appearance, carry eternal weight when done in faith and love. The practice of mindfulness in each encounter transforms routine moments into holy opportunities, revealing Christ in the face of friend and stranger alike. For in each act of kindness, we become conduits of God's transformative grace, and in each display of goodness, we testify to the enduring truth that His light dispels darkness.

This divine reflection also serves as a profound witness to the world, a living sermon that transcends spoken doctrine. In a time when skepticism and cynicism pervade many hearts, consistent kindness and goodness stand as irrefutable evidence of God's work within us. They attract the thirsty soul seeking refuge and offer tangible proof that the Gospel is more than words; it is life-changing power made manifest. As believers embody these fruits, they stitch together a community of faith where love reigns supreme and grace abounds. This sacred fellowship nurtures each member, allowing spiritual renewal to take deep root and flourish across generations.

Finally, we arrive at the prayerful surrender that both initiates and completes this divine cycle. To ask God for a heart that reflects His kindness and goodness is to invite His Spirit to dwell richly within, to kindle a flame that will outlast seasons of trial and triumph alike. It is to acknowledge our dependence on divine strength to cultivate virtues that surpass human effort. In the quiet of prayer, the soul yields to the Soft Voice that calls us to love without measure and serve without expectation, trusting that through such surrender, the invisible Kingdom becomes visible in acts of grace. It is here, in this holy communion, that our faith finds firm anchorage, steadfast and sure.

May we, then, be ever mindful to mirror God's own heart through kindness and goodness, allowing these fruits of the Spirit to bloom beside our feet as we journey forward. In so doing, we take part in the sacred artistry of grace, becoming living reflections of the eternal God, whose kindness never fails, whose goodness endures forever. Amen.

Faithfulness and Gentleness

In the quiet sanctuary of the heart, where the soul communes with the Divine, there emerges a profound interplay between faithfulness and gentleness, two virtues that together weave the fabric of steadfastness and humility in the believer's journey. Faithfulness, that unwavering constancy in trust and allegiance to God, stands as the bedrock upon which the sanctified life is built. It is a resolute anchor in the stormy seas of doubt and temporal trials, a candle that flickers not even in the darkest hour nor is extinguished by the fiercest winds of adversity. To be faithful, therefore, is to walk humbly before the Lord, maintaining an unwavering devotion that transcends circumstance, honoring the covenant of grace by steadfast obedience and unyielding trust. Yet, fidelity in the spiritual walk does not stand in proud isolation; it finds its harmonious accompaniment in gentleness, that quiet and tender strength born from a heart subdued by divine love.

The Apostle Paul, in his epistles, beckons the faithful toward this serene yet powerful union, advising that true strength is often veiled in humility and quiet patience. Gentleness is not weakness but a deliberate repose of the spirit, a controlled power wielded with mercy and grace. It tempers zeal with compassion and tempers zeal with wisdom, allowing the believer to respond to trials and provocations not with harshness or resentment but with a measured kindness, reflective of Christ's own tender heart. The balance of faithfulness and gentleness is akin to the olive branch borne in peaceful reconciliation, a symbol of spiritual maturity that neither wavers in truth nor forfeits the loveliness of meekness.

To cultivate this sacred harmony within oneself is to embark upon a profound inward journey, a daily crucible where pride is surrendered and replaced by a humble reliance on God's sustaining grace. The trials of life serve as the furnace in which the pure gold of faithfulness is refined, while gentleness tempers the refuse of anger, impatience, and pride that might otherwise sully the spirit. The believer's faith is thus not only demonstrated by an unwavering adherence to God's commands but also by the gentleness with which they embrace their fellow sojourners on the path of righteousness. The steadfast steadfastness of faithfulness intertwines with the yielding grace of gentleness, forming a radiant testimony that illuminates the Gospel's truth in an often harsh and unyielding world.

Scripture illumines this truth with majestic clarity. The Book of Galatians exhorts the faithful to cultivate the fruit of the Spirit, among which gentleness and faithfulness hold prominent place. The text reveals that these fruits are not mere abstract virtues but vibrant expressions of a transformed soul. Faithfulness enables the believer to persevere amidst the tumult of life, being "steadfast, unmovable, always abounding in the work of the Lord," as the psalmist declares. Meanwhile, gentleness embodies a softness of spirit that neither seeks to dominate nor to retaliate but is quick to forgive and slow to anger. These twin virtues, borne through the Spirit's indwelling, bring peace not only to the heart but also to those who witness their quiet power in the believer's conduct.

In the daily rhythms of existence, faithfulness manifests as the quiet choice to remain loyal to God's promises, even when the path grows steep and the destination obscured by shadow. It is the decision to trust in God's providence when the night seems interminable, the trust that the morning light surely follows the darkness. This faithfulness is often tested in the mundane, the seemingly inconsequential choices made in the furnace of routine, choosing prayer over despair, patience over frustration, obedience over convenience. To be faithful is to exhibit an unshakable resolve that does not falter because it is anchored in the immutable character of God, whose words are as sure as the everlasting hills.

Yet, faithfulness without gentleness risks growing rigid and unapproachable, a sternness that wounds instead of heals, a zeal that consumes rather than nurtures. Gentleness tempers faithfulness by wrapping it in a cloak of humility and love, reminding the believer that strength need not shout nor demand but can whisper and persuade. It is the gentle rebuke that calls the erring sister back to the truth, the soft encouragement that lifts the weary brother from despair, the patient listening ear that reflects Christ's love more than a harsh doctrinal proclamation ever might. Such gentleness flows not from human effort alone but is the fruit of abiding in the Vine, a Spirit-led disposition that chooses grace over judgment, tenderness over triumphalism.

Indeed, gentleness mirrors the very nature of Christ Himself, who, though divine, "made himself of no reputation," and came "not to be ministered unto, but to minister, and to give his life a ransom for many." The meekness and lowliness of heart that characterized the Savior's earthly ministry become the model for all who seek to walk in His footsteps. When we embrace gentleness, we walk in the humility that refuses to exert power for self-exaltation; rather, it reflects the servant-heartedness of the Lord who healed the brokenhearted and comforted the weary with a word and a touch. Thus, gentleness is a profound strength that reveals an inner character transformed by God's mercy, capable of bearing much, enduring wrongs, and responding with love even when provoked.

This union of faithfulness and gentleness, though deeply profound, is also intensely practical. It enables the believer to navigate the complexities of human relationships with grace, to endure life's afflictions without bitterness, and to stand firm amidst the world's temptation toward anger and despair. When trials beset the soul, faithfulness anchors it to God's immutable promises, while gentleness soothes the ripples of strife within, enabling the faithful to emerge not hardened but tenderened, not embittered but blossomed in spiritual maturity. Through this dynamic grace, believers find the grace to forgive others, to remain patient in waiting seasons, and to extend mercy freely, reflecting the divine mercy they have received so abundantly.

Prayer becomes the sacred avenue through which the soul nurtures these twin virtues, seeking divine empowerment to embody a faith that does not falter and a gentleness that does not fade. To pray for faithfulness is to ask for the perseverance to hold fast to God's Word, to trust His timing and sovereignty even when the heart trembles. To pray for gentleness is to beseech the Lord to soften the spirit, to subdue pride and impatience, and to clothe the spirit with His own tender compassion. As prayer becomes the lifeblood of this internal cultivation, the believer learns to surrender all to God's transforming work, inviting the Holy Spirit to shape a character pleasing in His sight and blessed to be a blessing to others.

Thus, the journey of faithfulness and gentleness is nothing short of a sacred pilgrimage, one where the soul is continually drawn into the deeper mystery of divine love manifested through steadfastness and humility. This pilgrimage reminds the believer that neither faithfulness nor gentleness stands apart as solitary virtues, but together they form a resilient and tender heart attuned to God's will. In a world often marked by harshness and uncertainty, this sacred balance offers a beacon of hope and peace, a testimony that God's grace is sufficient and His power perfected in weakness.

May we, therefore, embrace the call to be faithful and gentle, steadfast and humble, that our lives may shine as a fragrant offering before the throne of grace. Let us steadfastly hold fast the promises of God, allowing His Word to dwell richly within us, while manifesting toward others the tender compassion that reflects the very heart of Christ. In so doing, we anchor our souls deeply in the eternal Word, equipped to face life's adversities with a spirit both strong and meek, unwavering and kind. And in this holy symphony, the quiet power of faithfulness and gentleness becomes a melody that glorifies God and blesses humanity, a testament to the transformative grace that renews us day by day.

Self-Control

Amid the sacred tapestry of the Spirit's fruit, self-control stands as a sentinel of the soul's tranquility, a steadfast guardian over the restless desires that seek to rend the fabric of our inner peace. The mighty Apostle Paul, in his epistle to the Galatians, beseeches us to walk in the Spirit, that we shall not fulfill the lusts of the flesh; for self-control is not merely the abstinence from sinful cravings, but the divine mastery over the very impulses of the heart that threaten to eclipse the light of God's grace within us. To wield self-control is to embrace the gentle yet unyielding power of the Spirit who dwelleth in us, transforming frail human will into a conduit of heavenly strength, enabling us to say no to that which would bind us and yes to that which nurtures our sanctification. It is through this holy governance that the believer's desires are refined, tempered as gold in the furnace of patient submission, until they shine with the purity of Christlike character.

Consider the tempestuous nature of passion, how swiftly it rises like a storm within the untrained soul, sweeping away the moorings of peace and reason. Without the Spirit's aid, these desires, left unchecked, become chains that fetter the heart, leading from momentary pleasure to lifelong regret. Yet, when self-control is exercised, these same desires are brought low, not destroyed or denied, but brought into holy alignment with God's perfect will. Such mastery is not born of human effort alone; it is the fruit of a surrendered life, daily yielded to the Spirit's sanctifying work. The Psalmist's cry, "Create in me a clean heart, O God; and renew a right spirit within me," resounds here as a yearning not only for forgiveness but for empowerment to live governed by the Spirit's law of liberty. In this secret place of renewal, self-control blossoms as a natural outflow of a heart rooted deeply in the Word, nourished by prayer, and guided by the Spirit's whisper.

The Scriptures present self-control not as a burdensome restraint but as a glorious invitation to freedom, a freedom from the tyranny of impulse and the bondage of destructive desires. This freedom equips the believer to endure trials without yielding to bitterness or despair, to resist temptation with steadfastness, and to pursue holiness with diligent joy. The Lord Himself exemplified perfect self-control amid suffering and provocation, teaching us by His example that true power is found in gentle restraint rather than fierce aggression. He who could command the winds and waves offered Himself as the Lamb led to the slaughter, wielding obedience and patience as weapons of divine conquest over sin's dominion. Thus, self-control becomes a reflection of Christ's own life within us, a testimony to the world that the believer is no longer captive to the flesh but alive through the Spirit's renewing might.

Yet the path toward self-control is often steep and arduous, for it demands daily dying to self and a conscious turning away from worldly allurements. The flesh persistently clamors for gratification, whispering seductively of ease and fleeting pleasure. Here, the believer's faith is tried, and the soul is called to choose, moment by moment, whether to bow to desire or to stand firm in the Spirit's strength. It is a struggle not of brute force but of quiet endurance, an act of faith that trusts God's promises above immediate sensation. The Scriptures assure us that in this struggle we are not left alone, for the Spirit is our Comforter and our Guide, whispering wisdom and granting strength beyond our own frailty. To pray continually for the Spirit's filling becomes the believer's lifeline, inviting divine power to transform the heart and renew the mind, enabling us to master self rather than be mastered.

Moreover, practicing self-control fosters an inner peace that radiates outward, touching relationships and communities with the balm of measured response and thoughtful action. It tempers the tongue, stills the anger, curbs the excesses of appetite, and steadies the will, producing fruit that brings glory to God and edification to others. Without this fruit, faith risks becoming dry and brittle, vulnerable to the storms of passion and temptation. But with it, the believer shines as a beacon of steadfastness, a living epistle of God's grace and power at work within the transformed heart. Indeed, self-control is intimately linked with the other fruits of the Spirit, joy, peace, patience, as each supports and reinforces the other, creating a harmonious symphony of godly character. When the heart is controlled by the Spirit, it wells up with abiding joy, rests in unshakable peace, and endures with hopeful patience amidst trials.

Let us then, beloved, embrace self-control not as a mere moralistic duty but as a sacred calling to live in alignment with the divine rhythm of grace. Let us seek daily to be filled with the Spirit, that in all things our desires may be purified and our actions guided by heavenly wisdom. Let us pray earnestly for the Lord to create within us a spirit of self-control, that we may not be tossed to and fro by every wind of temptation, but stand anchored in the steadfast love and truth of God's Word. In this pursuit, we find a pathway to true freedom and a peace that passeth understanding, for when the soul is governed by the Spirit, it rests in the assurance of God's unfailing presence and power. May this divine mastery over the self draw us ever closer to the heart of God, where true life and lasting joy abide.

Renewal and Restoration

New Beginnings

In the quiet moments of dawn, when the world still slumbers beneath the soft veil of night's retreat, there lies a sacred invitation whispered from the heart of God, a call to new beginnings. The dawn, with its tender light casting away shadows, mirrors the eternal truth found in His word: that though our past may be marred by failures, wounds, and regrets, there exists an everlasting promise of restoration and fresh grace. The King James Bible breathes this timeless affirmation with regal eloquence and firm assurance, reminding the believer that the Lord is merciful and gracious, longsuffering, and abundant in goodness. In embracing new beginnings, we step into a divine rhythm where sorrow yields to hope, brokenness is mended by tender hands, and each soul is offered an unfathomable opportunity to arise anew, washed clean by the fountain of forgiveness.

How often in the scrolls of our own lives do we find parchments etched with errors, ink smeared by tears and faltered intentions? Yet, God's hand is never distant nor indifferent; it reaches into the depths of our past and, like a skilled potter, begins to reshape us into vessels of beauty and purpose once more. The psalmist declares, "Create in me a clean heart, O God; and renew a right spirit within me." This plea for renewal echoes across generations, resonating deeply with every soul burdened by the weight of guilt or despair. It is a sacred plea moved not by our merit but by the boundless grace of our Maker, who delights not in the destruction of His children but in their healing. The mercy extended toward us is not fleeting; it beckons us to lay down our fears and embrace the purity of new beginnings, for "old things are passed away; behold, all things are become new."

The journey into spiritual renewal is both gentle and profound. It calls us to surrender, not a surrender of defeat, but a holy yielding that opens the heart to receive the transformative power of God's forgiveness. In relinquishing the grip of past transgressions, we unshackle the soul from chains forged by regret and shame. The divine promise, radiant with hope, is that no sin is so great, nor any wound so deep, that God's grace cannot reach and restore. This restoration is not merely a return to the former state but an elevation into a higher realm of intimacy with the Almighty, where the scars borne from trials become testimonies of God's enduring love and faithfulness. The Spirit invites us to step boldly into this new terrain of grace, where every breath is a testimony to God's redeemer heart and every step a dance of victory over past bondage.

Embracing new beginnings also means learning to trust in God's timing and faithfulness in ways we have not dared before. It is a relinquishment of our frantic striving and a surrender to the gentle leading of the Spirit, who guides us through the fertile fields of renewal. The sacred scriptures hold many testimonies of individuals who, despite frailty and failure, experienced divine renewal and purpose. Consider the story of Peter, whose denial was steeped in fear yet whose restoration was wrapped in compassion. After his great fall, Christ did not condemn but lovingly restored him, commissioning him to shepherd His flock. Such divine encounters imbue new beginnings with dignity and hope, affirming that our God specializes not merely in starting over but in crafting holy purposes from the ashes of our lives.

The process of embracing this fresh start is not without its challenges; it requires courage to face the shadows within and patience to allow God's work to unfold in His perfect timing. Yet, as we meditate upon the words, "Behold, I will do a new thing; now it shall spring forth; shall ye not know it? I will even make a way in the wilderness, and rivers in the desert," our hearts are emboldened to hold fast to hope amidst uncertainty. The wilderness seasons, often perceived as barren and desolate, transform through God's promise into places of abundant possibility and divine provision. Like a river carving its path anew, God's grace flows relentlessly to refresh, restore, and revive the soul weary with the burden of past griefs.

To fully embrace new beginnings, we must cultivate an attitude of thankfulness, recognizing that each day born of God's mercy is a testament to His unwavering faithfulness. Gratitude turns our gaze upward, affirming that every sunrise is a sacred emblem of His steadfast love, illuminating even the darkest corners of our lives. It awakens within us a spirit open to change, eager to receive the new gifts God desires to bestow. In this posture, spiritual renewal blossoms, sprouting wings of hope and resilience that carry us beyond the confines of yesterday's mistakes. The transformation is not superficial but foundational, rooted deeply in the assurance that "if any man be in Christ, he is a new creature: old things are passed away; behold, all things are become new."

Prayer becomes a vital conduit in this sacred transformation, a divine dialogue where we pour forth our contrition and receive the salve of God's mercy. In moments of sincere prayer, the heaviness of guilt is lifted, and the heart is filled with peace that passes all understanding. The psalmist's cry reverberates as both lament and hope: "Restore unto me the joy of thy salvation; and uphold me with thy free spirit." Such prayers unlock the chains of the past, inviting a spiritual resurrection that replenishes the soul's wells with joy and courage. Through prayer, we align ourselves with God's redemptive purposes, allowing His Spirit to breathe new life into the fragile places of our being and weave tapestries of hope from threads of once-broken dreams.

Moreover, embracing new beginnings is an invitation to shed the old identity marred by sin and pain and to don the robes of righteousness bestowed through grace. It is the shedding of an old self that clings to despair and the embracing of a new self fashioned in Christ's likeness. The apostle Paul's words echo as a declaration of victory: "If any man be in Christ, he is a new creature." This transformation transcends mere superficial change, it engages the deepest parts of our soul, instilling in us a renewed purpose and a radiant hope. In this rebirth, the past is neither forgotten nor diminished; rather, it is transformed into fertile soil from which grows a harvest of spiritual fruit: patience, humility, love, and faithfulness.

It is through this lens of redemption that we can view our journey not as a series of broken attempts but as a sacred pilgrimage towards divine intimacy. Each setback becomes a stepping stone; each moment of weakness, an opportunity for God's strength to manifest. The steadfast hope in God's restorative power becomes the anchor that steadies us amid the storms of life, a beacon that guides us through the shifting tides of uncertainty. The promise that "He healeth the broken in heart, and bindeth up their wounds" assures us that God's healing touch is always near, ready to tenderly mend the fragments of our spirit and shape us anew.

In the embrace of these sacred truths, we find courage to release the past and to look forward with expectant hearts. We surrender our fears, our doubts, and our pain into the hands of the One who makes all things new. This surrender is not the end but the glorious beginning of a life lived in the fullness of God's grace and love. Like the sunrise that rises steadily and sure, illuminating the horizon with hues of promise, so too our souls are reborn each morning, anchored firmly in the unchanging Word of God. Herein lies the eternal hope: that by His mercies we are not consumed, because His compassions fail not; they are new every morning, and great is His faithfulness.

May this sacred truth dwell richly in your heart, so that with every breath you may rise anew, clothed in the righteousness of Christ, bathed in forgiveness, and strengthened by a hope that knows no end. Embrace these new beginnings as a divine gift, a sacred renewal that beckons you to cast aside all that burdens and to stride forward in faith, confident that the Lord who began a good work in you will bring it to perfect completion. Amen.

Healing Wounds

In the quiet recesses of the soul, where shadows of pain and memory entwine, there lies a sacred chamber yearning for the divine touch of healing. The wounds we carry, some visible, many veiled beneath the surface, bear the silent testimony of our journey through trials, betrayals, and losses that have etched themselves into the very fabric of our being. Yet, it is within this tapestry of brokenness that the radiant hand of Christ extends, inviting us not merely to endure but to be made whole again. The King James Bible, with its timeless cadence, assures us in Psalm 147:3, "He healeth the broken in heart, and bindeth up their wounds." This divine promise is not a mere whisper but a clarion call to all who suffer: restoration is not only possible but assured through the tender mercies of our Lord.

To be healed is to embark on a sacred pilgrimage from despair to hope, from fragmentation to unity, from silence to song. Such restoration is neither swift nor superficial; it is the deep working of grace that permeates the spirit, renewing the marrow and reawakening the life-force within. We often cling to our wounds as reluctant souvenirs, fearing that to let go is to lose a part of ourselves or to diminish the significance of our pain. Yet, Christ bids us release these burdens into His pierced hands, where they are transformed into testimonies of His enduring love and power. Just as the prophet Isaiah so tenderly declares, "He giveth power to the faint; and to them that have no might he increaseth strength" (Isaiah 40:29), so does He infuse renewed vigor into our weakest places, turning our afflictions into channels of His grace.

The journey toward healing calls for a profound surrender, not a resignation born of hopelessness, but a willing laying down of our woundedness at the feet of the Savior. This surrender is a quiet act of faith, an acknowledgment that our own strength is insufficient, and that true restoration flows only from the wellspring of divine love. It is within this sacred yielding that the balm of heaven descends, soothing our aching hearts and gently knitting together the torn fragments of our spirits. As we meditate upon the comforting words of Matthew 11:28, "Come unto me, all ye that labour and are heavy laden, and I will give you rest," we begin to sense the gentle invitation extended to each weary soul. In this divine rest, our brokenness finds not shame but sanctification, not despair but hope renewed.

The King James Bible draws us into vivid imagery that mirrors our experience of transformation. Consider the metaphor of a tree planted by the rivers of water, which "shall bring forth his fruit in his season; his leaf also shall not wither; and whatsoever he doeth shall prosper" (Psalm 1:3). This image speaks of steady, life-giving nourishment and growth, even after seasons of drought and devastation. So too, the soul, once parched and fragmented by pain, can be revived and made fruitful through the ceaseless grace of God. Healing is both a restoration and a blossoming, a sacred awakening that enables us to bear witness to God's redemptive power in a world longing for renewal.

Yet, healing from wounds is not without its struggles. There are moments when the pain resurfaces with uncanny vividness, when memories flood the heart and threaten to drown us in sorrow. These times test the very roots of our faith, challenging us to anchor ourselves ever more firmly in the truth that God is nearer than our own breath and that His healing presence is constant, even when hidden from sight. The apostle Paul's declaration echoes powerfully here: "But he said unto me, My grace is sufficient for thee: for my strength is made perfect in weakness" (2 Corinthians 12:9). It is precisely in our frailty that the glory of God shines most brilliantly, illuminating the dark corners of our woundedness with the light of hope and renewal.

Embracing this spiritual healing also invites us to extend grace to ourselves, to recognize that recovery is not linear nor immediate. We are invited to move gently, step by step, allowing the Holy Spirit to work patiently in the garden of our hearts. Each prayer uttered in humble trust, every tear shed in holy communion, becomes a seed planted in fertile soil. The apostle James reminds us of the power of persistent prayer: "The effectual fervent prayer of a righteous man availeth much" (James 5:16). Thus, our healing is nurtured not only through divine intervention but also through our own heartfelt engagement in this sacred dialogue with God.

Furthermore, spiritual and emotional restoration through Christ impels us toward a profound reconciliation, not merely with God but also within ourselves and, where possible, with others. While the process may demand confronting old wounds and releasing bitterness, it also offers the exhilarating promise of peace that surpasses understanding. As the Psalmist joyfully proclaims, God "hath not dealt with us after our sins; nor rewarded us according to our iniquities" (Psalm 103:10), so too does He invite us to mirror this mercy in our own hearts, opening the door to forgiveness and freedom. This cycle of receiving and extending grace becomes a wellspring of healing that flows beyond our individual lives, touching communities and generations with renewed hope.

In the stillness of reflection, as we bow before the altar of divine love, we discover that healing wounds is not merely about returning to a former state of being but about stepping into a new creation, one fashioned by the Father's hand, sealed by the blood of His Son, and breathed upon by the Spirit of life. Each scar becomes a mark of victory, a testament to the redemptive journey from brokenness to beauty. Thus, our faith is not anchored in the absence of suffering but in the profound assurance that Christ has conquered the very forces that seek to wound us.

May we, therefore, embrace this sacred invitation to healing with courage and hope, trusting that the God who "healeth the broken in heart, and bindeth up their wounds" is ever faithful to complete the good work He has begun. Let us surrender our pain into His loving hands, confident that through His grace, restoration is not a distant dream but a present reality, one that renews our spirits, revitalizes our faith, and anchors our souls in peace unshaken by the storms of life. In this holy healing, may we find the strength to walk forward with joy, bearing witness to the transforming power of Christ's abiding love.

Restoring Joy

Amid the quiet sanctuary of our souls, where the dust of yesterday's burdens settles and the shadows of sorrow seek to claim dominion, there lies an ever-present invitation: the restoration of joy. It is not a fleeting happiness tethered to circumstance, nor a brittle mirth swayed by the caprices of fortune, but a profound delight that springs forth from the wellspring of God's unchanging presence. To restore joy in the heart is to enter a sacred realm where the Divine breathes new life into that which is weary, where the shattered vessels of our past are mended with threads of grace, and where the soul rediscovers its original melody, unhindered by the cacophony of despair.

The King James Bible speaks with a majestic and tender voice to this truth, "Thou wilt keep him in perfect peace, whose mind is stayed on thee: because he trusteth in thee." This peace, intertwined with joy, does not come from the absence of trials but from the assurance that our God is ever near, sovereign over every circumstance and tender over every ache. When life has bruised us, when betrayal or loss has tempted our faith to faint, it is within the bosom of God's presence that the heart can find its balm. Joy, then, is the heavenly fruit harvested after the storms have passed, a symbol of resurrection not just for the body but for the spirit.

Consider the psalmist's cry: "Restore unto me the joy of thy salvation; and uphold me with thy free spirit." This heartfelt petition is not born from pride or presumption but from a deep recognition of human frailty mingled with divine mercy. To lose joy is to wander in a wilderness where the mirage of hope often dissolves into shadows; yet it is precisely in this wilderness that God prepares the way for restoration. The journey back to joy is thus a pilgrimage, an intentional turning away from the desolation of despair and a deliberate leaning into the sustaining arms of God's boundless love. Herein lies a paradox; surrendering control and admitting our brokenness opens the door for the joy we so desperately seek.

Restoring joy requires a gentle reckoning with the wounds that mar the spirit. The past, with its remnants of disappointment and grief, may seek to ensnare the heart with whispers of unworthiness or eternal loss, but these lies cannot survive the purifying light of divine truth. The Lord, whose mercies are new every morning, beckons us to lay down our burdens, those fetters of regret, bitterness, and despair, upon His altar. In the sacred act of surrender, the soul is set free. As the apostle Paul exhorts, "Rejoice in the Lord always: and again I say, Rejoice." This rejoicing is not a superficial cheer but a steadfast anchor, a deliberate choice to embrace the hopeful promise of God's restoration despite the lingering ache.

Within the embrace of God's promises, the heart finds courage to pursue purpose anew. Joy, restored, is not a passive state but a vibrant force that fuels the believer's mission in the world. It beckons us to lift our eyes beyond the pain of the moment and behold the grand tapestry of divine providence weaving redemption from our scattered threads. This joy empowers us to minister to others who bear their own shadows, sharing the light that has rekindled our own lives. It is in the giving and receiving of grace that joy flourishes, transforming our personal restoration into a communal blessing. Thus, the joy restored in our souls becomes a beacon of hope, proclaiming that no wound is beyond God's healing touch and no heart too broken to be made whole.

In this sacred renewal, prayer becomes both the vessel and the voice of restoration. To enter the throne room of grace with an open and contrite heart is to invite God's life-giving Spirit to breathe once again upon the embers of joy. The dialogue of prayer renews the believer's resolve, knitting faith and hope into a steadfast assurance that God's promises endure beyond the tumult of circumstance. It is within this communion that joy is nurtured, growing from a flicker into a flame that warms the coldest of nights and illuminates the darkest valleys. Prayer, then, is not merely a ritual but a lifeline, anchoring the soul firmly in the eternal, where joy's restoration is made complete.

Moreover, the contemplation of Scripture enriches this journey by revealing the character of God as both just and merciful, a Father who delights in the gladness of His children. The familiar cadence of King James English invites the reader to experience the sacred text as a hymn of renewal, each word resonant with divine promise and enduring truth. It is as if the ancient tongues themselves carry a melody that speaks directly to the broken heart, soothing and restoring with timeless wisdom. The poetic majesty of these words evokes a reverence that transcends mere understanding, stirring a deep, spiritual awakening that reaches beyond intellect into the very core of being. In this hallowed space, joy is not simply recalled but reborn.

To be anchored in such joy is to find a steadfast peace that no external turmoil can overturn. It is to stand upon the rock of God's faithfulness, immovable amidst the waves of uncertainty and sorrow. The soul that has tasted restoration bears witness to a profound truth, that God's grace is sufficient, and His power is made perfect in weakness. This joy, forged in the crucible of experience and tempered by divine love, enables the believer to face each day with renewed vigor, knowing that the God who redeems is ever watching, ever ready to restore even the deepest wells of sorrow into rivers of gladness.

Thus, the restoration of joy is simultaneously a gift and a sacred journey, calling us to a deeper trust and a greater surrender. It invites us to relinquish our grasp on the broken fragments and receive instead the abundant life that God freely offers. In this restored delight, the soul awakens to its true purpose: to live in harmony with the Creator, rejoicing always in the goodness of His presence and the fulfillment of His promises. Herein lies a peace that surpasses all understanding, a joy everlasting, a sanctuary where the heart is forever anchored in the Word.

Strength for the Journey

Amidst the winding paths of life's pilgrimage, there comes a sacred moment when the soul, wearied from the trials of the journey, turns in longing toward a source of unyielding strength, a strength not born of mortal resolve, but imparted from the very Spirit of God Himself. It is here, within the quiet sanctuary of the heart's surrender, that the Holy Ghost moves with gentle yet mighty power, emboldening the traveler to advance onward. The weary traveler, once beleaguered by the weight of past burdens and the scars of former wounds, finds rest not in human might, but in the abiding assurance of the Spirit's empowering presence, making possible what was once impossible: spiritual renewal, growth in grace, and the restoration of what had been broken. This strength, divine and ineffable, is neither fleeting nor superficial. It is the steady flame that kindles perseverance; the steadfast anchor in storms of doubt; the gentle hand that lifts the fallen and steadies the faltering step. To embrace such strength is to acknowledge the limitations of our own power and to trust wholly in the promise of God's sustaining grace.

The Scriptures, breathed forth by the inspiration of the Holy Spirit and preserved in the majesty of the King James Bible, speak repeatedly to this profound truth: "They that wait upon the LORD shall renew their strength; they shall mount up with wings as eagles; they shall run, and not be weary; and they shall walk, and not faint." (Isaiah 40:31). The imagery here is lavish and remarkably tender, yet it resounds with enduring hope. To wait upon the LORD is to relinquish haste and impatience, and to dwell in expectant trust. It is a posture of surrender that invites the divine strength to suffuse every fiber of being. The eagle, sovereign of the skies, becomes a symbol of that which is lifted above the mundane, drawing closer to the heavens, enabled by the Spirit to rise beyond earthly weariness and stagnation. This metaphor speaks not only to physical rejuvenation but to the soaring of the soul, empowered for a journey that stretches beyond mere survival into a realm of thriving and spiritual majesty. The promise of renewed strength is not reserved solely for select saints but for all who courageously lay down their own efforts and embrace the sanctifying power of God's comforter.

To comprehend the full measure of this empowerment is to recognize the nature of the Holy Spirit as an ever-present Advocate and source of divine enablement. It is He who breathes life into dry bones, He who anoints the heart with courage, He who teaches and reminds of all truth. The New Testament bears witness to this transformative presence. The apostle Paul, when confronted with his own weaknesses and afflictions, acknowledges a paradoxical strength: "And he said unto me, My grace is sufficient for thee: for my strength is made perfect in weakness." (2 Corinthians 12:9). Here, the Holy Spirit reveals the divine economy, our frailty, when surrendered, becomes the soil in which grace flourishes and strength is multiplied. This strength is not the stubborn will of flesh, but the power of God working within, enabling the believer to press forward despite opposition, hardship, and the shadows of the past. It is the divine lifeblood coursing through the soul, restoring vitality where despair once reigned.

The journey of spiritual renewal often involves confronting the deep reservoirs of brokenness and pain housed in the human heart. Past wounds, whether inflicted by others or borne of personal failure, have a way of whispering lies that stunt growth and breed a spirit of despondency. Yet, the sacred texts assure us that "He healeth the broken in heart, and bindeth up their wounds." (Psalm 147:3). It is in the intimacy of the Spirit's ministry that these wounds are attended with tender care, not merely to soothe but to restore. Restoration is more than a return to a former state; it is a transformation that shapes the believer into vessels of greater resilience, compassion, and thanksgiving. The shattered pieces, when gathered and held within the divine embrace, become instruments of beauty and purpose. Thus, healing is inseparable from strength, the two dance together in a divine choreography where the Spirit leads the soul toward wholeness and renewed purpose.

The empowerment derived from the Holy Spirit is vividly seen in the biblical narrative of obstacles overcome and mountains moved, not by human strength alone, but by divine intervention working through surrendered hearts. Consider the testimony of David, once a trembling youth, who faced the giant Goliath not by armor or sword, but by the Spirit's unshakable courage and faith. In moving beyond the limitations of fear and past failures, his strength was found and displayed in reliance upon God alone. This paradigm is repeated throughout Scripture and in the lives of saints across ages, beckoning the reader to find solace and aspiration. The Spirit is the wellspring of that courage, enabling believers to transcend the persuasions that seek to suffocate faith: doubt, discouragement, weariness. With such empowerment, the pilgrimage becomes not a path of endless struggle, but a sacred unfolding, a continual ascent where each step is fortified by divine grace.

Moreover, the Spirit's strength empowers not only endurance but transformation. The heart remodeled by the Spirit's presence comes to embody the fruit of the Spirit, love, joy, peace, longsuffering, gentleness, goodness, faith, meekness, temperance, qualities that radiate inward peace and outward testimony. It is through the Spirit's work that the believer's character is refined like gold in the furnace, and the trials of life become refining fires rather than consuming flames. This sanctifying strength fortifies the soul against despair and animates the believer to shine forth as a beacon of hope and love in a world too often shadowed by darkness and cynicism. In this way, the journey becomes itself a sacred ministry, a testimony to the abiding power of God to renew and restore, to lift and to revive.

To receive this empowerment calls for a heart posture of surrender and desire, a willingness to lay bare the hidden corners of the spirit and invite the Holy Spirit to illuminate and heal. It is an act of faith, trusting that God's promise to "renew thy strength" is not a mere consolation but a sure and present reality. Prayer becomes the gateway to this renewing encounter, a communion where the believer exchanges their frailty for divine might. It is in the silent whispers of the soul, in the stillness where recollection and confession meet, that the Holy Spirit breathes resurrection life into the dry bones of exhaustion and doubt. The power for the continued growth of the spirit is thus not a distant hope but a daily, moment-by-moment sustenance bestowed upon those who earnestly seek it. The life-giving presence of God becomes the well from which the traveler draws without ceasing.

Let us then approach this divine promise with gratitude and expectancy, allowing the words of holy writ to penetrate deep into our consciousness, stirring the embers of hope into a blazing flame. May we embrace the holy empowerment offered by the Spirit as the wellspring of our continued growth, the shield against faintness, and the anchor amid restless seas. In this divine strength, we find not only the power to endure but the courage to embrace the new life that awaits, shining bright and unshaken, a testimony to the mercy and mighty grace of Him who calls us onward. Thus, empowered and renewed, the journey continues, not in our own strength, but in the overflowing power of the Spirit, carrying us ever closer to the radiant vision of faith fulfilled and the eternal embrace of God's everlasting love.

The Way of Wisdom

Fear of the Lord

To begin the sacred pursuit of wisdom, the holy writ declares with unyielding clarity that the fear of the Lord is the very foundation upon which true understanding is established. This fear is not a trembling terror born from dread or anxiety, but a profound reverence that rises from the recognition of God's immeasurable majesty, His boundless holiness, and sovereign dominion over all creation. It is this awe-inspiring regard for the Almighty that guards the heart against folly and opens the spirit to the illumination of divine truth. In these opening breaths of spiritual reflection, we find ourselves drawn into a solemn covenant to place God at the center of our thoughts, our judgments, and our daily decisions, inviting His wisdom to become the lamp unto our feet and the light unto our path through the labyrinthine challenges of life.

When we embrace the fear of the Lord, we acknowledge that wisdom is not mere human cunning or cleverness, but the gift of insight granted by our Creator, who understands the depths of the soul and the universe alike. It is a wisdom that elevates the soul, steering it away from reckless pride and self-reliance toward humble dependence upon the Eternal. Such reverence transforms the heart's inclinations, turning the seeker away from the fleeting allure of worldly distractions and toward the enduring treasures concealed in the statutes and testimonies of the Lord. This fear sanctifies the mind, preparing it to discern good from evil and to navigate the tangled complexities of human existence with a grace that is both steady and sure. It is, in effect, the spiritual compass that guides us through every moral wilderness and decision-laden crossroads, teaching us that true wisdom begins and ends not in the wisdom of men, but in the profound submission to God's righteous will.

This reverent fear, therefore, becomes the bedrock of character development, shaping not only what we think but also who we are. It softens the heart to receive correction and instills a tender humility that acknowledges our limitations and the need for divine guidance. Character molded in the crucible of this holy fear becomes resilient, marked by steadfast integrity amid the tempests of temptation and trial. Such a person is not shaken by the shifting sands of circumstance nor seduced by the siren song of fleeting success, for their foundation rests upon the immovable Rock of Ages. The fear of the Lord cultivates in us a ceaseless respect for His commandments, enabling the transformation of our desires and actions so that they align with God's perfect purpose. It is this transformational power that acts as a sanctifying fire, purifying motives and refining the will, that we may walk blameless before Him in love and truth.

Consider, then, the divine promise that accompanies this sacred fear: "The fear of the Lord is the beginning of wisdom," and with it comes knowledge and understanding (Proverbs 1:7). These are not hollow words but a profound assurance that to walk humbly with God is to embark on a journey of ever-deepening enlightenment. Every decision becomes an opportunity to seek counsel from the Lord, every moment a chance to align our will with His divine plan. In the throes of uncertainty, when paths waver, and the future seems veiled, the fear of the Lord bids us to trust in His providential care, to rest in His sovereign wisdom that far surpasses our own. It compels us to pause amid the clamor of voices and opinions, turning instead toward the quiet whisper of the Spirit, who reveals truth with gentle authority. Such trust is no passive resignation but a vibrant confidence, anchoring the soul even as storm clouds gather and challenges press in from every side.

This holy fear does not breed hesitation or stagnation but rather emboldens the believer to act with courage grounded in divine assurance. The knowledge that God sees all, judges justly, and loves with unending faithfulness allows us to step forward with clarity and purpose, knowing that our lives are enfolded in His sovereign embrace. We are invited into a sacred dance of obedience and trust, where each choice becomes an act of worship, and every trial is transformed into a crucible of spiritual growth. The fear of the Lord is not a chain that binds but a sacred tether that secures us to the heart of divine love, enabling us to soar above fear itself with wings of faith.

In the tapestry of life's trials and triumphs, the fear of the Lord answers the deep, gnawing questions of meaning and direction. When faced with decisions that shape the course of our days, choices that demand discernment and courage, we find in this holy reverence a steady hand upon the helm of our souls. It teaches us to weigh our options not through the prism of personal gain or fleeting pleasure but by the lasting effects upon our soul's health and our witness for the kingdom. By orienting every thought and action towards God's will, the fear of the Lord liberates us from the tyranny of impulsiveness and short-sightedness. It dawns as the first light of wisdom, dispelling the shadows of confusion and crafting clarity where there was once only doubt.

Moreover, this sacred fear cultivates a heart attuned to grace, a heart that longs not only to avoid sin but to embrace righteousness joyfully. It beckons us beyond mere obligation to a place where reverence blossoms into love, and obedience becomes delight. Such a posture awakens the soul to the manifold blessings bestowed upon those who walk faithfully in God's statutes, enriching our lives with peace that surpasses understanding and hope that shines undimmed through the darkest nights. The fear of the Lord accompanies us, therefore, not as a heavy burden, but as a precious treasure, a pearl of great price that renews our sanctified vision and opens our ears to the wisdom flowing from Heaven's throne.

In our daily communion with God, we discover that the fear of the Lord stirs a profound and living prayerfulness within us, a devotion that shapes every breath and step. It softens the arrogance of self-will and replaces it with a yearning to know God more intimately, to walk evermore closely in His ways. This divine fear becomes the soil in which faith takes root and grows, reaching upward toward the light of God's countenance. It calls us to pause, to reflect, and to surrender our restless endeavors into the hands of the Almighty, trusting that His timing and purposes are perfect. Within this sacred surrender lies the true peace that the world cannot give, a peace born of reverent trust and obedient love.

Hence, beloved reader, as you contemplate the vast currents of life rushing around you, may you find solace in anchoring your soul with the fear of the Lord, the beginning of wisdom, and the foundation of a life richly blessed. Know that this reverence is not a call to withdrawal but an invitation to engage the world with a heart refined by grace and eyes enlightened by holy understanding. Each moment offers a fresh chance to choose wisdom's path, to embrace the fear of the Lord as the noble compass for your days. In this sacred fear, may your spirit find strength to face adversity, clarity in decision, and joy in obedience, for it is the very essence of true wisdom and the steadfast anchor of a soul renewed. Let us, then, walk forward in humble reverence and vibrant trust, certain that the God whose fear we embrace is ever faithful to guide, sustain, and uplift all who seek Him with sincere hearts.

Seeking Counsel

In the vast and intricate tapestry of life, the decisions we face often form crossroads upon which our destinies hinge, moments delicate and profound that require the discerning heart of one who seeks not only the wisdom of his own understanding but the guiding light of divine truth. To walk alone, relying solely upon human counsel without the counsel of God's word and the godly community, is to venture forth on a path fraught with danger and uncertainty. The King James Bible, with its timeless cadences and solemn reverence, repeatedly exhorts the faithful to seek counsel, for "in the multitude of counselors there is safety" (Proverbs 11:14). This ancient truth remains ever vital, reminding us that wisdom is not the solitary possession of pride but the collective treasure of those who walk humbly before the Lord and one another.

To value godly counsel is to acknowledge the exquisite interplay between divine revelation and human experience. The Spirit of the Lord moves through the lips of the wise, the hearts of the humble, and the steady hands of those seasoned in grace. It is no accident that David, a man after God's own heart, sought Nathan, the prophet, when in confusion or distress, thus embracing counsel from a source higher than his own impulse. This act of humility exemplifies the posture of faith that we, too, must cultivate. Wisdom flows not primarily from books or self-reflection but from the tender voices of fellow pilgrims who have learned, through trials and triumphs, the ways of righteousness. Indeed, the great men and women of Scripture attest to the power of counsel. Solomon's prayer for understanding was answered not just with personal insight but in the form of elders and advisors who shared the burdens and sharpened the discernment of the king's heart.

Yet beyond the practical necessity of advice, seeking counsel is an act of worship and obedience. To open ourselves to others' perspectives is to acknowledge that we are made for community, created to bear each other's burdens and to encourage one another in the sacred dance of sanctification. To close one's heart against the wise counsel of a brother or sister in Christ is to erect a wall that prevents the flow of God's grace through the means of His people. When we embrace counsel, we welcome the Lord's providence dressed in human speech, clothed in the humility and experience of the saints who seek to uphold us in truth and love. This communion of wisdom transcends mere advice; it becomes a participation in the divine economy of grace where each voice, inspired by the Spirit, is a thread woven into the fabric of our spiritual maturation.

Furthermore, the act of seeking counsel is not an admission of weakness alone, but a testament to the strength of character that knows when to lean on others instead of presuming all answers lie within oneself. Pride whispers the lie that we must navigate the treacherous seas of life alone, that our own reasoning should stand unchallenged. But the Word of God bursts forth like a clarion call, "Blessed is the man that walketh not in the counsel of the ungodly" (Psalm 1:1), contrasting the folly of unassisted pride with the blessing of guided wisdom. A heart anchored in the Word recognizes that true discernment emerges from a multitude of voices filtered through prayerful reflection, that the wisdom of the elders, the insight of the spiritually mature, and the comfort of the humble believer combine into a reservoir of revelation far deeper than any one mind could fathom alone.

Seeking godly counsel also serves as a crucible for character development, pressing and molding the soul as the master craftsman hammers the iron into shape. When we open ourselves to correction and guidance, we expose our imperfections to the light of Truth, allowing grace to proceed from the Word into the corridors of our mind and the chambers of our heart. This process, though at times uncomfortable, is blessed and sanctifying. Even Christ, the perfect Redeemer, submitted Himself to the counsel of the Father and the Spirit, setting us an example of dependence upon the divine community within the Godhead. Likewise, we must learn to bear one another's yoke with gentleness and patience, receiving the correction that builds up rather than tearing down, fostering a heart prepared to walk in righteousness all the days of the earth.

The sacred art of seeking counsel does not rely on mere human wisdom but is rooted first and foremost in prayerful dependence upon God, who grants wisdom liberally. The man or woman who approaches others with a heart bowed before the Lord creates space for the Spirit to speak through them, guiding both the seeker and the counselor in truths eternal and practical. In this communion, God's wisdom illumines the pathways of decision, strengthens the resolve of the wavering, and calms the tumultuous seas of the soul. The act of communal seeking is itself a holy ordinance, echoing the early church's practice of gathering in prayer and mutual exhortation, united in the common goal of glorifying God in all things.

Therefore, beloved reader, when you find yourself at the crossroads of life, beset by confusion or burdened with circumstance, do not shy away from the counsel of the godly. Lean into the fellowship of the saints, the sacred voices that God has placed in your life as instruments of His grace and wisdom. Welcome their insight with humility and gratitude, filtering it through the lens of Scripture and prayer, thereby guarding your heart against the counsel of the ungodly or the folly of impulsive decisions. Remember always that the community of faith is a sanctuary wherein the Spirit breathes wisdom anew, where burdens are divided, and where the soul finds anchorage in the certainty of God's unchanging promises.

May you be steadfast in the pursuit of such counsel, embracing the blessed safety promised to those who walk not alone but surrounded by the cloud of witnesses. And as you heed these godly voices, may the peace of God, which passeth all understanding, guard your heart and mind through Christ Jesus, nurturing your spirit until the day of Christ's return. The journey of faith is not solitary, but communal and sacred; to seek counsel is to honor the Lord's design for His people, to open wide the heart for mercy and guidance, and to be shaped ever more into the likeness of Him who is the Author and Finisher of our faith. Let this be your prayer and your practice, that in all your ways you acknowledge Him, and He shall direct your paths (Proverbs 3:5-6), with wisdom flowing like a river, and grace resting gently upon your soul.

Discernment in Choices

In the quiet moments when the mind wrestles with the necessity of choice, there arises a sacred opportunity for the soul to practice discernment, a divine skill granted not merely as a gift, but as a calling to commune deeply with the truths laid out in the eternal Word of God. To discern is to look beyond the surface murmur of circumstance and the seductive whispers of fleeting desire, anchoring instead in the steadfast light of Scripture that illuminates the path of righteousness. Each decision, whether monumental or seemingly trivial, demands more than mere human logic or fleeting intuition; it beseeches us to seek the heart of God's wisdom, to align our will with His sovereign purposes, and to cultivate a character molded by faith and grace.

Consider the majestic wisdom reflected in the Book of Proverbs, where the Psalmist reminds us, "Trust in the Lord with all thine heart; and lean not unto thine own understanding. In all thy ways acknowledge him, and he shall direct thy paths." These words are not a passive entreaty but a clarion call to active submission and prayerful surrender, inviting us to relinquish the precarious balance of human judgment for the sure foundations of divine counsel. To lean not upon our own understanding requires humility, a gentle breaking of pride and presumption, and an openness to the Spirit's gentle guidance that often speaks in the stillness between words, in the recesses of our hearts. Thus, true discernment is birthed in this sacred tension, as our minds and spirits strive to submit wholly to God's unfolding revelation through His Word.

When the believer stands at the crossroads of decision, each choice beckons with promises and potential pitfalls, a labyrinth of possibilities that can confound without divine insight. It is in this moment that the instruction of Scripture becomes both compass and map. The Apostle Paul, writing with urgency and reverence, beseeches the faithful to "prove all things; hold fast that which is good." Here lies a profound posture of inquiry balanced with steadfastness, first to test every option by the standards of Scripture, by the fruits it promises to bear in one's life and witness, and then to cling resolutely to what nurtures holiness, love, peace, and the glory of God. The pathway of discernment is not haphazard but deliberately wrought through intentionality, prayerful meditation, and the seeking of godly counsel, all grounded in the unwavering truth of God's promises.

In the crucible of decision-making, character emerges as the quietly forged artifact of one's spiritual resilience. It is not enough to choose rightly; we must choose rightly because our hearts are anchored in the sanctifying presence of God. Scriptural discernment acts as a mirror reflecting the character of the chooser, exposing motives, aligning intentions, and refining desires to echo the heart of Christ. James the Apostle exhorts believers to ask of God who giveth liberally and upbraideth not, but to do so with unwavering faith, lest wavering lead to instability and missteps. Hence, the act of discerning becomes a sacred dance between faith and obedience, trusting that God who commands wisdom will instruct and illuminate the unfolding path. Character, shaped by repeated acts of choosing God's way, becomes the foundation that sustains us through trials and multiplicities of decisions that life inevitably demands.

This process of seeking divine wisdom for decisions is not a hurried one; rather, it blossoms in a garden of prayer and reflection where the heart finds rest. It is in this slow unfolding that God reveals His will, often through the gentle layering of scripture passages that resonate with the believer's situation or through the quiet echo of a sermon, a whispered promise, or the counsel of another faithful servant of God. The seasoned soul learns to attune ears not only to the loud proclamations of the world but to the still, small voice of God, a voice full of grace and direction, echoing the ancient but ever-new whispers of sacred writ. In such moments, the believer surrenders the illusion of control, instead embracing the freedom found in the confidence that God's purposes prevail, and that our simplest acts of obedience are threads weaving into a rich and eternal tapestry.

Choosing in alignment with Scripture also necessitates that we wrestle with the tension between immediate gratification and eternal significance. The allure of instant rewards often entices the wayfarer to stray from God's path, yet the Word beckons us toward a deeper hope, an enduring prize that far outweighs the pleasures of the moment. Paul's exhortation to "set your affection on things above, not on things on the earth" invites believers to cultivate a vision that transcends temporal concerns, to allow the Spirit to transform the mind so that every decision bears the imprint of heavenly wisdom. This heavenly perspective imbues choices with purpose, turning even mundane decisions into acts of worship and faithfulness. The ineffable joy that ensues transcends human understanding; it anchors the heart, granting peace amidst uncertainty and clarity in confusion.

Moreover, discernment is not an isolated endeavor but is richly communal in nature. The wisdom of Scripture emphasizes the value of counsel and fellowship, recognizing that God often communicates His will through the shared experience and godly insight of the body of Christ. Proverbs declares, "Where no counsel is, the people fall: but in the multitude of counsellors there is safety." The believer, though called to a personal walk with God, is not left to navigate this labyrinth of choices alone. Within the sacred fellowship of godly friends, mentors, and pastors, the believer finds support and confirmation, encouragement and accountability, allowing discernment to be deepened and confirmed through testing in community. This shared journey of faith enriches the decision-making process, reminding us that God's wisdom is often revealed in the harmony and unity of the Spirit among His people.

In moments when the clarity of choice seems shrouded in fog, there is a profound solace in remembering that God's providence governs all things, even those apparently beyond human understanding. The Psalmist declares, "He that keepeth thee will not slumber," a promise that God remains vigilant, tenderly overseeing the paths of His children. This assurance does not absolve us from the need to make wise choices, but it enfolds us with the peace that our missteps are held in God's grace and that His mercy is new every morning. The believer, therefore, walks with confidence, not in self-reliance, but in a humble dependence on a God who is ultimately sovereign over all decisions, transforming even our faltering steps into instruments of His purpose.

Discerning choices aligned with Scripture also calls for vigilance against the subtle whispers of temptation and deception that can distort the soul's vision. The enemy's craft is often to disguise the counterfeit as good, the fleeting as lasting, the selfish as godly. Paul admonishes believers to "be not conformed to this world," a charge to resist the siren call of worldly wisdom that is often at odds with God's Word. This resistance requires not only knowledge of scripture but an intimate acquaintance with God's heart, cultivated through continual fellowship, worship, and obedience. It is in this ongoing sanctification that the believer gains the strength to reject the deceptive enticements and remain anchored in the truth. The armor of God, described eloquently in Ephesians, equips the soul to stand firm, girded with truth, righteousness, and the readiness that comes from the gospel of peace.

As the believer matures in faith, the practice of discernment transforms from a laborious exercise into a deeply ingrained rhythm of life. The Scriptures begin to shape instinct, the thoughts of the heart become aligned with God's perspective, and the Spirit's guidance grows more recognizable and beloved. This spiritual maturity is marked by a profound peace that surpasses understanding, an unshakable confidence that flows not from self but from the abiding presence of the Holy One. The landscape of decision-making becomes less a battlefield and more a sacred garden in which the fruits of the Spirit flourish, and choices become acts of worship, testimony, and embrace of God's transformative power.

Therefore, let us, in all our decisions, lean heavily upon the eternal Word, allowing its wisdom to permeate every corner of our hearts and minds. Let us approach each choice with a spirit of prayerful openness, a heart of humility, and a resolve to honor the God who guides us in righteousness. May our discernment not falter amid the clamor of the world but stand firm like a beacon in the night, rooted deeply in truth, shining forth with grace and love, that our lives may be living epistles, manifesting the glory of God in every step we take. As we ponder over the pages of Scripture and lift our voices in prayer, may the God of wisdom direct our paths, consecrate our decisions, and keep our feet from every snare, that we may walk onward with courage, hope, and unwavering trust in His holy name. Amen.

Patience and Understanding

In the quiet sanctuaries of our daily lives, where haste and clamor often threaten to drown the voice of reason, the virtues of patience and understanding emerge as twin pillars supporting a life rooted in steadfast faith and divine wisdom. The King James Bible gently exhorts us to "be swift to hear, slow to speak, slow to wrath," a divine counsel that invites the soul into a reflective calm before it moves to action. To cultivate patience and understanding is to embrace a holy pause, a reverent space in which we deliberately slow our hurried thoughts and judgments, allowing the Spirit of God to illuminate the deeper truths hidden beyond the surface of circumstances and human interactions. It is within this sacred stillness that we discover a profound capacity to respond with grace rather than impulse, with compassion rather than condemnation, and with thoughtful discernment rather than rash decision-making.

In the throes of life's complexities, when emotions run high and the tumult of immediate reactions beckon, patience serves as the anchor that steadies the soul, preventing us from being swept away by waves of frustration or anger. The biblical narrative offers countless examples where patience, intertwined with understanding, changes the course of human experience. Consider the story of Joseph, who endured betrayal, imprisonment, and years of waiting before his God-ordained purpose was fully revealed. His patience was not a passive surrender but an active trust in the sovereignty of the Almighty, enabling him to navigate hardships with a spirit of gracious endurance. Likewise, the apostle James admonishes believers to "count it all joy when ye fall into divers temptations," recognizing that the testing of our faith produces patience, and patience, when she hath her perfect work, makes us perfect and entire, lacking nothing. This divine sequence suggests that patience is both a product and a process of spiritual maturity, demanding our engagement and cooperation with God's timing and wisdom.

Understanding, closely allied with patience, deepens our ability to view trials and human frailty through a lens shaped by heaven's perspective. It is more than a cognitive recognition of circumstances; it is the heart's capacity to enter into the experience of others with empathy, to seek the root causes beneath troublesome behavior, and to discern the unseen struggles that may compel one's actions. The Psalmist prays, "Open thou mine eyes, that I may behold wondrous things out of thy law," a petition that mirrors our need for divine insight to comprehend the fuller tapestry of life's events. To cultivate such understanding requires humility, for it asks us to relinquish the presumption of immediate judgment and to acknowledge our own limitations in wisdom. It calls us to listen intently, to withhold quick criticism, and instead, to seek the guidance of the Holy Spirit who "will guide you into all truth." In this spiritual posture, our responses are softened and enriched, transcending mere etiquette to become expressions of Christ-like love and gentleness.

Thoughtful responses born of patience and understanding do not imply weakness or passivity but demonstrate a strength deeply rooted in self-control and spiritual discernment. Proverbs, inspired by divine wisdom, repeatedly extolls the benefits of measured speech: "A soft answer turneth away wrath: but grievous words stir up anger." Here lies the transformative power of our words and actions: to heal or to wound, to calm or to inflame. When patience governs our speech, we create a space where conflict can be defused and reconciliation nurtured. We also embody the image of Christ, who, though reviled and misunderstood, responded not with harsh retorts but with profound grace. This astounding example invites us to model our interactions on His divine pattern, especially in moments when our natural inclination might be to react with impatience or misunderstanding.

The process of cultivating these virtues is inexorably linked with daily communion with God's Word and prayerful dependence on His strength. As the psalmist declares, "Thy word is a lamp unto my feet, and a light unto my path," so too does meditation on Scripture illuminate the paths of patience and understanding. Each reflection upon God's promises and commands carves away impatience and hard-heartedness, replacing them with the tender mercies of the Spirit. Prayer becomes the fertile ground in which patience grows, as we lay before the Lord our desires for swift resolution, and in turn receive His assurance that His timing is perfect. In moments when we falter, God's grace is ever-present to restore and renew, reminding us that our journey toward patience and understanding is not a solitary endeavor but a divine partnership.

Moreover, the cultivation of these virtues profoundly shapes our character, transforming us into vessels of peace and wisdom amidst a world often marked by turmoil and misunderstanding. Through patient endurance, our faith is refined; through understanding, our relationships bear the fruit of genuine love and acceptance. In families, workplaces, and communities, this gracious disposition fosters harmony and builds bridges over chasms of conflict. It persuades the heart toward forgiveness and gentle correction, recognizing that every soul is precious in God's sight and deserving of tender care. As we grow in these qualities, we find ourselves better equipped to face life's uncertainties, equipped not with anxiety but with a deep-rooted confidence in God's providence.

In the complex decisions that weave the fabric of our daily existence, patience and understanding serve as the divine compass directing our steps. Whether facing personal challenges, relational tensions, or moments of societal unrest, these virtues allow us to deliberate with calm clarity, seeking God's guidance before we act. The psalmist's declaration, "I will both lay me down in peace, and sleep: for thou, Lord, only makest me dwell in safety," echoes the fruits of a heart anchored in patience and understanding, a heart unshaken by haste, untroubled by impulsivity, and sustained by trust in God's sovereign care. As we develop this holy restraint and insight, we mirror the eternal patience of our heavenly Father, who, with infinite understanding, meets us in our weaknesses and leads us gently toward His perfect will.

Thus, in every exchange, every decision, and every trial, may the Spirit grant us the grace to respond not according to the urgency of the moment or the stirrings of our flesh, but with the thoughtful patience and divine understanding that reflect the character of Christ Himself. So shall our lives become beautiful testimonies to the power of God's Word to transform hearts and make us nations of peace in a restless world. May our souls find rest in this sacred rhythm, anchored always in the promises of the Almighty, who instructs us, "But they that wait upon the Lord shall renew their strength; they shall mount up with wings as eagles; they shall run, and not be weary; and they shall walk, and not faint." In these holy moments of patient waiting and understanding, our spirits are not only renewed but also prepared to shine forth His glory in a world hungry for light.

Living Humbly

In the sacred tapestry of Scripture, humility emerges not merely as a virtue but as the very bedrock upon which divine wisdom is built and nurtured. To live humbly is to embrace a posture of soul that esteems others above oneself, recognizing that true understanding and discernment are gifts bestowed by the Almighty, not trophies of human pride or achievement. The words of the wise Solomon echo through the ages, "The fear of the Lord is the beginning of wisdom," and in this reverence lies the heart of humility. It is the sanctified acknowledgment of our limitations and the profound acceptance that, without God's guidance, our footsteps falter amid life's turbulent trials and shifting sands. When we approach the world with a humble heart, we open ourselves to the gentle instruction of the Spirit, who leads us into paths of righteousness and peace, far beyond the reach of our finite intellect or self-willed ambition.

Consider the quiet strength found in the life of our Savior, Jesus Christ, who "made himself of no reputation, and took upon him the form of a servant." This divine condescension reveals the power of humility not as weakness but as a chosen path of grace and victory over the entanglements of pride and self-exaltation. To pattern our lives after such holy humility is to cultivate a spirit sensitive to the needs of others, patient in adversity, and grounded in the confidence that God's wisdom will illuminate even the darkest corridors of our decisions. It is not a humility that shrinks beneath the weight of circumstance but one that stands firm, anchored in a trust that God's sovereign hand directs all things for the good of those who love Him. This posture frees us from the restless striving that so often leads to folly and regret because we cease to trust in our own understanding and instead lean wholly on the Lord's unfailing promises.

Yet, to live humbly is also a daily, sometimes arduous discipline that calls for self-examination and surrender. The world, with its clamorous call to self-glory and individual acclaim, tempts even the most devout to forget the inward meekness that honors God. The humble heart must fight a continual battle against pride's allure, which masquerades in many guises, self-righteousness, impatience, or a critical spirit that judges without mercy. In humility, the believer learns to listen with earnestness before speaking, to seek counsel in meekness rather than arrogance, and to rejoice in the successes of others without envy. This tempering of character refines the soul as gold in the furnace, producing a quiet confidence that refuses to be shaken by worldly approbation or rejection alike. A humble spirit is a sanctified retreat from the frantic noise of self-aggrandizement, a sacred space where wisdom can blossom like the lilies of the field, clothed with grace and dignity beyond human measure.

Moreover, biblical humility serves as a steadfast compass in navigating the complex decisions that daily surround us. Life's labyrinthine pathways are riddled with choices that demand discernment far deeper than surface reasoning or impulsive emotion. When crowned with humility, the mind is sharpened, receptive to the prompting of the Holy Spirit who "will guide you into all truth." This divine guidance is not the loud clamor of fantastical revelation but the whisper of peace and certainty that quietly affirms the soul's trust in God's perfect will. In practical terms, humility enables us to lay aside our stubborn preconceptions and selfish desires, opening our hearts to godly counsel and the scriptures' enduring truths. It reminds us that, although we may be tested, perplexed, or laden with care, God's wisdom suffices our every need and supplies the strength necessary to walk sensibly and securely amidst life's mercurial changes.

The wisdom manifest in humility is also profoundly relational. It colors not only private contemplation but community life, fostering bonds knit together in love and mutual respect. To live humbly is to embrace others not as rivals or burdens, but as fellow pilgrims on the journey of faith, bound in the shared experience of divine mercy. This spiritual disposition cultivates a tenderness that forgives readily, a gentleness that speaks life rather than condemnation, and a patience that endures trials without bitterness. Such qualities become the very salt and light of the world, manifesting the character of Christ in tangible ways that draw others to the hope we bear. The humble heart, therefore, is not isolated nor self-effacing to the point of invisibility, but vibrantly engaged in the kingdom's work with the assurance that all labor done in humble dependence upon God is fruitful and eternally significant.

In the quiet moments of reflection, when the soul comes to rest in the presence of the Almighty, humility breathes the deepest prayers of the heart. It is the sincere confession of our need for grace, the gratefulness for mercy undeserved, and the joyful submission to God's sovereign plan. Prayer flows naturally from such a posture, not as a transactional asking but as a communion of love and trust. Through humble prayer, we are continually reminded of our place before a holy God, a place of honor not because of our merit but because of His gracious invitiation. This sacred dialogue shapes us, softening stubborn edges and aligning our will with His perfect purpose. The psalmist's cry, "Teach me thy statutes," becomes the anthem of the humble soul eager to be fashioned into the likeness of Christ through surrender and obedience.

Living humbly is thus a radiant testimony of the life transformed by the Word of God. It affirms that true wisdom is discovered, not in the boastful accumulation of knowledge or accolades, but in the serene acceptance of our need for God's mercy and the joyful obedience to His voice. As humility anchors the believer, the complex storms of life reveal themselves less as threats and more as opportunities for faith to deepen and character to mature. Through the veil of humility, the dazzling light of divine wisdom shines with clarity, guiding each step, illuminating each choice, and bearing the soul safely to the everlasting shores of peace. Herein lies the sacred invitation to all who seek wisdom: to embrace humility fully, to walk humbly with God, and thereby to discover the eternal riches of His gracious counsel and unfailing love.

Gary E. Risenhoover

The Power of Praise

Praise in the Psalms

The Psalms, that sacred collection of divine poetry and heartfelt prayer, serve as an everlasting wellspring of praise, lifting the soul toward the heavens in reverent worship and adoration. Within their inspired verses, one encounters a tapestry woven with expressions of joy, solemn thanksgiving, and magnificent exaltation, each lifting God's name above all earthly powers. As we delve into these sacred hymns, we find that praise is not merely an act confined to moments of jubilation but a profound spiritual discipline that anchors the believer's heart in trust and gratitude. The Psalmist, through the breath of the Spirit, invites us into an intimate dialogue with the Almighty, where praise becomes the language of the redeemed, a song that resounds even amid affliction, transforming the very depths of our being.

Consider the opening declaration of Psalm 100, a clarion call to all the earth to "Make a joyful noise unto the Lord," inviting all living creatures to enter into His courts with praise and thanksgiving. This summons is not a mere ritual; it is a vibrant celebration of God's unfailing mercy and truth, a recognition of His everlasting covenant. Here, we see praise as an outward expression of inward joy, a deliberate act of worship that both remembers God's enduring faithfulness and anticipates His continued provision. As the heart echoes these words, it is drawn beyond the temporal into a sacred realm where God's presence is tangible, and the soul is refreshed. The Psalmist's call is thus both an invitation and a command: to lift the voice in heartfelt adoration, to affirm God's sovereignty in every season of life.

Yet the Psalms do not confine the language of praise to pristine moments alone. They acknowledge the shadows of sorrow and the heaviness of despair that often envelop the human spirit. Take, for instance, Psalm 42, where the writer's soul pants for God "as the hart panteth after the water brooks." Even in thirst and longing, the Psalmist clings to remembrance: "Why art thou cast down, O my soul? And why art thou disquieted within me? Hope thou in God: for I shall yet praise him for the help of his countenance." Such verses testify to praise as an act of spiritual resilience, rising in defiance against the tempests of doubt and weariness. Praise becomes the steadfast anchor that refuses to be severed, even when the night is dark and the heart is heavy. It is a declaration of faith that God's light will yet break through the gloom, a trust that his presence surpasses the pain.

The Psalms also reveal the multifaceted nature of praise, embracing not only spoken acclamations but the whole being's participation , the lifting of hands, the beating of drums, the sounding of trumpets, as well as the silent reverence of bowed knees. Psalm 150 triumphantly proclaims, "Praise him with the sound of the trumpet: praise him with the psaltery and harp. Praise him with the timbrel and dance: praise him with stringed instruments and organs. Praise him upon the loud cymbals: praise him upon the high sounding cymbals." Here, praise is a vibrant symphony where every instrument and every movement becomes an expression of worship. The physicality of praise draws the worshipper into an embodied encounter with God, melding spirit and flesh in harmonious adoration. It reminds us that worship transcends intellectual assent; it is an outpouring of the soul, a joyous surrender that enlivens faith and uplifts the heart.

Moreover, the Psalms teach us that praise is inherently rooted in the knowledge of God's character and mighty works. Psalm 145 affirms the greatness of the Lord with vivid descriptions: "Great is the Lord, and greatly to be praised; and his greatness is unsearchable." The Psalmist elaborates upon myriad divine attributes , the Lord's righteousness, mercy, faithfulness, and graciousness toward all He hath made. Praise arises not from circumstance alone but from the profound recognition of who God is in His eternal glory. This understanding nurtures a worship that is unshakable and pure, rising above fleeting emotions and external conditions. As the Psalmist meditates on the omnipotence and benevolence of the Almighty, praise blossoms as a natural response, a sacred melody springing forth from the well of divine truth.

The daily practice of praise found within the Psalms becomes a vital spiritual balm, replenishing the wearied soul and erecting a fortress of hope. It is through this sacred habit that believers find the strength to endure trials and the courage to face each new dawn with confidence. When the Psalmist declares in Psalm 34, "I will bless the Lord at all times: his praise shall continually be in my mouth," we perceive praise as a spiritual discipline that transcends mere expression and becomes a way of life. To bless the Lord continually is to maintain a heart fixed upon the divine, to cultivate an attitude of gratitude despite the shifting sands of circumstance. In doing so, worshipers lock their souls into the eternal purposes of God, drawing comfort and renewal even when the storms of life rage.

Within these psalms of praise, we also find the profound mystery of corporate worship , a communion of hearts united in adoration. The Psalms were penned not only as private prayers but as hymns for the congregation, offering a template for collective praise that binds God's people in unity. The harmonies of voices raised together create an atmosphere thick with divine presence, where faith and hope are strengthened by shared testimony. Such communal worship echoes the eternal assembly of heaven where angels and saints alike join in a ceaseless anthem to the Lamb. Participating in this ancient tradition, believers across time step into a sacred rhythm that transcends generations, linking every heart in one great chorus of praise.

Praise in the Psalms is thus a luminous thread weaving through the fabric of spiritual renewal. It rekindles the flame of faith where it may flicker low, infusing the weary with a fresh breath of joy and peace. It positions the heart to receive God's blessings anew, cleansing the mind of doubt and fear. When the psalmist cries, "Praise ye the Lord. O give thanks unto the Lord; for he is good: for his mercy endureth forever," it is a summons to embrace gratitude as the foundation of trust. This eternal goodness, anchored in unchanging mercy, becomes the bedrock of our confidence amid an ever-changing world.

As we allow the Psalms to shape our praise, we are invited to enter a sanctuary of spiritual intimacy where worship ceases to be an external act and becomes the very language of the soul. Here, praise is not an escape from reality but a courageous affirmation of hope and steadfastness in the midst of it. It draws the believer into an exalted posture of humility and joy, where the heart, though pressed by trials, rises with the assurance that God's presence is near and His purposes prevail. Thus, praise becomes a sanctuary, a refuge, and a weapon, empowering the faithful to rise above despair and proclaim God's sovereign love with unwavering confidence.

May our hearts be conformed to the spirit of the Psalms, echoing their timeless melodies of adoration and thanksgiving. Let our voices join the ancient song that transcends time and circumstance, lifting the holy name of God on high. In the quiet moments of reflection and the exuberant outpourings of worship, let praise be our constant companion, an anchor for the soul that secures us in the everlasting arms of our Creator. Through praise, may we find renewal, fortitude, and the unshakable peace that springs from resting wholly in the sovereign goodness of the Lord. Amen.

Gratitude as Praise

There is a sacred majesty in the expression of gratitude that transcends mere words, ascending as a celestial incense before the throne of the Almighty. Gratitude, when embraced as an attitude of the heart, becomes far more than a fleeting response to blessings received; it is the very essence of praise itself, woven deeply into the fabric of our spiritual affections and a wellspring of divine communion. To give thanks is not simply to recount our mercies, but to embed within our souls a posture of worship, an acknowledgment of the unchanging goodness and sovereignty of God that elevates faith, renews the weary spirit, and fortifies our resilience against the storms of life. In the hallowed pages of the King James Bible, we encounter the luminous glow of thanksgiving shining forth from saints of old, their hearts aflame with worship that stirred heavens and earth alike, and beckoned us to join in this timeless liturgy of praise.

Consider the psalmist's jubilant declaration: "O give thanks unto the Lord; for he is good: for his mercy endureth for ever" (Psalm 107:1). In these words lies the profound wisdom that gratitude springs first from the recognition of God's unyielding mercy, an eternal fountain of kindness that never wanes despite our failings. The psalmist invites us into a practice whereby thanksgiving is not an occasional utterance but a perpetual state, "for his mercy endureth forever" declares a truth unwavering and sure, a banner beneath which the soul finds refuge in times of travail and peace in moments of joy. In structuring gratitude as praise, the heart is drawn heavenward, its gaze lifted from temporal cares to eternal certainties, allowing faith to grow robust and hope to flourish even amid affliction.

The attitude of gratitude is a sacred sanctuary where the spirit can repose, a place where the tumultuous waves of doubt and despair are calmed by the recognition of God's providential hand. When we perceive every breath and every circumstance through the lens of thanksgiving, we awaken to the reality that even trials are channels of grace, appointed by a loving God to refine and strengthen us. The Apostle Paul, imprisoned and beset by hardship, exemplifies this spiritual alchemy when he exhorts: "In every thing give thanks: for this is the will of God in Christ Jesus concerning you" (1 Thessalonians

5:18). These words unveil a remarkable command, gratitude is not contingent on ease or triumph but is to remain steadfast in all, becoming a testament of trust that acknowledges God's purpose beyond the veil of suffering. Thus, thankfulness forged from faith becomes an unshakable refuge, a fortress built not on circumstances, but on the immovable rock of divine truth.

To cultivate gratitude as praise is to awaken a daily reverence for the manifold mercies bestowed upon us, whether grand or small. It is found in the dawn light that bathes the earth in hope, the quiet repose of evening's sweet embrace, the tender touch of fellowship, and the abiding presence of God's Spirit whispering peace amid solitude. This practice nurtures an inner song, a melody woven through the fabric of our days that testifies to God's faithfulness and invites the soul to join in heavenly symphony. Just as Jesus, our Redeemer and exemplar, lifted eyes and hands in grateful worship before the Father, rendering thanks for the bread and the chalice (Luke 22:19), so too are we called to lift our hearts in unceasing praise, acknowledging that all good things flow from Him who is the fountain of life and love.

The biblical narrative teems with instances where praise and thanksgiving are inseparable companions, each feeding the other in an eternal dance of devotion. When Hannah was heard by God and granted a child in her old age, her response was one of exuberant thanksgiving turned into prophetic praise: "My heart rejoiceth in the Lord, mine horn is exalted in the Lord: my mouth is enlarged over mine enemies; because I rejoice in thy salvation" (1 Samuel 2:1). In her song resounds the victorious power of gratitude that lifts the soul above earthly sorrow, transforming past anguish into triumphant hope. Praise arises not only from abundance but from the recognition that God's salvation, His deliverance and sustaining presence, is the ultimate blessing worth celebrating. Thus, gratitude rooted in the heart blossoms into praise that unmasks the glory of God, offering Him the highest exaltation.

In this light, praise is not an occasional ritual but a constant liveliness of spirit, an ever-flowing river of thanksgiving that irrigates the soul with joy and peace beyond comprehension. The prophet Isaiah calls out with resplendent clarity: "Sing unto the Lord a new song; his praise from the end of the earth, ye that go down to the sea, and all that is therein; the isles, and the inhabitants thereof" (Isaiah 42:10). Here, the summons transcends all boundaries, conveying the universal call for creation itself to join in the chorus of praise, a divine symphony orchestrated by grateful hearts acknowledging God's creative power and sustaining grace. We, as believers, are invited into this cosmic hymn, our gratitude becoming a vital note that reverberates with the very heartbeat of heaven.

To approach gratitude as praise also means to cling to hope when shadows lengthen and the night threatens to overwhelm the day. When Job, amid his anguish and loss, declared, "The Lord gave, and the Lord hath taken away; blessed be the name of the Lord" (Job 1:21), he illuminated the sublime courage inherent in praise that springs from faith. This sacred declaration is not a denial of grief but a triumphant affirmation of trust in God's inscrutable wisdom and abiding goodness. Gratitude, anchored in such faith, enables the soul to sing when silence seems the easier choice and to offer praise when confusion and pain loom large. The resilience fostered by this spiritual discipline is a holy bulwark, sustaining the soul even when the heart falters.

Moreover, gratitude as an attitude of the heart reshapes our perception of daily living, inviting us to a perpetual awareness of grace woven through every moment. It calls us to recognize God's fingerprints in our relationships, our work, and the very breath that sustains us. As the Psalmist declares, "This is the day which the Lord hath made; we will rejoice and be glad in it" (Psalm 118:24), we find in each day a wellspring of thankfulness that reorients our souls away from complaint toward jubilant celebration. This practice draws us deeper into intimacy with our Creator, each act of thanksgiving a step along the pathway of worship, aligning our hearts with the divine purpose and filling us with a peace that surpasses understanding.

Indeed, to render thanks with a heart fully engaged is to meet God in sacred encounter, a moment where the veil of the earthly falls away, and the soul glimpses the eternal. Prayer becomes infused with praise, not as a mere formality but as a breath of life, a spiritual anthem rising from the depths. "Enter into his gates with thanksgiving, and into his courts with praise" (Psalm 100:4) summons us into the very presence of God, where gratitude is the currency of communion and the fragrance of worship. Here, praise elevates faith beyond the trials that seek to ensnare it, lifting the soul on wings of hope toward the everlasting embrace of divine love.

May we, therefore, cultivate in our hearts this holy attitude of gratitude, allowing it to transform our daily journey into an ongoing act of praise. Let thanksgiving become to us what breath is to the body, a continuous, life-sustaining rhythm that draws us nearer to God and strengthens us for every trial. In the quiet moments of reflection, may we find the grace to proclaim with the psalmist, "I will praise the name of God with a song, and will magnify him with thanksgiving" (Psalm 69:30), knowing that such praise is a balm for the soul, a light unto the path, and an anchor for the spirit amidst the ever-changing tides of life.

Praise in Adversity

In the crucible of adversity, when the storms of life unleash their fiercest tempests upon our souls, praise emerges not as a fleeting sentiment but as a steadfast anchor that holds us fast in the unyielding grip of God's grace. It is within these moments of trial that the heart's true posture is revealed, and though the path may be shadowed with suffering, the soul finds refuge in the act of worship. The sacred texts of the King James Bible resound with voices that lift up hymns of adoration not with a clamor of ease, but from the depths of hardship and ache. Consider the psalmist who, amidst the valley of the shadow of death, proclaimed, "I will bless the LORD at all times: his praise shall continually be in my mouth" (Psalm 34:1). This declaration is not one of convenience but a bold testament that praise in adversity transforms the very fabric of our experience, knitting our fears into trust and our sorrows into songs of hope. To praise God in hardship is to testify to the unfailing sovereignty and providence of the Almighty, acknowledging that even in the furnace of affliction, He is working to refine, restore, and redeem.

The act of praise in adversity is both a defiant declaration against despair and a sacred surrender to divine purpose. It transcends the superficial melioration of mood and reaches deep into the spiritual reservoir where faith is replenished. From the ancient prophet Habakkuk, who wrestled with the perplexities of injustice and ruin, we hear a song rising from the throat of lament: "Though the fig tree shall not blossom, neither shall fruit be in the vines... yet I will rejoice in the LORD, I will joy in the God of my salvation" (Habakkuk 3:17-18). Here is a portrait of faith unwavering, a willful delight in God's presence that does not depend on the flourishing of earthly circumstances. Praise becomes the vessel of resilience, a sacred fortification that empowers the soul to face the bleakest desolation with a heart uplifted and a voice exalted. In these moments, worship is no longer a response conditioned by ease but a spiritual modality that actively shapes and sustains the sufferer, illuminating the path forward with the light of divine hope.

Moreover, praise in adversity reorients our vision from the temporal to the eternal, shifting focus from what is lost to what is secured in Christ. The Apostle Paul, even imprisoned and persecuted, exhorted the early church to "Rejoice evermore. Pray without ceasing. In every thing give thanks" (1 Thessalonians 5:16-18), underscoring the transformative power of continuous praise and thanksgiving as a means of spiritual perseverance. Paul's life itself stands as a monumental example of rejoicing amidst trials, for his chains were not merely physical bonds but opportunities to magnify God's name, proving that adversity need not silence the worshipper. Praise, therefore, is not the crown of success but the fortitude in failure; it is the river that does not run dry when drought threatens but flows in richness when strength wanes. Through the lens of worship, hardship is refracted into a divine tapestry of purpose, where even the sharpest thorns serve to deepen our dependence and delight in God.

Immersed in this sacred practice, the believer is invited to articulate a prayerful song that weaves praise and lament into a singular tapestry of trust. The Psalms abound with examples of this divine paradox, hearts broken yet hopeful, voices trembling yet triumphant. David's cry, "The LORD is my shepherd; I shall not want" (Psalm 23:1), resonates with steadfast assurance even as he navigates the valley of death. This melody of confidence amid chaos invites us to join in a worship that transcends feeling, grounded instead in the steadfast nature of God's covenant love. Praise in adversity teaches us to lift our eyes beyond the immediate pain, fixing them upon the beauty and faithfulness of the One who guides through darkness. It becomes a sacred exercise in spiritual vision, training our hearts to see the invisible hand that upholds us and to sing even when the music around us has been silenced.

In practicing praise, we cultivate a resilience that is both spiritual and psychological, knitting the fractured soul back into wholeness through the recognition of God's goodness. The Hebrew word for praise, "halal," encompasses not just words of exaltation but joyous clapping, shouting, and celebration, expressions that energize the spirit and transform the atmosphere. When we praise in adversity, we embody this vibrant worship, declaring with all our might that God's love is more powerful than any trial. Our words become lifelines cast into the stormy sea, binding us to the promises written in holy scripture. Praise thus becomes a revolutionary act of faith; it is the sacred choice to trust and honor God when circumstances scream otherwise. The spiritual discipline of praise recalibrates our hearts, reminding us that in every difficulty, the Creator remains supremely worthy of adoration, His presence our unfailing refuge.

Yet, praise in adversity is not a shallow platitude or forced cheerfulness; rather, it is a profound engagement with God's truth that validates our pain while refusing to be defined by it. This delicate balance is witnessed in the prayers of Hannah, who poured out her soul in anguish and then rejoiced in the Lord's faithfulness (1 Samuel 1:27-28). Her story teaches that supplication and praise are not mutually exclusive but are threads woven together in the tapestry of spiritual endurance. By bringing our struggles honestly before God and then choosing to worship, we participate in a divine dialogue that heals and sanctifies. Praise softens the hardness of hardship and sharpens the vision of faith, an alchemy that turns our trials into testimonies of grace. It is in this sacred rhythm of lament and exaltation that the soul is strengthened, and the believer learns to rise each day renewed, anchored in the eternal Word.

As you traverse your own valleys and wrestle with your burdens, may you find in praise a refuge as profound as the shadow of the Almighty. Let your songs be a balm to your spirit, a melody that rises above despair, affirming that even in the darkest nights, the dawn of God's mercy will break forth. To praise in adversity is to embrace the paradox of faith: rejoicing not because the storm has passed, but because the Shepherd walks with us through it. This holy practice nurtures a soul fortified by grace, steadfast in hope, and unmovable in love. May your heart be ever lifted in worship, finding strength not from circumstance but from the boundless promises of the King eternal, whose Word is a lamp unto your feet and a light unto your path. Amen.

Joyful Noise

How sweet and melodious is the sound that rises from a heart truly awakened to the presence of the Almighty! To make a joyful noise unto the Lord is not merely the cacophony of hurried song or vain repetition but the sincere, unabashed lifting of soul and voice in exaltation. It is the deep, resounding echo of gratitude and worship, unrestrained by the trivialities and burdens of the world, yet anchored firmly in reverence and truth. The psalmist bids us, "Make a joyful noise unto the Lord, all ye lands," reminding us that praise is not for the elite or the solemn alone, but for all creation, inviting every tongue, every heart, every breath to join in a chorus of thanksgiving that transcends time and trials. To praise God with enthusiasm is to embrace a divine appointment where the mundane fades and the spirit is lifted into realms of wondrous delight.

When our hearts break free from the shackles of sorrow and doubt, the joy of the Lord becomes our strength, prompting a spontaneous outpouring of praise that mirrors the heavens rejoicing at the salvation of a soul. Praise, when it rises sincerely and fervently, is a powerful spiritual act, one that enlivens the weary and fortifies the faint. It kindles a glow in the soul, a fire that consumes despair and crafts hope anew upon the altar of trust. The act of making a joyful noise is not rooted in perfect melody, nor is it contingent upon the grandeur of the voice, but is rather born of a heart that understands the depth of God's mercy and chooses to respond with gladness. This noiseless joy within overflows in vibrant outcry, echoing the jubilation of the Psalmist who danced before the Lord with tambourine and harp, his countenance radiant with the light of divine delight.

Consider the vibrant worship witnessed in the temple courts, where priests and people alike lifted their voices in harmonious adoration, their songs woven into the fabric of Scripture and the breath of the Spirit. The inspired hymns proclaimed God's mighty acts, His steadfast love, and His faithfulness that endureth forever. These were not empty rituals but heartfelt affirmations of God's unchanging nature. When the walls of Jericho fell, it was the joyful noise of praise that heralded victory; when Hannah's barren heart was finally blessed with fruitfulness, her song of thanksgiving ascended in holy triumph. Their praises serve as living testimony that in the depths of surrender lies the highest form of exaltation. To emulate this spiritual practice of enthusiastic praise is to open ourselves to a sacred communion wherein our souls find restoration and our faith is emboldened.

Sincerity enshrines the joy of praise with authenticity. The Lord hath no pleasure in the lip-service of the hypocrite, who offereth words with a heart far from Him. True worship demands a heart laid bare, a spirit willing to pour forth the fountains of thanksgiving with authenticity that the Lord delights to behold. When we lift our voices with honesty and fervor, we honor not only the grandeur of God but the intimate relationship that draws us nearer to His heart. It is in these moments of genuine praise that we find our burdens lightened and our spirits refreshed. For the Lord inhabits the praises of His people; His presence is manifest where joy is expressed in truth and love. Such praise becomes a refuge, a sanctuary wherein the soul is renewed and anchored in eternal hope.

Let us not forget that praise is also a spiritual weapon. The enemies of the soul, be they doubt, fear, or despair, are silenced before the sound of exultant acclaim to the King of kings. For when the tongue confesses the goodness of God, it summons heavenly hosts to our defense and casts down the strongholds that seek to bind us. The psalmist's declaration, "Praise ye the Lord: for it is good to sing praises unto our God; for it is pleasant; and praise is comely," reminds us that praise is a fitting response to the goodness of God, transforming our circumstances and renewing our resilience. This divine ordinance grants the believer strength to endure afflictions and emerge triumphant. As the early church sang hymns and spiritual songs even in prison, so today, we are called to make a joyful noise, not merely in times of abundance but likewise in trials, knowing that God's presence is most palpably near amid our praises.

In expressing praise with enthusiasm and sincerity, our worship embraces not only the voice but the totality of our being. The heart rejoices, the hands are lifted, and the feet dance in homage to the Creator. Each act of praise becomes a living testimony of our allegiance and a celebration of the grace that sustains us daily. As we repeat the ancient songs, we connect with a vast cloud of witnesses who have gone before us, the prophets, apostles, and saints who found refuge and joy in God's promises. To join their ranks through heartfelt praise is to participate in a sacred tradition that renews the soul across generations. It is here, in the joyous noise of worship, that the listener meets the Lord, and the eternal love of God envelops the weary pilgrim, breathing strength and peace anew.

Therefore, to cultivate praise as a spiritual practice is to invite a rhythmic renewal that shapes our entire walk of faith. It encourages the believer not only to remember the mercies of the past but to anticipate the fullness of joy yet to come. When the clouds of sorrow gather or when the path grows steep, the joyful noise of praise becomes a beacon of light, guiding the way with radiance. It is an assurance that God remains sovereign and gracious, that His purposes are unchangeable, and that His love endureth forevermore. As our lips declare His goodness with boldness and our hearts swell with gladness, we are transformed from within, strengthened, restored, and beautifully anchored in the unshakable truth of the Scriptures.

Let every believer resolve to embrace this divine invitation: to make a joyful noise unto the Lord with a heart full of sincere praise, letting our worship be an unceasing melody that rises above trials and speaks boldly of hope. May our voices join the eternal chorus that celebrates the majesty of God and the richness of His grace. And as we sing, may our souls be lifted higher in the knowledge that the Lord delighteth in our praise, and that with every joyful noise, we draw nearer to the heart of our Redeemer, finding rest, strength, and everlasting peace.

Living a Life of Praise

To live a life of praise is to embrace an ongoing harmony with the Divine, weaving worship into the very fabric of our daily existence so that our hearts continually resound with gratitude and adoration. Consider the psalmist's declaration, "O praise the Lord, all ye nations: praise him, all ye people" (Psalm 117:1), where the call to worship transcends time and circumstance, inviting every soul to raise a song of thanksgiving irrespective of the trials that surround. Praise, therefore, is not reserved for moments when blessings overflow or triumph is sweetest, but is rather the steady flame that illumines the shadows of our days. It becomes a lifeline, offering refuge when burdens are heavy and anthems of joy when spirits soar. To integrate praise into our daily journey is to root our souls in the awareness that God's goodness remains constant, an unshakable foundation beneath life's shifting sands.

The sacred scriptures overflow with vivid portrayals of worship, testifying to the transformative power of praise when it rises from sincere hearts. The prophet Habakkuk commands, "Though the fig tree shall not blossom, neither shall fruit be in the vines; the labour of the olive shall fail, and the fields shall yield no meat; the flock shall be cut off from the fold, and there shall be no herd in the stalls: Yet I will rejoice in the Lord, I will joy in the God of my salvation" (Habakkuk 3:17–18). Here lies a profound lesson , praise is not contingent upon the abundance of earthly circumstances but is a deliberate act of faith that affirms God's sovereignty and steadfast love even in scarcity and suffering. To praise in hardship is to cast a luminous net over despair, gathering hope that sustains; it is the soul's audacious rebellion against discouragement, anchoring itself in trust when the storm rages fiercest.

Incorporating praise into our daily experience invites us to perceive the mundane as sacred, transforming ordinary moments into offerings of worship. We awaken to the melody in the morning's first light, the whispering wind that caresses our faces, the harmonious chorus of birdsong that proclaims God's handiwork. The Apostle Paul exhorts, "Be careful for nothing; but in every thing by prayer and supplication with thanksgiving let your requests be made known unto God" (Philippians 4:6), linking the practice of gratitude and prayer to a heart that chooses praise in all things. To cultivate a life of praise is to cultivate a spirit that finds reasons for thanksgiving not by ignoring hardship, but by framing every experience within the embrace of divine grace. It invites a revolution in perception, where trials become teachers, and even wounds are canvases for God's redemptive artistry.

The act of praise also strengthens our resilience by shifting the focus from our limitations and frailty toward the boundless might and mercy of God. Praise acknowledges that no circumstance, no matter how pressing, holds ultimate dominion over our souls. When the writer of Psalms declares, "Praise ye the Lord. Praise, O ye servants of the Lord, praise the name of the Lord" (Psalm 113:1–2), it is a summons to remember that worship empowers us to transcend the transient in favor of the eternal. Worship is the soul's courage to affirm life's goodness even when drenched in tears, a quiet strength that sets us upon solid rock. This spiritual posture nurtures patience, endurance, and hope, which flourish as pillars supporting us through tribulation. Thus, praise is not simply an expression of joy but a fortress of faith, an unyielding declaration that God reigns sovereign over both triumph and trial.

Moreover, living a life of praise invites a dynamic conversation with God, where words of adoration and thanksgiving form a sacred dialogue. Prayer becomes a tributary flowing into worship's great river, washing the soul clean, refreshing faith's flame, and nurturing intimacy with the Divine. The psalmist's words, "I will bless the Lord at all times: his praise shall continually be in my mouth" (Psalm 34:1), embody this continuity of communion. Worship then transcends mere ritual or duty; it is the spontaneous outpouring of a heart captivated by God's beauty and truth. It is singing in the night, dancing in the dawn, and silent awe in the noonday sun. It colors every act, blessing each breath, infusing even the smallest service with grace. When we carry the fragrance of praise with us, we become vessels of hope and encouragement to those we meet, emanating the peace that surpasses understanding.

To integrate worship as a constant companion is to live with an immortal song upon our lips and a sanctuary within our spirits. The story of the children of Israel, encamped between Pharaoh's chariots and the Red Sea, illustrates this vividly. Miriam took the timbrel in her hand, and all the women went out after her with timbrels and with dances, singing and praising the Lord for their deliverance (Exodus 15:20–21). Praise birthed joy in the midst of uncertainty and transformed fear into fearless celebration. Such praise is revolutionary; it defies circumstance by proclaiming victory before the battle's end. To echo this in our daily walk is to invite God to be the center of every triumph and every trial. Our lives thus become living psalms, echoes of heavenly worship that testify of God's enduring covenant with His people.

Yet the pursuit of a life rich in praise calls for intentionality, lest the noise of daily demands drown out the sacred music within our hearts. It requires us to establish rhythms of worship, to cultivate moments of stillness where we might listen as well as offer song. The King James Bible's poetic cadence becomes a balm in these pauses , "My praise shall be continually of thee" (Psalm 71:6) , guiding us back to the sanctuary of sacred words that uplift and renew. Through breathing deeply in meditation upon these ancient passages, we find renewal of spirit and clarity of purpose, rekindling the flame of worship that might otherwise flicker and falter. It is in these sacred moments that praise becomes not just an act but a state of being, an enduring posture of thanksgiving and trust that colors every thought, stretch of the day, and encounter.

The living of such a life also stirs the heart toward creativity in worship. Praise need not be confined to spoken word or song; it manifests in acts of kindness, service, and sacrifice, becoming an offering that embodies God's love and glory in the world. When the Lord Jesus said, "By this shall all men know that ye are my disciples, if ye have love one to another" (John 13:35), love itself becomes the highest form of praise, a living testimony of God's grace active among us. The hands that serve, the heart that forgives, the eyes that see the good in others, all sing the silent chorus of praise that delights heaven's ear. In this way, worship expands beyond the sanctuary walls and permeates the mundane and the miraculous alike, consecrating the ordinary as sacred.

Therefore, to live a life of praise is to embody a continual offering of the soul to God, a persistent melody that rises higher with each breath, undimmed by circumstance, unwavering amid change. It transforms our worldview, anchors our hope, and nurtures a deep and abiding joy that defies fleeting happiness. As the psalmist reminds us, "Praise the Lord, O my soul: and all that is within me, praise his holy name" (Psalm 103:1), praise is not only a spontaneous reaction but a deliberate choice, an act of will aligned with the heart's deepest truth. It invites us into a sacred dance, steps guided by faith, and a rhythm pulsing with divine love. Through this sacred practice, the believer is continually lifted toward the heavens, anchored in the Word and fortified against the tempests of life, finding in praise both sanctuary and strength. May this journey inspire us to enfold worship into every moment, to anchor our hearts in the eternal melody of God's praise, and to echo His glory forevermore.

Faith in Action

Serving Others

To serve others is to breathe life into our faith, transforming belief from mere words spoken in quiet moments into vibrant acts lived out in the world's bustling arena. The Apostle James declares, "Faith without works is dead," echoing the profound truth that faith must find its expression beyond the confines of the heart and mind, into the hands and feet, into tangible deeds of love, kindness, and mercy. As followers of the King of kings, we are called to mirror the life of our Lord Jesus Christ, who, though He was in the form of God, humbled Himself to serve, wash the feet of His disciples, and give His life for the salvation of many. Serving others becomes the sacred bridge connecting divine grace to human need, the living proof that God's love within us is neither dormant nor theoretical but active and alive. Every small action of compassion, be it a word of encouragement, a helping hand, a shared meal, or a listening ear, resonates with eternal significance when done out of love.

To live a faith rooted in the Word is to carry within us the imprint of Christ's servant heart, a heart moved not by selfish ambition or fleeting desires but by the eternal call to love our neighbor as ourselves. This love is not an abstract ideal but a practical, daily commitment to see beyond ourselves, to bear one another's burdens, and to offer kindness where hardness abides. The scriptures abound with examples of this holy posture, our Lord reaching out to the lepers, embracing the outcasts, healing the broken, and speaking tender words to those scorned by society. The Good Samaritan's story is etched deep into the fabric of sacred teaching as a clarion call that service transcends boundaries, barriers, and prejudices: the neighbor is not merely the familiar or the convenient but every soul in need, crafted in the very image of God. Thus, serving others dismantles the walls our pride builds, inviting us into the unfolding kingdom where mercy and justice flow like a mighty river.

Yet serving others requires more than mere reaction; it is the fruit of a heart anchored in God's Word, nourished by prayer and steeped in humility. We do not serve to earn favor or to seek recognition, but from a deep wellspring of gratitude for the unmerited grace bestowed upon us. The King James Bible's majestic cadence reminds us that even the humblest servant is exalted in the eyes of Heaven: "Whosoever exalteth himself shall be abased; and he that humbleth himself shall be exalted." In this divine economy, the act of service is never wasted or overlooked but transforms both giver and receiver. Serving softens our hearts, breaks the chains of selfishness, and leads us closer to our Creator, who inhabits the humble contrite spirit. When we wash the feet of others, whether literally or figuratively, we partake in a holy rite of surrendering our pride, following Christ's example, and entering into the rhythm of grace.

Imagine the world as a vast sea, sometimes calm and soothing, other times storm-tossed and perilous. Our acts of service become anchors cast amidst the waves, securing hope in places of despair, light where darkness threatens to overwhelm, and warmth where cold isolation dwells. For the weary, the lost, the broken-hearted, service is a tangible manifestation of God's unfailing love. When we fill the hands of hunger with food, tend the wounds of the afflicted, comfort the lonely, or simply offer our presence with genuine attentiveness, we embody the hands and feet of Christ. It is in these moments that faith is not an ethereal doctrine but a vivid reality, visible, tactile, and deeply felt. By serving others, we bring to life the promise that the kingdom of God is not merely future but present, among us, within our hands and hearts.

The call to serve also invites us to a profound spiritual transformation, challenging us to move beyond ourselves and our comfort zones. Service often requires sacrifice, of time, resources, and personal desires, and yet, it is in these sacrifices that God's grace shines most brightly. The Lord Himself said, "It is more blessed to give than to receive," and therein lies a sacred paradox of the Christian life: by losing ourselves in the love of others, we find our truest selves and deepest joy. The voluntary relinquishing of control and convenience cultivates a faith that is adventurous, courageous, and deeply rooted in trust. We come to understand that our hands are instruments of divine purpose, our lives woven into a greater tapestry of redemption and hope. The servant's path may be narrow and challenging, but it leads to the heights of spiritual intimacy and fulfillment.

Moreover, serving others cultivates community and unity, knitting disparate hearts together into the body of Christ. When we serve, we recognize the imago Dei, the divine image, in each person we encounter. This recognition births respect, compassion, and a longing for justice that extends far beyond individual acts. Through service, walls of division crumble, prejudices dissolve, and the church becomes a living testament to the reconciling power of God's love. As Paul exhorted the Corinthians, "Now ye are the body of Christ, and members in particular," so too does every act of service remind us that our faith is communal, interconnected, and meant to ripple outwards, touching families, neighborhoods, and nations. We are not mere solitary believers but a covenant people, called to embody the gospel in tangible, transformative ways.

In the stillness of prayer, we seek divine strength and wisdom to serve well and love abundantly. We pray for open eyes to perceive needs hidden beneath surfaces, hearts softened to respond with grace, and hands eager to labor without count or complaint. The sacred practice of service flows from a well of spiritual vitality sustained by constant communion with God, for true service is never our own endeavor but the outworking of the Spirit within us. The King James Bible's stately phrases offer us a balm and fortification: "I can do all things through Christ which strengtheneth me." This promise emboldens us to step beyond hesitation and fear, knowing that each humble act of service is empowered by God Himself. Our faith is anchored, not in fleeting human strength, but in the mighty hand of the Almighty.

To embody a living faith through serving others is to weave the threads of hope and healing into the fabric of everyday life. It transforms ordinary moments into sacred encounters where heaven touches earth. It challenges us to see beyond our own concerns and to respond with the generosity reflective of our Father's heart. Serving becomes a sacred dialogue where our hands articulate the silent prayers of love, our footsteps trace the pathway of Christ, and our lives bear witness to the abiding truth that God's kingdom is among us now. May we be found faithful in this high calling, vessels of mercy and agents of grace, ever ready to serve, to uplift, and to love, as Christ has served us, with an everlasting, boundless heart. Amen.

Walking the Narrow Path

To walk the narrow path is to embrace a pilgrimage of holiness, a journey that calls for unwavering commitment amidst the tempests and seductions of this present world. The King James Bible, with its solemn cadence and majestic resonance, beckons us to venture forth where few dare to tread, the narrow way that leadeth unto life, straight and narrow, unlike the broad path that spreadeth to destruction. This path is no mere metaphor but a tangible and demanding course of righteous living, a deliberate choice to embody the doctrines of faith in every waking moment, pressing onward with steadfastness, courage, and humility. To follow Christ is to take up the cross, to deny the self with passion and resolve, and to pour forth love not as a fleeting sentiment but as a firm foundation of daily action. The narrow path is defined not only by its exclusivity in doctrine but more so by the call to incarnate the living Word through acts of kindness, sacrificial service, and an unyielding dedication to the will of our heavenly Father.

The world around us, with its clamorous allurements and enticing distractions, invites many to opt for convenience, to settle for the easy route where righteousness is but a casual thought, and compromise becomes the currency of survival. Yet, the Scriptures admonish us, saying, "Enter ye in at the strait gate: for wide is the gate, and broad is the way, that leadeth to destruction, and many there be which go in thereat." The narrow path demands attention, not to mere ritual or external piety, but to the transformed heart that perfuses intentions and outward deeds with sincerity. This sacred journey is etched in the daily choice to seek holiness not as a burden but as a blessing, to love our neighbor as ourselves, and to embody a mercy that faithfully reflects the ineffable grace bestowed upon us through Christ's sacrifice. It is here, in this crucible of tested faith, wherein the believer's character is refined, tempered by adversity, polished by kindness, and strengthened through perseverance.

To walk this narrow way is to confront the paradox of Christian life: that strength is found in weakness, joy in tribulation, and victory in surrender. Each step taken in righteousness must wrestle with the forces of temptation and the shadows of doubt. Yet, the assurance of the Spirit's presence provides an unshakeable anchor, bidding the pilgrim to press forward, emboldened by the promises of Scripture. The psalmist declares, "Thy word is a lamp unto my feet, and a light unto my path." It is the illumination of God's truth that steels the heart and softens the will to obey, even when such obedience demands sacrifice or invites misunderstanding. The narrow path, therefore, is not an escape from suffering but a deliberate embrace of it, for suffering borne in faith produces an exalted testimony, a witness that proclaims the abiding power of God's redeeming love.

Moreover, the walk along this path is inseparably linked to the life and example of Jesus Christ, who embodied the perfect obedience we strive to emulate. Christ's footsteps were marked by compassion for the downtrodden, patience amidst persecution, and a tender yet firm resolve to accomplish the Father's will. His life vividly illustrates that commitment to righteousness is not a solitary endeavor but a communal outpouring of love expressed in tangible acts, feeding the hungry, comforting the afflicted, and serving the least of these as if serving Christ Himself. As followers of the narrow way, we are called to mirror this servanthood, reflecting the heart of God by extending grace and kindness beyond measure. In doing so, our faith transcends abstract belief and becomes a living, breathing testament to the transformative power of divine love.

This journey on the narrow path thus demands a full-bodied faith, one that moves beyond personal salvation to encompass acts of justice, mercy, and humility. Our lives are not meant for self-centered pursuits but for the advancement of God's kingdom here on earth. Every decision to honor God in speech, deed, and thought reinforces the path's exclusivity, shaping a life that stands in stark contrast to the secular drift around us. Indeed, the narrow way requires courage, the audacity to resist cultural conformity, to remain resolute in prayer, and to cherish the counsel of Scripture as the compass by which we navigate life's complexities. This courage is not born of human strength alone but is nurtured in the quiet moments of devotion where the soul is drawn near to the heart of God. In these sacred hours, fortified by prayer and meditation upon His word, the believer is renewed, empowered, and equipped to continue the pilgrimage with fresh resolve.

Yet, let us not be weary in well-doing, for the narrow path is also marked by an unending supply of grace. When faltering occurs, as it inevitably will in the frailty of our humanity, God's mercy meets us mercifully, inviting repentance and restoration. The journey is progressive, a steady crescendo of sanctification wherein each step forward aligns us more fully with Christ's image. It is a divine dance of surrender and renewal, wherein the soul grows attentive to the Spirit's whisper and sensitive to the needs of others, thus expanding the horizon of faith from the self to the community. Through this grace, every act of obedience, no matter how small, ripples outwards with eternal significance, weaving a tapestry of holy living that glorifies God and bears witness to the world.

In the quietude of reflection, the call to walk the narrow path compels us to examine the texture of our own lives, to prayerfully consider how our thoughts, words, and deeds echo the character of Christ. Are we willing to be counted among the few who choose righteousness over ease, light over darkness, truth over falsehood? The narrow path is not a pathway of isolation but a journey shared with the communion of saints who encourage one another to hold fast the profession of faith without wavering. It is a sacred invitation to embody the goodness of God daily, to allow His love to overflow through us, and to stand as a beacon of hope and faithfulness in a world hungry for divine light.

So let us rise each day with a heart inclined to obedience, a spirit ready to serve, and a mind fixed upon the eternal promises of God. Let our feet be planted firmly upon the narrow way, walking in the footsteps of Christ with humility and zeal. May our lives be living sermons, echoing the majesty of the King James Bible and the timeless truth it proclaims. In steadfast commitment to this journey, we find not only a sanctified path but a transformed life, anchored in the unchanging word and guided by the enduring love of the Almighty. Henceforth, let no trial or temptation dissuade us from this sacred course, but let us press onward, rejoicing and enduring, knowing that those who walk the narrow path shall inherit eternal life, and find rest for their souls in the everlasting kingdom of our Lord.

Courage in Witnessing

To stand boldly as a witness to the faith that dwelleth within us is not merely to utter words borne of belief, it is to embody the very essence of Christ's love and grace in all our dealings and to carry forth His light in a world oft obscured by shadows of doubt and despair. The sacred trust bestowed upon each believer is to be a living testimony, a beacon that doth not waver in the tempest, nor falter amid the clamour of a wayward generation. Scripture admonisheth us in the book of Acts, "But ye shall receive power, after that the Holy Ghost is come upon you: and ye shall be witnesses unto me both in Jerusalem, and in all Judaea, and in Samaria, and unto the uttermost part of the earth." This divine promise affirmeth that the courage to bear witness doth not spring from human will alone but is empowered mightily by the Spirit of God, who emboldens the timid and strengthens the faint-hearted to proclaim the truth in the face of opposition and indifference alike.

Many a soul is stifled by fear, for fear of rejection, of ridicule, or the loneliness that often attendeth those who lift up the name of Christ openly and without apology. Yet, the Lord calleth us from this hesitance, beckoning us to step forth with unwavering conviction. Consider the Apostle Peter, who, though he was once impetuous and uncertain, did rise and speak with boldness before the councils and rulers, emboldened by the Spirit that had descended upon him at Pentecost. Such courage is not born of human bravado but of the deep-seated assurance that one is upheld by the Almighty. The knowledge that in testifying of God's redeeming love we serve a cause eternal, that our words can breathe life anew into weary hearts and lift many from the abyss of despair, is a wellspring of strength. To witness, therefore, is to be a vessel of hope and a bearer of light, steadfast amid the flickering shadows.

Yet, the courage required for this sacred task transcendeth mere verbal proclamation; it is mirrored in our actions, in lives sanctified by kindness, patience, and humility. Jesus Himself, the author and finisher of our faith, doth not only command us to speak but to serve, opening the mouths of our witness through tangible acts of love and mercy. When we clothe the naked, feed the hungry, tend the sick, and comfort the brokenhearted, our service doth become a sermon, even to those deaf to words. In the gentle touch of compassion and the silent sacrifice of our time and resources, the gospel is made resplendent, more convincing than the loftiest of speeches. It is in such humble, Christlike service that the bravery of our faith journey is most profoundly displayed, for to serve unconditionally requireth strength to set aside selfishness and to elevate another's need above our own. This is the truest form of courage, bearing the marks of Christ not only on our tongues but etched deeply upon our hands and hearts.

The world, in all its clamorous distraction and darkness, doth hunger for this very light. In towns and villages, in the bustling cities and in the quiet countryside, the Lord's ambassadors are called to unveil faith as a living reality, radiating hope that transcendeth circumstance. When we dare to live out the gospel boldly and lovingly, we invite others into a sacred place of renewal, where doubts can be laid down and faith rekindled. The boldness to witness often requires that we confront not only external challenges but internal doubts that linger at the borders of our confidence. It is a continual struggle to lay aside our fears and embrace vulnerability, trusting that the Spirit will guide our words and deeds. Yet, each act of courage in witnessing enriches our spiritual walk, drawing us nearer to God as we rely on His strength rather than our own. The moments when we step forth despite trembling hearts are the very moments when God's power is most clearly made perfect.

In the weaving of this faith narrative, prayer is the loom that binds our courage with divine purpose. It is imperative that each believer, before venturing into the field of witness, seek the mantle of the Holy Spirit through fervent supplication. Prayer aligns our hearts with God's will and arms our spirits with peace that surpasseth understanding. As we lift up our voices in prayer, so do we prepare our hearts to listen, to hear the promptings of the Spirit that lead us when words falter or situations grow complex. In prayer, we find the fortification needed to persevere, the gentle boldness to speak truth in love, and the patience to endure misunderstanding and opposition. The courageous witness is therefore not an act of impulsive zeal but the fruit of a soul deeply rooted in communion with God, steadfast amidst the trials and uncertainties of this earthly pilgrimage.

Moreover, bold witnessing extends beyond personal encounters and spills into the fabric of daily living. To be courageous in our faith means that we refuse to isolate our spiritual walk from the mundane and ordinary, weaving the testimony of God's love through all that we are and do. It calls us to exhibit integrity in our work, kindness in our speech, forgiveness in our relationships, and perseverance in hardship. Each deed, each small act of grace, whispers to the world "Herein is love," and fortifies the witness of Christ's transforming power. Sometimes, the most profound testimonies arise not from grand proclamations but in the quiet consistency of godly living. Such courage is often met with awe, stirring the curiosity and yearning of hearts thirsting for truth and assurance amid life's uncertainties.

It is vital, too, to remember that witnessing is not a solitary venture but one conducted in the fellowship of believers, a communion of saints who uplift, encourage, and strengthen one another. The courage to witness is multiplied in the gathering of God's people, where prayers intercede, testimonies inspire, and love manifests tangibly. When the brothers and sisters in Christ stand shoulder to shoulder, sharing their faith like a quiver full of arrows, the impact receiveth a potency that no one arrow alone could achieve. The mutual encouragement found in such fellowship rekindles the flame of boldness when it groweth dim, reminding each soul that they are part of a divine movement propelled by the Spirit's might.

Ultimately, to embrace courage in witnessing is to enter into the sacred dance of faith and action, trusting that while our voices and hands may be small and imperfect, they are instruments in the hands of the Almighty. It is to surrender wholly to the cause of Christ, knowing that in every humble act of bearing witness, the kingdom of heaven is advanced and lives are eternally touched. The path of boldness is steep and oft strewn with trials, yet the reward is immeasurable: a heart anchored in the unchanging truth of God's word, a soul bathed in the peace that only He can give, and the joy of seeing lives transformed by the very gospel we declare. In this divine calling, the believer finds not only the courage to witness but the deep fulfillment of walking faithfully in the footsteps of the Savior, who commissioned us to go forth and make disciples of all nations, teaching them to observe all things whatsoever He hath commanded.

May this courage be born anew within us, that we might arise each day clothed with strength and humility, ready to testify by word and deed of the boundless love that hath redeemed us. And in that courage, may we be found faithful to the very end, our lives a testament to the glory of God and a wellspring of hope to a world yearning for light. Amen.

Humility in Service

To embrace humility in service is to walk the very path trod by our Lord and Savior, Jesus Christ, who, though being the Son of God, manifested the most profound example of lowliness and love. In the pages of the Holy Scripture, He teaches us not by mere words alone, but by the sacred virtue of action, that true greatness lieth not in rulers or riches, but in the contrite heart that giveth itself wholly unto the service of others. The King James Bible, with its majestic cadence, proclaims this with clarity and solemnity: "Whosoever will be great among you, let him be your minister; And whosoever will be chief among you, let him be your servant" (Matthew 20:26-27). This divine paradox, exalted above worldly wisdom, calls us to invert our natural inclinations, that we might find true honor only in laying down our own desires and ambitions for the sake of our brethren. In this holy exchange, humility sacrificeth self-glory and embraceth the quiet dignity of service, becoming the guiding light that shapes a faith alive in deeds.

The heart of humility in service is unfettered by pride or the craving for recognition; it is a sacred yielding to the needs of another, reflecting the self-emptying (kenosis) of Christ who, being rich, became poor for our sakes (2 Corinthians 8:9). This mystery of divine humility invites us to ponder deeply the stations of Christ's earthly ministry, from washing the feet of His disciples with tender care, to healing the broken, uplifting the weary, and comforting the forlorn. Each act stands as a monument to the servant's heart, a call to clad ourselves not with garments of pomp and pretense but to clothe ourselves with compassion, patience, and gentle mercy. To serve humbly is to imitate the Master who bore our infirmities and sorrowed with the afflicted, teaching us that service is not a mere task but a sacred vocation wherein the soul doth find its renewal and purpose.

In our modern world, rife with the temptation to exalt self and seek personal gain, the call to genuine humility and service grows all the more urgent. The devil's cunning often whispers that our worth is measured by achievements, applause, or power. Yet, the Bible firmly rebukes such vanity, inviting us instead into a liberating grace: being "clothed with humility: for God resisteth the proud, and giveth grace to the humble" (1 Peter 5:5). The humble servant's journey is not a path of ease, for it demands the surrender of ego and a willingness to stoop low in love and kindness. It is through these acts, small and great, done not for our glory but for the joy and blessing of others, that our faith breathes anew and is anchored in the living Word.

Consider the way Christ's humility illumines our understanding of service: He did not come to be ministered unto, but to minister, and to give His life a ransom for many (Mark 10:45). This ultimate example compels us to re-examine our own hearts and actions. Are we prepared to serve without counting the cost, to love without limits, to give without expectation? To serve with humility is to recognize that every opportunity to aid another is a sacred moment to reveal the face of God's love in this broken world. The very act of humbling ourselves for service transforms us, breathing sanctity into our every gesture and word. It teaches us patience when weariness tugs at our spirit, endurance when our sacrifices seem unacknowledged, and joy in the mere act of obedience to God's will. It is here, in the quiet surrender to service, that we find the sanctifying fire of true discipleship.

Humility in service is also a mirror reflecting the nature of the Church itself, a body called not to exalt itself, but to serve one another in love. The epistle to the Philippians exhorts us to "look not every man on his own things, but every man also on the things of others" (Philippians 2:4), echoing the Christlike pattern of selflessness. As members of this sacred body, we are bound in fellowship and mutual care, inviting us to embody the humility of Christ in our daily walk, that our faith may manifest in practical love and widen the horizons of our spiritual growth. Through acts of kindness, the giving of time, resources, and presence, we build the kingdom of heaven on earth, each moment an offering poured out in fealty and grace. This communal service, born from a humble heart, becomes a vessel of light and hope in the dark places of despair and loneliness.

Moreover, to serve humbly is to cultivate a spirit of gratitude and reliance upon God's grace rather than our own strength. The King James Bible reminds us that "I can do all things through Christ which strengtheneth me" (Philippians 4:13), a promise assuring us that in the weakness of service lies the power of God made perfect. When our hands grow weary or our hearts falter, this divine strength reneweth and sustaineth, enabling us to persevere in love that looks beyond itself. Prayer becomes a sustaining balm for the servant's soul, a sacred dialogue in which we lay bare our fears and ask for the grace to continue. Humility directs us to this dependence on God, foreclosing the arrogance of self-sufficiency and opening wide the heart's door to divine guidance and sustenance.

In this journey of humble service, we encounter the sweet fruits that nourish both giver and recipient: peace that passeth understanding, joy that is not fleeting but deeply rooted, and love that heals and unites. To serve as Christ taught is to draw nearer to the heart of God, to experience the profound union with Him who stooped low for our sake. Each act of kindness, no matter how small or unseen, is woven into the eternal tapestry of grace and redemption. As we cultivate this spirit of humility, we are transformed by the renewing power of the Holy Spirit, who sanctifies our actions and inflames our souls with love divine. And so, the humble servant is both baptized by trial and anointed with blessing, ever growing into the likeness of Christ and becoming a beacon of His eternal light.

May our hearts be ever tender to the call, and our hands ready to serve, that we too might tread the sacred road of humility in service. Let us bow low in spirit even as we lift up the weary, giving not for applause but from a heart that seeks to honor God through loving action. Let us remember that our Lord Himself hath said, "He that is greatest among you shall be your servant" (Matthew 23:11), and by this standard alone shall we judge the measure of our own faithfulness. May the grace of the Almighty empower us to lay aside pride and selfishness, clothing ourselves in the garments of compassion as we journey forth in humble service, reflecting the shining image of Christ to a world in need. In this sacred calling, may our souls find rest and our faith be anchored ever deeper in the unchanging Word. Amen.

Faith That Works

Faith, in its purest and most vigorous expression, is not a mere whisper within the heart or a silent witness in the soul; it is the living, breathing force that compels the man or woman after God to step forth boldly into the world, girded with the armaments of conviction and steadfast love. The sacred writ declares unto us that faith, without works, is dead, being alone. This solemn admonition reverberates through the corridors of time, challenging the complacency of mere belief and beckoning us instead to the vibrant realm where belief and deed intertwine, where the unseen conviction finds its eloquence in acts manifest and tangible. To possess faith that works is to embrace a divine paradox: unseen yet powerfully visible, ethereal in origin but concrete in expression, a pearl of great price that enriches not only the soul but the very atmosphere in which we dwell.

Consider, beloved, the example of our Lord Jesus Christ, the ultimate exemplar of faith in action. In His sojourn upon this earth, He did not merely speak of love; He lavished it with healing hands, with tender mercies towards the downtrodden, and with unyielding courage confronting darkness. His faith was not a static monument but a living river, flowing outward, transforming barren hearts and fractured lives. Likewise, our journey of faith beckons us beyond the threshold of silent assent to doctrine, calling instead to the marketplace, the hospital bedside, the weary neighbor's door, and the barren field of everyday toil. A faith that does not move the feet and stretch forth the hand is like a lamp hidden beneath a bushel, deprived of its purpose and robbed of its beauty. It is thus that faith becomes sanctified, not only within the enclosures of Scripture and prayer but in the soil tilled by works of kindness, in the fabric woven through sacrifice and the amber glow of service.

The epistle of James provides a stirring discourse: "Show me thy faith without thy works, and I will show thee my faith by my works."

Here is not a repudiation of faith's primacy but a profound symphony of unity. Faith and works dance together in holy cadence, each incomplete without the other. To pray for the hungry, to sing praises in the sanctuary, to confess the saving power of Christ, these are the bones and sinews of faith. Yet, to feed the hungry, to embody worship in humble service, to manifest confession in the welcoming embrace of brotherly love, these are the flesh and blood, without which faith languishes like a root deprived of moisture. How then does one cultivate such faith that works? The answer springs forth like water from a spiritual well: by anchoring the heart firmly in trust, and by casting the net of obedience wide upon the sea of grace.

To anchor faith in the word and pour it out through deeds demands a daily renewal of the mind's commitment and a heart tenderized by mercy. It requires that we look beyond ourselves, for faith is not a solitary treasure but a communal covenant. The commandment to love one's neighbor as oneself is the very heartbeat of faith in action. It bids us to labor in humility, crossing the boundaries of race, class, and culture, embodying the universal reach of God's love. Each act of kindness, whether it is sharing bread with the hungry, comforting the afflicted, or simply offering a listening ear, becomes a living epistle, read by all men. These are the tokens of a robust, resilient faith that prove our beliefs are not idle musings but foundations laid on the rock of divine truth. This faith that moves into the world is like a tree planted by the rivers of water, that bringeth forth fruit in its season, whose leaf also shall not wither.

The presence of works accompanying faith also serves to strengthen the believer's reliance on God. As we labor in love and step out in service, the evidence of God's providence and power becomes manifest, engendering deeper trust and a fortified spirit. The trials we endure in the pursuit of righteous deeds do not weaken faith but, through the refining fires of perseverance, sharpen it like the whetstone to the blade. It is in the crucible of living faith that our character is formed and tested, mettle proved by the furnace of obedience. Hence, faith that works is not merely measured by the quantity of deeds but the quality of the heart that engenders them, motives pure, intentions aligned with God's will, reflections of Christ's humility, and earnestness toward the glory of God. Such faith quickens the soul, bringing joy in sacrifice and peace amid labor.

Moreover, faith enacted through works extends beyond personal edification; it is an outward proclamation to the world of the transformative power of the Gospel. The hands that serve the poor, the lips that speak comfort, and the feet that journey to distant fields proclaim a truth that reason alone cannot capture: that God's kingdom is present where love is manifested in action. It stands as a testimony against the cynicism of a world beleaguered by doubt and despair, unveiling a faith that is living, active, and mighty to save. Through this faith, the Church is not merely a gathering of believers but a beacon of hope, a refuge for the weary, and a force for justice and compassion. It is faith incarnate, a testament to the boundless and enduring grace of God.

Yet, beloved, let us be mindful that the works wrought by faith are not for the glory of man but for the praise of God alone. The temptation to seek recognition or to perform out of obligation rather than genuine love must be vigilantly guarded against. True faith works in the secret places of the heart, untethered by the need for acclaim but motivated by a profound gratitude for the mercy received. In this sacred humility, our actions are sanctified, becoming fragrant offerings rising like sweet incense before the throne of heaven. The Lord trieth the hearts and reins, and it is this sincere devotion that breathes life into faith's works, rendering them pleasing and acceptable unto God.

In closing this reflection, let us embrace the call to a faith that works, a faith vibrant and unfeigned, grounded in the eternal truths of

Scripture and vivified by deeds inspired by divine love. Let us not be content with mere profession but press onward into the realm of demonstration, that our lives may be a living testimony of God's grace. As we endeavor to embody Christ's example, may the Spirit kindle within us a fervent desire to serve with joy, to love without condition, and to labor unceasingly for the advancement of His kingdom. Thus shall our faith become a mighty force, an anchor sure and steadfast, holding us firm amid the storms of life and beckoning others to partake in the abundant life found only in Him. O Lord, grant us grace to walk in this holy calling, to manifest our faith through deeds, and to glorify Thy name in all the earth. Amen.

Persevering in Good Works

In the weariness of days that stretch beyond measure, when the spirit grows faint, and the road appears endless, there lies an unyielding call to persevere in good works, a divine summons that beckons the soul to press onward, to labor faithfully in that sacred vineyard where the seeds of kindness, charity, and grace are sown. It is not enough, dear reader, to confess the truths of our faith with mere words or to cherish the promises of salvation in the silence of the heart; no, the Father who looketh upon the heart desires that our faith be worked out in steadfast action, an enduring testament to Him who hath called us out of darkness into His marvelous light. The Apostle Paul exhorts us, "Not slothful in business; fervent in spirit; serving the Lord." In this exhortation, there resounds a clarion charge to ensure that our deeds do not languish or grow cold, but blaze with the fervency of a flame kindled in eternal purpose, burning ever brighter through the storms and trials of life.

To persevere in good works is to walk the narrow path that Christ Himself traversed, a journey marked by humility, compassion, and self-sacrifice, holding fast to the resolve that our actions, though oft unseen by the eyes of men, are precious offerings laid upon the altar of divine service. The earthly realm is filled with temptations to grow weary and faint-hearted, for the enemy seeks diligently to snatch away every spark of kindness and wilt every act of mercy through the deceit of discouragement, weariness, or neglect. Yet the Word assures us that the reward of such perseverance is not vain: "In due season we shall reap, if we faint not." How often the toil of love and service seems to go unnoticed, like the gentle rain that falls unseen upon the thirsty earth, yet it is this very faithfulness that nourishes the garden of God's kingdom and prepares the soil of many hearts to receive the saving knowledge of the Lord.

The pathway of persevering good works is neither swift nor crowned with worldly applause, for it is measured rather by the constancy of the heart and the devotion of the soul. To lay hold of this calling is to embody the very footprint of Christ's own ministry: feeding the hungry, clothing the naked, visiting the prisoner, and consoling the afflicted, all in quiet, sincere humility. Consider the Master's words, "Inasmuch as ye have done it unto one of the least of these my brethren, ye have done it unto me." Each act of tenderness, each labor of love, is an encounter with the living Christ incarnate, and therein lies the sacred impetus to endure. When the hands grow tired from lifting others, when the eyes grow dim from weeping with those who suffer, remember that such endurance is itself a fragrant offering to God, a powerful witness against a world that often measures worth by triumph and immediate reward. To persevere is to fix the gaze not on transient gain but on the eternal fruit that comes through patience and unshaken fidelity.

It is paramount to grasp that perseverance in good works is nurtured by a continuous flow of divine grace, sustaining the weary and infusing strength where human resolve falters. The Spirit of God who dwells within us is the wellspring of this unending courage, empowering each act of mercy with heavenly vitality. We are reminded in the sacred scriptorium that "the fruits of the Spirit" include love,

acts of kindness, your generous giving, your faithful service be the living verses of Scripture inscribed upon the world's narrow path. Embrace the daily disciplines of mercy and charity, knowing that these are prayers of action, worship manifested in deeds that transcend time. For in such perseverance, the soul is anchored beyond the tumult of circumstance, and the heart finds peace in the knowledge that it laboreth not in vain but for a crown of righteousness, which the Lord, the righteous judge, shall give at that day.

In closing, lift up your eyes unto the hills, from whence cometh your help. Remember that perseverance in good works is no mere human endeavor but a sacred partnership with the Almighty hand that orders our steps and strengthens our souls. Press onward, therefore, with joy and humble confidence, assured that every act of faithfulness wrought in love and patience is stored in the heavenly treasury and will shine forth as a beacon for generations yet unborn. Rest not until the goal is reached, until the lasting kingdom is fully won, and your good works culminate in eternal praise and divine fellowship. May this resolve anchor you in storms and sunshine alike, strengthening your faith, quickening your hope, and deepening your love as you walk steadfastly in the footsteps of the Savior, who endured all things for our sakes and now intercedes for us at the right hand of God.

God's Promises

Everlasting Covenant

In the vast tapestry of divine revelation woven throughout the sacred pages of the King James Bible, one truth shines with unwavering radiance, the certainty of God's everlasting covenant. This covenant, not forged by mortal hands nor subject to the frailties of human endeavor, stands as an eternal testament to the unfathomable faithfulness of our Almighty God. From the dawn of creation to the final promise of restoration, the Scriptures resound with declarations of God's steadfast commitments, echoing through the chambers of the heart and soul as a balm for the weary and a beacon for the hopeful. It is in the knowledge of this unbreakable bond that the believer finds solace amid tumult, strength in the face of despair, and the assurance that no shadow of doubt may ever rightly linger where the sure word of God reigns.

Consider the covenant God made with Noah, that solemn vow to never again drown the earth beneath waters, inscribed not in fragile paper, but in the very arcs and colors of the rainbow stretching across the heavens. "And I will establish my covenant with you; neither shall all flesh be cut off any more by the waters of a flood," the Lord declared, His voice cascading like a mighty river of mercy (Genesis 9:11). There, in the covenant with Noah, we discern a divine pledge woven into the fabric of nature itself, a promise that the cycles of destruction shall yield to cycles of renewal, and that even the fiercest storms shall bow to the enduring grace of God's word. Such a covenant reassures the believer beyond transient fear, reminding us that despite the roaring tempest and the battering waves of life's afflictions, God's protective hand is ever present, unyielding in its commitment to preserve and restore.

But the covenant extends far beyond the waters; it dwells deeply in the narrative of God's chosen people, Israel. With Abraham, the Lord made a covenant that would thread through history, time, and eternity, a covenant sealed not by human merit, but by divine grace alone. "And I will make my covenant between me and thee, and will multiply thee exceedingly" (Genesis 17:2), God proclaimed, promising descendants as numerous as the stars of the firmament and the sands upon the shore. This covenant, marked by the sign of circumcision, was no mere contract of earthly convenience but a sacred bond of promise that God Himself would be the God of Abraham's seed. It was a declaration that transcended generations, a promise so steadfast it would come to find its fullest expression in the Messiah, the Seed through whom all nations would be blessed. Herein lies the beauty of God's everlasting covenant: it is alive, dynamic, and fulfilled through the ages, a living promise that breathes hope into the hearts of all who trust in His word.

The prophets of old echoed this immortal assurance, each utterance a thread in the glorious tapestry of holiness and fidelity. Jeremiah, in the depths of exile and despair, conveyed the profound covenant of peace that God extended to His people, a covenant not like the fragile tablets of stone broken by human hands, but a covenant inscribed upon the heart. "This is the covenant that I will make with the house of Israel after those days, saith the Lord; I will put my law in their inward parts, and write it in their hearts" (Jeremiah 31:33). What infinite tenderness shines through this promise, that God's law, His very will, would no longer be distant or external, but internal, intimate, a living force of transformation from within. This is the covenant of grace, sealed by the blood of the Lamb, that renews and sustains the soul, forging a bond so intimate that the believer may walk each moment in the light of divine communion and unshakable trust.

As we journey through the New Testament, the covenant of old is magnificently unfolded in the person and work of Jesus Christ, the

Mediator of a new and better covenant. The sacred words of the Savior at the Last Supper echo through the corridors of time: "This cup is the new testament in my blood, which is shed for you" (Luke 22:20). Herein lies the heart of the everlasting covenant, the sacrificial love of God manifested in the Son, whose blood cleanses from iniquity and restores fellowship with the Father. This new covenant is not merely a renewal of past promises but a triumphant consummation, a covenant that guarantees eternal life, unfailing mercy, and the indwelling presence of the Holy Spirit. It is a covenant sealed with love so deep that death could not sever it, a covenant that promises everlasting reconciliation and peace for all who are called according to His purpose.

The apostle Paul, in his inspired epistles, further illumines this wondrous truth by reminding believers that they are not bound by the condemnation of the old law but are free in the grace of this new covenant. "Now the God of peace, that brought again from the dead our Lord Jesus, that great shepherd of the sheep, through the blood of the everlasting covenant" (Hebrews 13:20), he writes, exposing the power and permanence of Christ's sacrifice. This is the covenant that assures us no adversary or circumstance can nullify God's promises. Whether in joy or suffering, our hope is anchored by this covenant, a bond that anchors the soul firmly in unchanging love, securing the believer in the tender hands of the Almighty through every trial of existence.

Let us, then, embrace this everlasting covenant with a heart wide open to the fullness of God's faithfulness. Our earthly lives teem with uncertainties, our paths often shrouded in the mists of sorrow, worry, and doubt. Yet in the sovereign promises of God's covenant, we find an unassailable rock, a refuge steadfast and sure. When despair would seek to overshadow our spirit, let us recall the assurance of God's word, "For I am the Lord, I change not" (Malachi 3:6), an eternal declaration that His promises endure beyond the changing tides of time and circumstance. Within this faith lies a peace that surpasses understanding, a quiet confidence that even in the darkest valley, we walk beside the Good Shepherd whose covenant with us remains unbroken.

This covenant invites us to rest, to lean wholly upon the divine assurance that God's purposes will not falter. It compels us to live in the light of this promise, trusting not in human strength but in the unfailing power of His word. As we meditate upon the grandeur of this sacred bond, let us allow the tender currents of grace to wash over our souls, renewing our spirits and restoring our weary hearts. The everlasting covenant calls us into a deeper fellowship, a spiritual intimacy crafted by divine promise and sealed by Christ's blood, eternal and unyielding.

May the contemplation of this unbreakable covenant inspire within us a faith that does not waver, a hope that does not fade, and a love that reflects the enduring love of God who has loved us with an everlasting love. In the quiet of our devotion, may we cling to this holy trust, that no matter the storms which assail us, no matter the shadows that seek to obscure our pathway, the covenant of God remains as a steadfast anchor for our soul, keeping us grounded in the eternal truth of His promises. Thus, with hearts illumined by Scripture and spirits renewed by prayer, we walk forward, ever anchored in the Word, embraced by the everlasting covenant, and forever secure in the loving arms of our faithful God.

Promises of Provision

In the tapestry of our lives, woven with threads of uncertainty and moments of scarcity, the promises of God's provision stand as a steadfast beacon of hope and assurance. There is a profound comfort in resting our souls upon the unshakeable declaration that our Heavenly Father, who clothes the lilies of the field and feeds the myriad birds of the air, is ever mindful of our needs. The sacred scriptures of the King James Bible echo with the voice of divine providence, urging us to lift our eyes beyond the transient shadows of want and fear, and to behold the eternal faithfulness of God who is our shepherd, our refuge, and our supply. When the heart is heavy with doubt, the soul finds solace in the sacred word that "my God shall supply all your need according to his riches in glory by Christ Jesus" (Philippians 4:19). It is in this assurance that trust is not only invited but beckoned with a holy insistence, for the God who has promised to provide never falters nor delays.

To trust God for provision is to surrender the turmoil of anxious striving and to embrace a divine economy far beyond mortal understanding. It requires a faith that transcends mere hope, a faith that stands firm when the cupboards seem bare and the days grow lean, revealing the profound truth that our sustenance is not measured solely by earthly abundance but by the rich grace that flows inexhaustibly from the throne of heaven. The Lord declares through the prophet Isaiah, "Fear thou not; for I am with thee: be not dismayed; for I am thy God: I will strengthen thee; yea, I will help thee; yea, I will uphold thee with the right hand of my righteousness" (Isaiah 41:10). These words are not simply poetic encouragements but the very lifeblood of a promise that enshrines our needs within the unfailing power of God's righteousness. To lean on this promise is to exchange the restless striving of the flesh for the peace of resting in a divine embrace that upholds and sustains.

It is often in the wilderness of waiting, amid seasons of barrenness or hardship, that the fullness of God's provision is revealed in ways spiritual and tangible. Consider the children of Israel fleeing bondage, their footsteps marked by thirst and hunger, and yet gathering manna each morning, a miracle of daily provision that taught dependence and faithfulness. Such profound lessons remind us that provision is not always the abundance we imagine but the nourishment divinely appointed, sufficient and timely for every purpose ordained by the Almighty. Similarly, Jesus' own ministry abounds with demonstrations of God's providential care, feeding the five thousand with loaves and fishes, restoring the hand of the sick, granting grace to the brokenhearted, each sign pointing to the truth that God's love and provision are inextricably bound. He who feeds the sparrows assures the care of His children, and this sacred reality invites us to lay down our worries, trusting that He who clothes the heavens with stars will not neglect one who calls upon His holy name.

Yet trusting in divine provision calls for a surrender that often challenges the pride of self-reliance. The temptation to grasp and bargain for security with mere human effort can cloud the heart's vision and obscure the gentle voice of God's promise. The Psalmist exhorts us to "Commit thy way unto the Lord; trust also in him; and he shall bring it to pass" (Psalm 37:5), reminding us that provision flows most richly when aligned with the soul's submission to divine will. This commitment is not passive resignation but active faith, walking forward with confidence that every step is served and supplied by the One who holds all things in sovereign hands. Such trust fosters a spiritual resilience that enables the believer to rejoice even in scarcity, knowing that God's provision may come in forms unforeseen, through friends, unexpected opportunities, or a quiet peace that surpasses understanding. The true riches of provision often lie not in gold or grain but in the sustaining grace that empowers, comforts, and steadies the soul.

As we meditate on the promises of provision, we are drawn toward a deeper realization that God's supply is holistic, caring not only for our physical needs but for our emotional, spiritual, and eternal well-being. The Lord Jesus reminds us not to be anxious for our lives, what we shall eat or drink, nor for our bodies, what we shall put on, for the very hairs of our head are numbered, and heavenly Father knows our needs before we ask (Matthew 6:25-30). This profound recognition invites a tranquil heart that rests on the divine omniscience and loving care that governs all creation. Provision thus becomes a sacred partnership where our faith meets the faithfulness of God, creating a sanctuary of trust amid the storms. In this sacred space, prayer flows as the vessel through which we present our petitions, seeking not only what is needed in the moment but also the wisdom to discern the eternal purposes behind every provision.

The journey of faith, anchored in the word, assures us that God's promises are not vague hopes but firm foundations that can withstand the tempests of doubt and difficulty. When the pantry is bare and the future uncertain, the soul may draw deeply from the wells of scripture: "The young lions do lack, and suffer hunger: but they that seek the Lord shall not want any good thing" (Psalm 34:10). This assurance is a heavenly covenant of care that infuses our ordinary lives with divine significance. God's provision is a living promise, breathing hope into the weary heart, and an invitation to rest in Him, who is the giver of all good things. As we embrace this truth, may we be transformed by a faith that is not shaken by circumstances but firmly rooted in the immutability of God's word, trusting that His provision will ever be abundant and sufficient, guiding us gently from moment to moment to the fullness of life in Him.

Let us then, with grateful hearts, lift our prayers as an offering of trust, beseeching the Lord that in every season He might reveal His provision, not only in bread or water but in peace that quieteth the soul and strength that anchors the spirit. May the sacred promise of divine supply renew our hope, kindle our faith, and deepen our communion with God, ever faithful and ever true. In this divine assurance, we find a sanctuary, a holy refuge where our needs are met, our fears dispelled, and our faith anchored securely in the unchanging word of God.

Promises of Protection

In the midst of life's ever-shifting storms, when shadows lengthen, and the tempest howls with fierce abandon, the soul seeks refuge, a sanctuary untouched by the tumult that assails the heart and mind. It is in these sacred moments of vulnerability that the promises of protection offered by Almighty God stand as steadfast bulwarks, unyielding and sure against the whirlwind of our tribulations. The King James Bible, with its majestic cadence and ancient reverence, whispers eternally to the earnest believer: "The Lord is my refuge and my fortress: my God; in him will I trust" (Psalm 91:2). This divine assurance is not merely a poetic phrase but a bedrock truth, declaring that beneath the outspread wings of God, we find shelter impenetrable, a sacred haven where fear gives way to peace, and despair is swallowed by hope.

To be anchored in the Word is to grasp this celestial promise with the trembling hands of faith. The God who fashioned the heavens and the earth, who commanded the seas to roar no more, who clothes the lilies of the field in royalty without labor or strife, extends His protective arms over His children. When the adversities of life rise as mountains before us, be they anguish, loss, illness, or the insidious whispers of doubt, His covenant stands inviolable. He is our bulwark against the cunning snares of the enemy and our fortress amid the fierce onslaught of every trial. The apostle Paul, confined and battered in his earthly journey, could yet proclaim with unwavering confidence, "I can do all things through Christ which strengtheneth me" (Philippians 4:13), for this strength was born from the Savior's faithful guardianship, a shield that neither fatigue nor torment could shatter.

Consider the imagery of Psalm 91 in all its profound comfort: "He shall cover thee with his feathers, and under his wings shalt thou trust." What tender shelter is here depicted! The Creator likened to a magnificent bird, its majestic feathers stretched wide to protect the vulnerable within the nest. It is a powerful symbol of God's loving vigilance, watchful, tender, and resolute. In a world rife with rampant uncertainty, where shadows of fear can so easily eclipse the human spirit, the believer is invited to abide under these feathers, to wholly trust in the divine covering that repels every fiery dart hurled by malice and misfortune. This is no passive protection; it is active, living, breathing, a constant embrace that never loosens nor wanes.

Yet, this promise of protection does not presume exemption from hardship. Rather, it declares that in the midst of even the cruelest trials, God remains a sanctuary. The rocks of our endurance are forged not in times of ease, but in adversity, tempered by the faith that God's shelter is real and reachable. When Job lost all he possessed, when friends turned cold, and his own flesh suffered torment, he clung to the knowledge that though God's ways are inscrutable, His justice and mercy endure forever. "Though he slay me, yet will I trust in him" (Job 13:15). This profound declaration echoes through time, encouraging believers to place their hope not in fleeting circumstances but in the eternal hand that upholds the universe. For God's protection is not a shield that prevents the storm but a refuge that makes the storm bearable and ultimately victorious for the soul anchored in His Word.

The New Testament further illuminates this sanctuary of divine protection through the person of our Lord Jesus Christ, who bore our infirmities and carried our sorrows, that we might find true rest beneath the shadow of His wings. "Come unto me, all ye that labor and are heavy laden, and I will give you rest" (Matthew 11:28) speaks not only to weary bodies but to troubled spirits crying out for relief. In Christ, the promises of protection unfold in tender compassion and supernatural power; He is the Good Shepherd who neither loses nor forsakes His sheep, guiding them securely through dark valleys. This Shepherd leads beyond fear, beyond pain, to the pastures of peace and the streams of consolation. To trust Him is to trust unconditionally in the shield He provides, an impenetrable fortress not wrought by human hands but fashioned in divine love.

The assurance of God's protection also carries a sacred call to faithfulness and vigilance. To abide in His shadow, to dwell in the secret place of the Most High, is to nurture a living, breathing relationship sustained by prayer, worship, and the meditation of His holy Word. Scripture exhorts the believer: "Be sober, be vigilant; because your adversary the devil, as a roaring lion, walketh about, seeking whom he may devour" (1 Peter 5:8). This caution is not a summons to fear but a reminder that divine protection is both grace and responsibility. The armor of God described by Paul (Ephesians 6:10-18) reminds us that while God's hand shields us, we must stand in spiritual readiness, clothed with truth, righteousness, and faith. This partnership with the divine ensures the believer is not passive but actively engaged in defense of the soul, standing firm upon the rock of faith amidst raging seas.

Moreover, the promises of protection extend beyond mere survival; they are laden with transformative hope. To be protected by God is to be preserved for a purpose, to be carried through the furnace of trial, cleansed and refined as pure gold. These promises ignite a sacred resilience that refuses to bow beneath despair's yoke. The psalmist affirms, "No evil shall befall thee, neither shall any plague come nigh thy dwelling" (Psalm 91:10), a declaration that affirms God's sovereign power to guard not only the body but the very essence of our being. This promise echoes in the deepest chambers of the heart, offering a sanctuary where fear is dismantled and courage blooms forth, where hope is kindled anew with the certainty of His abiding presence.

In our daily pilgrimage amid the perplexities of life, these promises become living realities through prayer, conversations with the Almighty who hears and answers. To approach Him with trust is to invite His protection into every corner of our existence, granting peace that surpasses all understanding, even when circumstances are fraught with peril. This sacred dialogue nurtures the soul, weaving a tapestry of comfort and strength that clothes the believer through every season. It is here, in the silent moments of reflection and communion, that the heart discerns the unbreakable cords of God's faithfulness, holding us fast when the world threatens to upheave us.

The unfolding of God's protection is also manifest in the communion of the saints, the body of Christ that stands as a fortress of prayer and love around the individual believer. The scriptures teach that none who call upon the Lord shall be forsaken, and this divine promise is often experienced through the kindness and steadfastness of His people. Together, believers find mutual encouragement as they share testimonies of God's sheltering grace, reinforcing the truth that the Lord's protection is not distant or abstract but tangible and near, a balm for weary hearts.

Finally, the greatest promise of protection culminates in the eternal hope found in Christ's resurrection and the life everlasting. The earthly trials, though arduous, are but brief passages in the grand tapestry of redemption and glory. "The eternal God is thy refuge, and underneath are the everlasting arms" (Deuteronomy 33:27), a verse that bridges the temporal with the eternal, reminding us that the God who shields now will carry us home to perfect peace beyond the veil of this world. This final promise encourages the weary pilgrim to press on, filled with courage and hope, anchored unshakably in the Word that endures forever.

Thus, amidst life's trials and shadows, to dwell in the shelter of God's promises is to find a peace that transcends understanding, a hope that never falters, and a strength that rises eternal. As the soul anchors itself in these sacred truths, the restless waves of fear and doubt grow still, and the believer stands secure, cradled within the everlasting arms of divine protection, now and forevermore.

Promises of Peace

In the restless tides of our daily lives, beset by turmoil and uncertainties that no mortal eye can foresee, there stands a radiant bastion, a fortress laid not in stone but in the eternal promises of God. The sacred Word, as given unto us in the King James Bible, proclaims with unwavering certainty that amidst the tumult and the clamor of the world, there exists an inner wellspring of peace reserved for those who place their trust in Him. "Peace I leave with you," saith the Lord, "my peace I give unto you: not as the world giveth, give I unto you. Let not your heart be troubled, neither let it be afraid." These words echo through the chambers of the soul with a gentle yet powerful assurance that transcends the fleeting comfort of earthly reprieves. They call forth a tranquility rooted not in circumstance but in the steadfast character of God Himself. How often do we find ourselves grasping desperately for repose, only to be met with the storm's unrelenting fury? Yet, the divine promise invites us to cease from our striving and to anchor our spirits in Him whose faithfulness endureth forever. This peace, bestowed as a sacred gift, overflows not from human endeavor but from the tender heart of a loving Father, who desires not the anxiety of His children but their repose in His sovereign care. It is a peace that passeth all understanding, an enigmatic calm that saturates the very marrow of our being, shielding us in moments when the shadows lengthen, and fear would seek dominion.

To dwell in this peace is to embrace a vision beyond the immediate, to see with eyes unclouded by the petty vexations of time, and to rest in the unshakable truth of God's covenant. The psalmist, yearning for such serenity, affirms, "Thou wilt keep him in perfect peace, whose mind is stayed on thee: because he trusteth in thee." Herein lies a divine paradox: peace is not the absence of trouble but the presence of God's sustaining nearness. When the heart is anchored to the Almighty, it need not be tossed like a ship upon the stormy seas. Such assurance demands not a religious stoicism but a heartfelt surrender, a quiet yielding that allows the Spirit to weave serenity within our tempest-tossed soul. It is the peace that enveloped the disciples when their Master calmed the storm with but a word; it is the whisper that stills the clamoring of anxious thoughts and grants rest where none seemed possible. In embracing these promises, we find that the turmoil around us loses its dominion, for the greater reality of God's abiding presence emerges as the anchor of hope that holds fast through every trial and tribulation.

Moreover, the promise of peace extends beyond the personal to touch the very fabric of our relationships and interactions. The apostle exhorts us, "Let the peace of God rule in your hearts," urging us to permit His tranquility not only to soothe but to govern, transforming the often chaotic interplay of human emotions into a symphony of divine harmony. This ruling peace cultivates forgiveness where anger might have risen, patience amid provocation, and love that surpasseth understanding. It is the peace born of reconciliation with our Creator and with one another, a testimony to the power of God's grace to mend what is broken and to restore what is lost. As readers and believers journey through the reflections offered here, may they be gently carried into the sanctuary of this peace, invited to rest not in their own might but in the everlasting arms of Him "whom the winds and the sea obey." The promise is sure, the invitation tender: come unto Him, all ye that labor and are heavy laden, and He will give you rest.

Yet, the peace promised is not passive or distant but dynamic and living, intertwined with the faith and hope that sustain us. It is the calm that arises when we cast our cares upon the Lord, knowing He careth for us, even when circumstances seem dire and the night is dark. The wise man counsels us, "Be careful for nothing; but in every thing by prayer and supplication with thanksgiving let your requests be made known unto God." This profound instruction directs the weary soul from anxious contemplation to prayerful communion, where the burdens of the heart are laid before the throne of grace and replaced with celestial calm. Thus, the peace that God imparts serves as the very breath of the spirit, renewing, strengthening, and quieting our restless hearts. It is both refuge and fortress, an impenetrable stronghold amid an uncertain world. And so, as we meditate upon these promises, may the well of divine peace spring forth within us, nurturing a confidence that transcends circumstance and a calm that withstands every storm. In God's perfect peace, our souls find their true home, unshaken and ever anchored in the eternal Word.

Gary E. Risenhoover

Peace in God's Presence

Still Waters

Like a gentle stream flowing through a quiet valley, the soul yearns for stillness amidst the tumult of earthly cares and ceaseless demands. The psalmist's ancient voice carries a balm for the restless heart: "He maketh me to lie down in green pastures: he leadeth me beside the still waters." In these words, wondrous peace is found, a promise that reaches beyond the ordinary grasp of human understanding, hinting at the divine refuge available to the weary and burdened. To find rest in God's care is to enter a sacred sanctuary where the clamor of the world dissipates, and the spirit is refreshed by the quiet assurance of His presence. This rest, unlike the fleeting respite offered by the world, is profound and all-encompassing, inviting the believer to release anxiety and weariness into the hands of the One who governs all creation with perfect wisdom and tender love.

Dwelling in God's presence is an invitation to embrace stillness, not as mere inactivity, but as a deliberate posture of surrender and trust. When the noise of life threatens to drown the soul's song, the faithful are beckoned to quiet their minds and open their hearts to the divine whisper that offers comfort and strength. Prayer, in this sacred dance, transcends mere words; it becomes a sacred communion where the anxious heart can lay down its weapons, where fears dissolve in the light of divine assurance. Through prayer, the restless spirit finds a harbor from the storm, a place where tumult is transformed into tranquility by the gentle hands of the Almighty. It is here that true rest is discovered, not as a distant goal to be achieved but as a present reality nurtured by continual fellowship with God.

Meditation on Scripture serves as the water from which the soul drinks deeply, anchoring hope in the truths of God's unchanging promises. The King James Bible, with its majestic and poetic language, enfolds the reader in a rich tapestry of spiritual beauty, each verse a window opening onto the eternal. When the heart contemplates passages such as "The Lord is my shepherd; I shall not want," or "He restoreth my soul," an inner peace blossoms, rooted not in circumstance but in the steadfast character of God Himself. These ancient words carry an enduring power to soothe the troubled mind and invigorate the weary spirit. By immersing oneself daily in the sacred stream of Scripture, the believer is drawn beside still waters, where life's frenetic pace pauses and the soul is renewed in quiet depths. This sacred space becomes a wellspring of strength and contentment, a refuge where the storms of life lose their grip.

The promise of rest in God's care extends further, offering restoration and healing beyond human comprehension. When the world presses hard, and burdens grow heavy, the divine invitation beckons, "Come unto me, all ye that labor and are heavy laden, and I will give you rest." This rest is not the absence of trials but the presence of divine peace amidst them, a peace that guards the heart and mind by the power of Christ Jesus. To embrace this rest is to acknowledge that ultimate security does not come from one's own efforts but from surrendering to a loving sovereign who holds all things in His hands. By trusting in His providence, the believer's soul is unshaken, anchored in the knowledge that God's care is constant and His mercies are new every morning. In the quiet assurance of this care, the heart finds the strength to endure, to hope, and to bloom afresh.

Moreover, rest in God's care fosters an inner tranquility that extends beyond personal solace, shaping the believer's character to reflect divine calmness even amid external storms. As one dwells in the still waters of God's presence, patience deepens, grace flourishes, and love expands, producing a peacefulness that radiates outward into daily life. This peace transcends mere ceasefire with turmoil; it becomes a powerful testimony to others, a beacon of hope and comfort for those tossed upon life's rough seas. The believer, having found solace beside the still waters, becomes a conduit of God's peace, sharing this sacred tranquility through words, deeds, and quiet confidence. Thus, the transformative power of God's rest not only renews the individual soul but also blesses the community, weaving a tapestry of peace amidst a fractured world.

It is in the gentle rhythm of resting and trusting that the soul learns the art of abiding in God's care. This abiding is not passive; rather, it is a vibrant relationship characterized by continual seeking and intimate dwelling in the heavenly presence. The practice of daily prayer, meditation on His Word, and mindful surrender crafts a life anchored in unwavering faith. Even in moments when the heart is overwhelmed, these spiritual disciplines draw the believer back to that peaceful shore, reminding the soul of the everlasting covenant that God has made with His people. The metaphor of still waters becomes vivid and real when the believer, amidst life's trials, recalls that God is not distant, He is nearer than the breath and closer than the beating heart. This nearness sustains, comforts, and restores with a tenderness that surpasses all understanding.

To rest in God's care is ultimately to find one's true home, a place of perfect peace that the world cannot give nor take away. The journey to this sanctuary begins with a willing heart, one that chooses daily to step away from anxiety and busyness to enter quietly into the Lord's presence. There, beside the still waters, the soul is healed and made whole, renewed in strength and purpose. This sacred rest nourishes every aspect of life, infusing it with divine serenity and hope. The believer who drinks deeply from these waters is transformed, no longer tossed by every wind of doctrine or shaken by the trials that threaten the spirit. Instead, they are anchored firmly in God's steadfast love, upheld by His sovereign care, and empowered to walk the days ahead with confident peace.

Let us, then, embrace this divine invitation with hearts open and spirits willing. May we find rest beside the still waters, immersing ourselves in prayer and scripture, allowing God's presence to hush the clamor within. In this holy stillness, may our faith be rekindled, our hope restored, and our souls anchored in the eternal peace that only He can provide. For in God's care, truly, there is rest, a rest that revives, sustains, and anchors us through every season of life.

Quiet Confidence

In the sacred stillness where our souls are gently invited to rest, there blooms a quiet confidence, born not of human strength or understanding, but of an unshakable trust in the Lord's perfect timing and sovereign will. To dwell in this peace is to embrace a divine assurance that transcends all earthly tumult, a serene anchor amid life's relentless storms. The psalmist's words echo through the corridors of our heart: "Be still, and know that I am God" (Psalm 46:10). In this holy stillness, noise and distraction fall away, and the soul arises to meet the eternal calm of God's presence. It is here that confidence takes root, a confidence not loud or brash, but steady and steadfast, like a river deep beneath the surface, flowing surely according to God's divine plan.

The wisdom of the ages teaches that human eyes see only a fragment of the grand tapestry God weaves through time. Where we perceive delay or frustration, He ordains purpose and perfect timing. As the prophet Habakkuk cried out, "O Lord, how long shall I cry, and thou wilt not hear? even cry out unto thee of violence, and thou wilt not save?" (Habakkuk 1:2), so do many hearts wrestle with the space between prayer offered and answer revealed. Yet God's ways are higher than ours, His thoughts lofty beyond our grasp; He calls us to humble ourselves beneath His mighty hand, that in due season He may exalt us (1 Peter 5:6). Trusting in God's sovereignty means surrendering the urge to control or hasten outcomes, resting instead in the truth that His providence governs all, and His timing is flawless. When the night lingers long and hope flickers, the believer learns to draw strength from the promise that "all things work together for good to them that love God" (Romans 8:28), even when the path is hidden from sight.

To cultivate this quiet confidence, we must dwell intentionally in God's presence, weaving prayer and meditation into the fabric of our days. Prayer is not merely the utterance of words but a sacred communion, a respiration of the spirit where burdens are cast, and hearts unfold before the Almighty. In these moments, the heart whispers its deepest longings, the soul confesses its frailties, and yet remains poised on the firm foundation of faith. Meditation on Scripture breathes life into this prayerful posture, as the promises of God form a fortress of hope within. The psalms overflow with divine assurances: "Thou art my hiding place and my shield: I hope in thy word" (Psalm 119:114). To meditate upon such truths is to draw water from the wellspring of grace, refreshing weary bones and rekindling a spirit willing to trust beyond the seen and known.

Consider the story of the patriarch Abraham, whose faith rested not in the immediate fulfillment of God's promise but in the certainty of God's nature. Though his seed seemed barren, though years passed without the fruit of his hope, he held steadfast to the assurance that God would perform what He had spoken (Romans 4:20-21). His confidence was a quiet lamp burning in the dark, a testament to the power of unwavering belief in God's timing. We, too, are called to nurture such confidence, a patience that endures, a hope that does not waver, grounded in the knowledge that the Lord is never late, never powerless, and always good.

In the quiet chambers of the heart, where doubt and fear often conspire to steal peace, the believer may plead, "Lord, grant me the serenity to accept the things I cannot change." This prayer, humble and profound, opens the soul to rest beneath the shadow of the Almighty. God's sovereignty is a refuge: He holds all things in His hands, our past, our present, and the future yet unseen. His reign is eternal, and His faithfulness unchanging. To trust in Him is to release the tension of anxious striving, to stand firm on the rock of His promises even when the tempest rages. This confidence honors God's omniscience and omnipotence, affirming that He who began a good work in us will perfect it according to His divine purpose (Philippians 1:6).

Yet this quiet confidence is not passivity; it is active surrender. It calls for a heart attuned to the Spirit's leading, a disciplined stillness that watches and waits, ready to respond when the time appointed by God unfolds. The believer embraces the present moment with gratitude and peace, knowing that God's hand is weaving intricate designs beyond what the eye can discern. This trust bears witness to a heart that has been shaped by grace, a grace that teaches us to relinquish control and to rest in the benevolent sovereignty of our Creator.

As we cultivate this confidence, let our prayers be suffused with thanksgiving, even in the waiting, for the faith that blossoms in patience is precious unto God. We pray not in vain but pray in hope, leaning on the sacred words of Scripture as our compass: "Wait on the Lord: be of good courage, and he shall strengthen thine heart: wait, I say, on the Lord" (Psalm 27:14). This waiting is an act of trust, a devotion that refines the soul and prepares it to receive the fullness of God's blessing at His perfect hour.

In this divine stillness, where time yields to eternity, our spirits find rest. The quiet confidence birthed there is not a fragile hope but a mighty fortress, a spiritual stronghold impervious to the barrages of fear and uncertainty. Rooted deeply in the knowledge of who God is, faithful, wise, and loving, it sustains us through seasons of trial and seasons of waiting, reminding us that "He that keepeth Israel shall neither slumber nor sleep" (Psalm 121:4). In the comprehensive embrace of His sovereignty, we discover a calmness that surpasses all understanding, a peace that steadies the heart, and a confidence that is both humble and bold.

Thus, to stand in quiet confidence is to trust the Lord not only with our future but with our present. It is to carry within us a sanctuary of peace, a holy anchor to which we cling when tempestuous winds assail our lives. In the scriptures, in prayer, and in meditative silence, we lay hold of this gift, a confidence that rests not on human measure but on the unchanging word of God, who governs all things with wisdom and love. As we journey onward, may this quiet confidence be our shield and our song, a testimony to a faith firmly planted in the sure foundation of God's sovereign grace.

Shelter in the Storm

In the midst of darkness and the tumultuous tempests of life, there exists a sanctuary unlike any earthly fortress, an unshakable refuge that no storm can penetrate. The King James Bible calls it the Rock of Ages, a stronghold where the weary and the burdened may find solace and restoration. When the winds howl and the waves rise, threatening to overturn the fragile vessel of our souls, God's presence stands as a shelter that neither time nor trial can erode. To dwell in this sacred refuge is to immerse oneself in a wellspring of peace, a tranquility that surpasseth all understanding, guarding the heart and mind through the assurance of divine care. It is not a fleeting hiding place, but a steadfast fortress built in the eternal promises of Scripture, where faith clings tightly, unyielding against the fiercest gale.

As we embark upon this journey of seeking shelter in the storm, our hearts incline toward the prayerful communion that draws us near to the Almighty. Prayer becomes the lifeline cast into the depths of God's mercy, a humble lifting of hands and soul that cries out amidst the thunderous trials. The psalmist's words ring true: "God is our refuge and strength, a very present help in trouble." In these sacred declarations, we find the unassailable truth that no affliction is too grievous to pierce the veil of God's vigilant gaze. The storms of life, be they sickness, loss, loneliness, or fear, do not conquer those who rest their hope in Him; rather, they become the crucibles in which faith is refined and perfected. To shelter in God's presence is to experience a sacred reprieve, where the tumult of the world grows dim and the soul is cradled in the arms of everlasting love.

Contemplation of God's word reveals the tender care with which the Creator guards His children. The imagery of an eagle, spreading her wings to bear her young, evokes a profound picture of divine protection. "He shall cover thee with his feathers, and under his wings shalt thou trust." Herein lies the essence of our refuge, a place beneath the outstretched wings of grace, where fear flees and hope ascends. This metaphor not only comforts but invites us to a posture of trust, to yield our anxieties and weariness into the sacred embrace of a Father who is ever attentive, never slumbering nor weary. The storm outside may roar like a lion, yet within the sanctuary of His presence, we abide in perfect peace, shielded from despair.

The true challenge in seeking shelter in the storm lies in the surrender of control. The tempest of life often stirs a desperate desire to steer through its chaos by our own strength or wisdom. Yet the King James Bible gently admonishes, "Commit thy way unto the Lord; trust also in him; and he shall bring it to pass." To find refuge is to relinquish the futile grasping for certainty and to anchor firmly in the unfailing promises of God. It is to recognize that even when the path is shrouded in shadow and the outcome unseen, the One who holds the cosmos in His hands is also carrying our fragile hearts. In mingling prayer with scripture meditation, the soul receives renewal, a calm that quiets the restless unrest. This practice becomes a sacred rhythm, a breathing in of divine assurance and a breathing out of burdens that would otherwise drown us.

Amid these realities, the devotional journey takes on a deeper texture, transforming moments of fragility into opportunities of grace. When wearied, the longing for rest is answered in the stillness of God's word, a balm to the troubled spirit. The sacred text whispers, "Thou wilt keep him in perfect peace, whose mind is stayed on thee." How profound the promise that peace is not the absence of storms, but the presence of God, steadfast and unmovable. This peace steadies the wavering heart, firming the foundation beneath life's shifting sands. Further, it cultivates resilience, not through our own might, but by the overflowing strength bestowed by the Shepherd who neither slumbers nor sleeps. To shelter in the storm is thus to be wrapped in a garment woven from the threads of divine faithfulness, woven to withstand the fiercest onslaught.

Moreover, worship enfolds the sheltering soul in a sacred embrace that transcends circumstance. Through praise, the heart ascends beyond the immediacy of trouble, lifting eyes heavenward and fortifying trust in God's sovereign plan. The music of prayer and the sweetness of meditation become a fortress within the fortress, a spiritual refuge where joy and hope rise aloft on wings of exaltation. When the heart's tumult threatens to drown out the still small voice of God, worship reorients the soul, drawing it back to the sure foundation of grace and mercy. It is in this elevated place that fear dissolves and faith takes root anew, nourished by the precious promises embedded in the pages of Scripture.

In this sacred refuge, prayer is not only supplication but dialogue, a heartfelt exchange where the troubled spirit finds comfort in God's responsive love. Within the words of Scripture and the unspoken yearnings of our heart, prayer anchors us firmly to the divine presence. Each petition or quiet whisper draws us deeper into the sheltering shadow of the Almighty, reminding us that we are not alone in our distress. In these moments of sacred intimacy, God meets us where we are, healing the wounds inflicted by pain and anxiety. His word becomes both shield and song, enabling us to endure with grace when the storm's fury seems relentless.

It is also in this refuge that the community of faith becomes a beacon of shared strength. Though the shelter is found first in the presence of God, the fellowship of believers offers mutual encouragement and support. The prayers, testimonies, and shared Scriptural truths of fellow sojourners carry us across difficult valleys, reminding us that we are part of a larger body, upheld by collective grace. The apparent solitude of trial yields to the warmth of connection, and the fortress of God's love manifests through the hands and hearts of others who share in the divine promise to never leave nor forsake.

Ultimately, to find shelter in the storm is to cultivate a heart anchored in divine truth amidst life's uncertainties. It is to develop a spiritual posture that chooses daily to abide in the presence of a God who is unmovable and faithful. In turning to the King James Bible for meditation, we encounter the richness of language that stirs the soul and elevates the spirit, drawing us deeper into reverence and trust. These ancient words, luminous and powerful, invite us to rest beneath the canopy of God's care, assured that no matter the tempests that arise, there is a refuge eternal and unfailing. Here, amidst the noise and chaos, the soul finds its sanctuary, a place where peace flows like a river, where hope is renewed, and where the heart is anchored forever in the boundless love of the Almighty.

Peace Beyond Understanding

In the midst of a world often restless and filled with turmoil, there exists a profound and still delight that surpasseth all human comprehension, a peace not fashioned from external circumstances but birthed within the heart by the divine presence of God Himself. This peace, so beautifully described in the sacred pages of the King James

Bible, is an anchor for the troubled soul, a sanctuary where the spirit findeth refuge despite the storms that rage without. It is a transcendent peace, not mellowed by the fleeting blows of worldly strife, but established on the immovable foundation of God's eternal truth and unchanging grace. To dwell in such peace is to enter a realm where fear looseth its grip and anxiety is silenced, where the heart is calmed beneath the shadow of the Almighty, and the mind findeth rest in the everlasting arms.

The Apostle Paul, in his epistle to the Philippians, enjoins believers with this divine promise: "And the peace of God, which passeth all understanding, shall keep your hearts and minds through Christ Jesus." How strange, yet wondrous, that the peace God imparts is described not as a product of reason or human intellect, but as a sacred mystery that transcends understanding! It cannot be dissected by philosophy nor grasped by the wisest of men; rather, it is a gift dispensed when the heart yields its worries and surrenders to the sovereignty of Heaven's King. It is here, in the quiet surrender and humble submission to divine will, that the soul's tumult is stilled, that anxious thoughts fall away like autumn leaves before the steady breeze of God's unfathomable love.

To experience this peace is not to deny the reality of affliction, but to walk through affliction adorned with a serene confidence. It is to gaze upon the darkest nights with the assurance that dawn is appointed by the everlasting God. The psalmist's words echo in our spirit as a balm: "Thou wilt keep him in perfect peace, whose mind is stayed on thee: because he trusteth in thee." This peace, perfect and unshaken, flows forth from a mind fixed, resolved, and enveloped in the contemplation of God's goodness and faithfulness. It arises when the heart is set on the Creator, acknowledging His sovereign reign over all creation, and resting in the knowledge that no circumstance can thwart the divine purpose or overthrow the tender hand of providence.

Prayer emerges as the sacred pathway into this peace. It is the sweet communion of the soul with its Maker, a sacred dialogue where the burdens are cast upon the Lord and the spirit is lifted into heavenly realms. When fervent prayers ascend like incense before the throne of grace, they dissolve the chains of fretful thoughts and kindle a holy calm within. It is in the quiet space of prayer that the heart receives the whispered assurances of divine love, as the Spirit intercedes with groanings unutterable, renewing the inner man and setting the captive mind free. Meditating upon the holy word nourishes this peace, as the precious promises of Scripture resonate over the quiet waters of the soul. Verses such as Isaiah's comforting oracle, "Fear thou not; for I am with thee: be not dismayed; for I am thy God", imbue strength and quietude, as the believer anchors in the rock of ages with unshakable resolve.

This peace is no mere cessation of external disturbance but a profound harmony that chords the heart with the eternal melody of God's presence. It is a peace that steadies the trembling hands and soothes the sorrowful spirit, transcending the ebb and flow of transient troubles. The world's tumultuous clamor may rage on, yet the believer, anchored in the Word and bathed in prayer, retains a serene core, a calm center amid chaos. This secret of peace is revealed in the lifework of the Son of God Himself, who in Gethsemane's garden prayed not to escape the coming anguish but to submit to the Father's will, revealing that true peace is found in obedient trust even unto suffering.

To abide in this peace, therefore, is to foster an intimate walk with God, to commune daily with His presence, and to steep oneself continually in the fountains of Scripture. It sanctifies the weary heart, refreshing it as the dew that falls silently upon the morning grass, renewing strength and inspiring hope. It is a peace that imparts courage to face opposition, consolation in sorrow, and joy in trials. When the soul tastes this peace, it is as if an invisible hand gently clasps the heart and whispers, "Be still, and know that I am God." In that sacred stillness, the believer is fortified, equipped to navigate the wilderness of life with a steadfast spirit unbroken by despair.

Thus, divine peace bestowed transcends all human understanding because it is not subject to the fluctuations of circumstance. It is a sacred rest that enables the faithful to journey through valleys of shadow with unwavering confidence and to stand upon the mountaintop rejoicing, knowing that God's presence enfolds them in every step. It is the peace that keeps the heart and mind, guarding them as a celestial sentinel against the invasion of fear and doubt. It renews, restores, and reorients the soul toward the glorious hope of redemption, ever whispering of the eternal day when sorrow and sighing shall flee away.

In the practice of seeking this peace, may the reader be encouraged to turn often to the wellsprings of prayer and meditation, to immerse deeply in the inspired words of the King James Bible, where the timeless promises reside and the living God speaks anew. Let the heart rise like the morning sun, dispelling shadows with the radiant light of divine assurance, and drink fully from the cup of salvation that quenches all unrest. Through this sacred journey into the heart of God's peace, may the soul find its rest not in the fragile securities of the world, but in the unshakable trust and boundless love of the eternal Word, forever anchored and unmovable.

Joyful Living

Joy in Salvation

The radiance of joy in the soul is a divine melody, born not of fleeting circumstance but of a steadfast hope rooted deep within the sanctuary of the redeemed heart. To rejoice in salvation is to embrace a new creation, for as it is written, "Therefore if any man be in Christ, he is a new creature: old things are passed away; behold, all things are become new" (2 Corinthians 5:17). This transformation is the wellspring from which a perennial joy flows, a joy that transcends the mutable tides of life's trials and tribulations. It is a rejoicing not of superficial delight but of a profound, abiding gladness infused by the Spirit of God, who maketh the heart leap with a gladness that no earthly trial can diminish. To celebrate redemption is to lift one's eyes beyond the temporal cloak of present weakness and see the eternal tapestry woven by the hand of the Almighty, whose mercies are new every morning and whose covenant of love endureth forever.

Joy in salvation is, at its very essence, a choice, a discipline of the spirit akin to the firm anchorage of a ship's keel in the depths of a storm-tossed sea. Though winds may blow with fierce adversity, the soul anchored in the knowledge of God's redeeming grace remains buoyant and unstirred. The apostle Paul bade the Philippians, "Rejoice in the Lord alway: and again I say, Rejoice" (Philippians 4:4), exhorting believers to cling to joy as an act of faith that defies the natural inclinations toward despair. It is in choosing joy, even amid sorrow and struggle, that the redeemed manifest the victorious power of salvation. This selection of joy is not a denial of pain but a refusal to allow pain the final word. It is to proclaim, in the strength of God, that the light of redemption outshines the shadows of grief, and that a heart fixed upon Christ is fortified against the tempests of a weary world.

In the tender chambers of the believer's soul, joy blossoms as the fruit of the Spirit, nurtured by continual communion with the Word and prayerful dependence on divine grace. Like the olive tree, whose leaves retain a verdant hue despite the harshness of the season, the believer stands resilient, fed by the enduring promises of Scripture. The joy that springs forth is not merely an emotional response but a sacred disposition, given and sustained by the indwelling presence of the Holy Spirit. As Jesus Himself declared, "These things have I spoken unto you, that my joy might remain in you, and that your joy might be full" (John 15:11), so too is our rejoicing a reflection of His own perfect joy imparted to us. Through meditation on the blessed assurance of salvation , that sins are forgiven, that death holds no dominion, and that everlasting life awaits , hearts are flooded with a joy that renews strength and kindles hope.

Yet, the cultivation of joy requires deliberate tending; it demands a vigilant guarding of the heart against the encroachment of bitterness, anxiety, and worldly distraction. The psalmist exhorts, "Rejoice in the Lord, O ye righteous: for praise is comely for the upright" (Psalm 33:1), reminding us that the upright heart finds its rightful expression in rejoicing. To cultivate joy is to dwell daily within the courts of thanksgiving, recognizing the manifold blessings yet confided to our stewardship , the breath of life, the whisper of grace, and the fellowship of saints. It is a mindful discipline to turn the heart upward when the shadows lengthen, to fix upon the surpassing riches of Christ's love rather than the parching deserts of circumstance. This conscious choice becomes a shield, a bulwark against despair, and a sweet incense rising before the throne of grace.

Sustaining joy through all seasons of life is a pilgrimage marked by many trials and yet crowned by a faithfulness that does not waver. Life's autumns may strip away the outward splendor of earthly joys, but within the soul of the believer, a springtime perpetual lingers, nourished by the unchanging promises of the Lord. A faithful heart knows that tribulations, though grievous, work patience; patience, experience; and experience, hope (Romans 5:3-4), thus the path of sorrow itself becomes a means whereby joy is refined and made perfect. It is a paradox, holy and mysterious, that in the furnace of affliction the fragrance of joy grows sweetest, for it testifies to a trust unwavering and to a salvation secured. The joy of the Lord becomes a banner that waves courageously above the darkest valleys, proclaiming victory even before the final triumph is fully revealed.

When we consider the joy of salvation, we witness its expression in the celestial realms and on the earthly pilgrimage alike. The very angels rejoice over a soul delivered from death (Luke 15:10), a heavenly chorus that echoes the gladness of the Father who rejoices over His children. This divine rejoicing invites us to partake in a joy that is sacred and communal, correcting the misconception that joy is a private or solitary matter. Indeed, joy multiplied within the body of Christ becomes a testimony to the world of the hope that lies beyond temporal sorrow. The redeemed, as a chosen generation, a royal priesthood, bearers of light amid darkness, radiate this joy through acts of love, worship, and steadfast witness. Their countenance reflects the inward joy that countless trials cannot quench, a joy that shines with the brilliance of the morning star.

Moreover, the joy of salvation fuels the believer's strength to serve, to labor in hope, and to await patiently the glorious consummation of all things. It is the wellspring that refreshes the weary, "Thou hast put gladness in my heart, more than in the time that their corn and their wine increased" (Psalm 4:7), and the song of the soul that rises even in the silent watches of the night. This joy is not passive but active; it compels us to extend grace, to comfort the afflicted, and to bear one another's burdens. In this way, joy becomes a sanctifying power, transforming not only the inner life but rippling outward into the community of faith and the world. Through such joy, the believer shines as a beacon of hope, a living testament to the power of redemption to renew and restore.

As we reflect deeply upon the blessed theme of joy in salvation, let us entwine our hearts more intimately with the eternal truths of the

Word. May we continually choose joy, not as a mere feeling but as the fruit of a soul anchored in the gospel, abiding in the presence of the Father who redeems and sustains. May we cultivate this sacred rejoicing by dwelling daily on His promises, by walking humbly in His light, and by lifting our voices in praise, so that the peace which surpasses all understanding guard our hearts and minds through Christ Jesus. In so doing, we participate in the heavenly joy that awaits us, a joy surpassing any fleeting delight, a joy immortal and everlasting. And as we journey forth, may the well of this joy overflow, refreshing our spirits and drawing others unto the magnificent light of salvation, unto the boundless grace of our Lord, forevermore. Amen.

Rejoicing Always

In the midst of life's ever-shifting tides, where trials rise unbidden, and shadows lengthen over the paths we tread, the call to rejoice always is both a solemn charge and a radiant promise. To rejoice not merely when the sun shines bright upon our faces, but in every season, through every tempest, is a profound testament to the indwelling Spirit within us. Scripture declares, "Rejoice evermore" (1 Thessalonians 5:16), an exhortation that resonates beyond mere comfort and veers into the realm of divine empowerment, a joy not anchored in circumstances, but rooted deeply in the unchanging character of God Himself. This joy is not a fleeting feeling born of fleeting moments but a steadfast flame, kindled by faith and nourished by the eternal truths of the Word.

To rejoice always is to embrace a sacred paradox: rejoicing even when the world seems to crumble, when sorrow presses close, and the heart feels heavy laden. Yet, as believers, this rejoicing is no vain or hollow sentiment but a chosen posture of the soul, a deliberate act of trust in the God who reigns sovereignly over all things. The apostle Paul's own life bears witness to this truth, for he found joy not in the absence of hardship but in the presence of Christ that sustained him amidst persecutions, imprisonments, and afflictions unnumbered. His declaration that he "glories in tribulations also" (Romans 5:3) reveals that joy and suffering are not mutually exclusive but intricately woven threads in the tapestry of a Spirit-filled life. It is this joy that lifts the spirit above despair, that infuses hope where darkness threatens, and that anchors the soul in the steadfast love of the Father.

Cultivating this joy requires a heart attuned to the Spirit's gentle whispers and a mind saturated with the promises of Scripture. It begins in the silent chambers of contemplation where we consider the manifold blessings bestowed upon us, not the fleeting or the superficial, but the eternal and intangible gifts that no trial can steal: the mercy that renews each morning, the peace that surpasses understanding, the love that never fails. When we fix our eyes upon Jesus, the author and finisher of our faith, joy is born anew; for in Him, all sorrows find their balm and every wound is wrapped in grace. The psalmist aptly testifies that the joy of the Lord is our strength (Nehemiah 8:10). Thus, joy is not a luxury reserved for the untroubled but a wellspring of power to endure and overcome.

Moreover, this lasting joy emerges from gratitude, an aware and thankful heart that refuses to overlook God's faithfulness amid adversity. The choice to rejoice is often found in a conscious redirection, away from the clamoring of fear and complaint, toward the quiet affirmation of God's sovereignty and goodness. It is a restoration of perspective, recalling that trials serve a holy purpose, refining faith as gold in the fire, shaping us into vessels fit for divine use. Though our flesh may falter, the Spirit's fruit is nurtured within us when we recognize that our suffering is never wasted but worked into a greater good that surpasses human understanding. The Lord's promise to work all things together for good to them that love Him (Romans 8:28) forms the bedrock upon which joy rests unshaken.

Joy in trial also blossoms when fostered through prayer and worship, the twin disciplines that draw us nearer to the heart of God and enliven our spirits. In prayer, we pour out our fears and despair, and receive peace that quiets the tempest within. Worship lifts our eyes from earthly woes to heavenly realities, enchanting the soul with songs of praise that declare God's majesty and unfailing care. This sacred dialogue between the believer and the Divine rekindles the embers of joy that sorrow would seek to quench. Through prayerful surrender and reverent adoration, the atmosphere of our inner sanctuary becomes charged with hope and gladness, enabling us to rejoice not because all is well in the world, but because our King is enthroned in glory and His promises endure forever.

Yet, the journey of rejoicing always is neither facile nor free from struggle. The tension of life's battles may press heavily, and the flesh's natural inclination toward despair can threaten the stability of joy. It is in these moments that perseverance is most vital, for joy is a fruit that grows deep roots in the rich soil of steadfast faith. Each choice to praise, each act of trust, each refusal to succumb to bitterness nourishes this fruit, enabling it to withstand the storms. The community of believers also plays an invaluable role, as fellowship fosters encouragement, mutual exhortation, and shared rejoicing that buoy the spirit. Together, the body of Christ reflects the multifaceted beauty of joy, demonstrating that rejoicing is not solitary but communal, a vibrant expression of the Spirit's work within the whole.

In this divine economy of joy, nothing escapes the transformative touch of God. His love and grace infiltrate every sorrowful place, transfiguring pain into praise, mourning into dancing. The sacred refrain of Scripture echoes unceasingly, "Weeping may endure for a night, but joy cometh in the morning" (Psalm 30:5). This hope is the beacon that guides us through darkness, a joy that is sure, steadfast, and secure, abiding beyond the reach of circumstance. The believer anchored in this joy rises each day renewed, equipped not only to bear their own burdens but to be a wellspring of encouragement to others walking through their own valleys of shadow. In this way, rejoicing always becomes a powerful testimony that illuminates the gospel truth: that our joy is found in Christ alone, and in Him, we are fully satisfied.

Therefore, to walk the path of rejoicing always is to adopt a sacred rhythm, one that dances between the anguish of the present and the glory to come, anchored in the blessed assurance of God's unchanging character. It is a daily surrender that embraces hope, a posture that refuses despair, and a declaration that, despite the trials that bruise and batter, our souls remain anchored in joy. This joy, borne of the Spirit and rooted in faith, is an unquenchable fire, a divine delight that transcends understanding, shining brightly in the darkest nights and whispering to the weary soul that all things are held within the boundless hands of a loving God. It invites us, beloved, to rejoice evermore, not as a fleeting fancy, but as a steadfast song, rising eternally from our hearts, proclaiming the glory of our King through every season, in every circumstance, forevermore. Amen.

Joyful Generosity

In the tender dance of the soul's engagement with the divine, joy emerges as a radiant fruit blossoming not merely from circumstance but from a wellspring of faith, a choice that transcends fleeting emotion and anchors itself deeply in the promises of God's eternal covenant. This joy, whose source is heavenly, manifests outwardly in acts that mirror the lavish generosity of our Creator, for to give with an open heart is to partake in the abundant life proffered through Christ Jesus. When the Apostle Paul extols the virtues divine within the tapestry of the Spirit, joy is proclaimed not simply as a feeling to be grasped in moments of triumph but as a steadfast companion that traverses the valleys of sorrow and the heights of gratitude alike. Within this sacred fellowship between giving and joy lies a profound truth: generosity is a sacrament of gladness, a testament to the soul's willingness to reflect the bounty it has received rather than to hoard it selfishly.

To give joyfully, then, is to declare trust in God's providence, a joyful offering that acknowledges the Lord as the ultimate Provider who requites all with blessings beyond measure. It is a sanctified act, one that enkindles the flame of grace within the giver's heart and binds the giver to the recipient in divine union. There is a sweetness in this mutual exchange that rebounds upon the spirit, transforming the act of giving from a mere transaction into an expression of worship, a tangible demonstration of the heart's delight in God's goodness. Indeed, the Psalmist's declaration that blessed are the hands that give freely is a timeless echo reverberating through the corridors of the believer's life, urging a continued embrace of generosity as a conduit of joy. When one gives without reluctance, unshackled from the grip of fear or calculation, it is as though the soul dances in the light of God's presence, reflecting the exuberance of the Creator whose very nature is to give life and hope without measure.

Moreover, joyful generosity functions as a remedy for the insidious creeping of discontent and selfishness, which so often dampen the spirit's gladness. When we look through the lens of faith, the act of giving eagerly becomes a remedy for the soul's hunger, a balm that restores and invigorates spiritual vitality. To share one's blessings, be they material, emotional, or spiritual, is to acknowledge that all things are gifts from above, entrusted to our stewardship rather than possession. This humility fosters an ongoing awareness of God's hand in our lives and cultivates a disposition where joy is not contingent upon abundance alone but upon a heart yielded to the divine economy of grace. The early church, as described in the book of Acts, offers a sterling example of this principle in motion: believers selling possessions and laying the proceeds at the apostles' feet did so out of profound gladness and unity, their generosity both fueling the community and drawing them into deeper communion with Christ's body.

Yet joyful giving does not imply a careless scattering of resources or an abandonment of wisdom; it is a spirited act, deliberate and borne of discernment, enlivened by love, and rooted in hope. It arises from the assurance that by investing blessings in the lives of others, one participates in a holy cycle where goodness begets goodness, and seeds sown in faith reap a harvest beyond human comprehension. The words of the Lord Jesus, "It is more blessed to give than to receive," remain a luminous beacon calling believers to venture beyond self-interest into a realm of joy perfected by sacrificial love. It is here, in this generous overflow, that the heart finds true rest, a solace untouched by scarcity's shadow, and a jubilance that defies circumstance. When joy pulses through the veins of generosity, the soul is anchored in a divine rhythm pulsating with hope fulfilled and promise kept.

Furthermore, to cultivate joyful generosity in seasons of plenty is relatively easy; the soul rejoices openly, and the giving flows naturally as an outpouring of thanksgiving. Yet, the truest test of this joy is found in the darkened periods of hardship and loss, when resources are scarce, and the heart's desires are unmet. It is in these profound moments that faith must fortify the spirit against despair, whispering the assurance that God's provision is unfailing and His love unwavering. To give under such circumstances is to offer not only material aid but also a profound testimony of trust, a living sermon of hope that the receiver may cherish and the giver may hold fast unto. Each act of kindness in these moments shapes the contours of spiritual renewal, reminding the believer that generosity is not measured by the quantity given but by the quality of the heart's intention. Even a cup of water offered in Christ's name becomes a vessel carrying the transformative power of joy flowing from a well-tended faith.

The reciprocity of joyful generosity thus becomes a sacred dance between giver and Receiver, the human soul and the divine. Prayer intertwines with action as the giving heart communes with God, inviting the Spirit to manifest not only in the material gift but also in the invisible blessings bestowed upon both parties. This continuous exchange nurtures spiritual intimacy and anchors the soul more firmly in the Word. It is in these moments that the soul reaps a glimpse of heavenly reality, where all labor done in love is noble, and all gifts rendered from cheerfulness are remembered before the throne of grace. Herein lies the secret joy that endures beyond the fleeting delights of the world, an anchored peace rooted in the unfailing generosity of Christ Himself, who gave His all for the redemption of many.

To nurture this disposition daily, the believer is exhorted to adopt a posture of gratitude and mindfulness, allowing the Spirit to cultivate a heart that delights to give. Meditation upon scriptures such as 2 Corinthians 9:7 , "Every man according as he purposeth in his heart, so let him give; not grudgingly, or of necessity: for God loveth a cheerful giver" , illuminates the path to a life enriched by joy through generosity. It becomes evident that the lavishness of God's love is mirrored in the cheerful abundance of the giving heart, and that through these acts, believers align themselves with the divine character. The more one practices this joy-infused giving, the more the soul is saturated with peace, and the less it is troubled by the world's pursuit of gain or glory. This deliberate cultivation of joyful generosity sustains the believer's spiritual vitality across the seasons of life, consecrating each gift as a fragrant offering acceptable and pleasing unto the Lord.

Thus, to give joyfully is to live in harmony with the divine nature, to embody the grace and magnanimity that flows from the heart of God and courses through the veins of Christ's body on earth. It is a clarion call to trade the fleeting trappings of selfishness for a life marked by the sublime joy of sacrificial love and grace. In this giving, the soul is renewed, faith is affirmed, and hope is kindled anew, a holy cycle where joy perpetually renews itself in the giving of God's gifts to others. This joy, firm and unwavering, becomes a sure anchor in the shifting tides of life, inviting the believer to walk boldly in the path illuminated by the Word, steadfast in trust, rich in grace, and surrounded by the peace born from a heart that gives without hesitation and rejoices without measure.

Community and Joy

Among the many rich blessings bestowed upon us through the Spirit, the sweetness of joy stands as a testament to the abiding presence of God within the heart of the believer. Joy, as a fruit of the Spirit, is not a fleeting sentiment dependent on the shifting circumstances of life; it is a deep wellspring of gladness that overflows from a soul that remaineth steadfastly anchored in the promises of the Almighty. Yet, this joy is not meant to be hoarded or concealed in solitary chambers of the spirit, but rather it is designed by the Divine Architect to be shared and multiplied within the sacred fellowship of the body of believers. When God's children gather together, bound by the cords of love and united in faith, the joy that springs forth is magnified beyond measure, it becomes a radiant light that dispelleth the darkness and sends forth a melody of praise that uplifts every heart present.

The communal experience of joy is thereby an essential expression of our walk with God. It is in the company of the saints that our rejoicing findeth voice and strength, a sacred echo that resonates through the corridors of time and eternity. The Apostle Paul exhorteth us to "Rejoice with them that do rejoice, and weep with them that weep," thereby calling us into a mutual participation in each other's spiritual condition. The joy we share is a powerful testimony to the world, a manifestation of the peace and hope that transcendeth understanding, which the world cannot give nor take away. In the gathering of believers, laughter mingles with song, tears blend with encouragement, and hearts are knit together in bonds that reflect the heart of Christ Himself. Within such a community, the burdens of life are lightened, and the soul findeth strength anew to endure the trials that would otherwise threaten to rob us of our gladness.

Moreover, this joy is not a reflection of perfection or the absence of hardship, but a conscious choice rooted in faith and the assurance of God's goodness. The Psalmist declareth, "Thou wilt shew me the path of life: in thy presence is fulness of joy; at thy right hand there are pleasures for evermore." It is an acknowledgment that true joy doth not depend upon outward conditions, but upon an inward alignment with the Will of God, who giveth abundantly to those who seek Him. Cultivating such joy requires a deliberate turning of the heart towards gratitude, praise, and trust, even when shadows lengthen and sorrows press upon us. The fellowship of believers aids us greatly in this sacred task, for in sharing testimonies of God's faithfulness and in lifting one another in prayer, we are reminded afresh of the foundation upon which our joy is built. Each shared experience of God's deliverance, each account of mercy, serves to rekindle the flame of gladness in our souls.

In times of trial, the communal joy becomes all the more poignant and necessary. When afflictions assail and hope seemeth distant, the presence of a joyful, loving congregation is a balm to the weary spirit. The joy that springs from shared worship, united song, and collective prayer is a fortress that no enemy can breach. It anchors the soul amidst the tempest, reminding us that we are not alone, and that the God who hath called us into His marvelous light remaineth unchanging. In such moments, the act of rejoicing together is itself an act of faith. It proclaims that no matter what the world may bring, be it sorrow, loss, or uncertainty, there is a joy unspeakable and full of glory which the believer may claim and share. This joy is a testimony not only to the reality of God's kingdom but also to the transforming power of His Spirit within our midst.

The joy of community is also a wellspring of strength that nourisheth the individual believer's journey in profound ways. It is within the living tapestry of the body of Christ that we find encouragement to persevere, counsel for discernment, and comfort in moments of weakness. The laughter of brethren around a table, the smile of a sister in prayer, the hand extended in compassion, these simple expressions of shared joy breathe life into the weary and ignite hope in the heavy-laden heart. It is through these interactions that the joy of the Lord becomes a tangible reality, no longer abstract but alive and palpable. The body of Christ, united in joy, becomes a sanctuary wherein the soul may be refreshed, the spirit renewed, and the burdens of life exchanged for the peace which surpasseth all understanding.

Indeed, the joyful fellowship of believers serves as a foretaste of heaven itself, where the redeemed will unite in unending praise and gladness. Here on earth, our shared joy is a glimpse of that eternal communion, a blessed harmony that echoes the song of the angels and the redeemed throng before the throne of God. As we partake in this joy, we are spiritually strengthened, our faith deepened, and our hope fortified. This noble fellowship also nurtures humility, for in rejoicing together, we acknowledge our dependence upon one another and the grace that sustaineth us all. We bear one another's burdens and thereby fulfill the law of Christ, manifesting the love which is the very essence of joy and life eternal.

It is thus both a privilege and a sacred responsibility to cultivate a community marked by the fruit of the Spirit's joy. This endeavor calls for intentional acts of kindness, patience in relationships, the sharing of burdens, and the adopting of spirits that seek to uplift rather than to diminish. A community rich in joy is a sanctuary from despair, a beacon of hope in a weary world. Its members are knit together not by mere sentiment but by the powerful working of grace that transformeth hearts and maketh us one. In such a fellowship, joy is not only experienced but also multiplied, rippling outward to touch lives far beyond the walls of any gathering place. Here, the love of Christ is made manifest, and the joy of the Lord becomes our strength.

Beloved reader, as you journey through the seasons of life, may you find refuge and renewal in the joyful fellowship of God's people. Let the words of Scripture kindle within you a desire to not merely receive joy but to give it generously as a sacred gift to those around you. Remember that joy shared is joy multiplied, and that in the communion of the saints, the heart is enlarged and the soul singeth praises unceasingly. May your spirit be enlivened by the sweet assurance that you are part of this living body, called to rejoice together and bear witness to the unchanging love and faithfulness of our Lord. May the light of communal joy guide your steps, strengthen your faith, and lift your heart into the celestial realms where true joy hath its eternal home. Amen.

Joy as Strength

In the vast tapestry of the Christian life, joy emerges not merely as an ephemeral feeling, but as a formidable and steadfast strength, a celestial fortification granted by the Spirit of God that sustains the soul amid the vicissitudes of mortal existence. To behold joy in this light is to perceive it as the radiant fruit borne from the deep roots of faith, ripening through trials and triumph alike. The King James Bible, resplendent in its majestic cadence, declares with solemn beauty that "the joy of the Lord is your strength" (Nehemiah 8:10). Herein lies a divine paradox, the recognition that strength is not wrought through mere human exertion or temporal success, but flows abundantly from the wellspring of divine joy, an enduring rejoicing anchored in God's eternal promises and unshakable presence. This joy is no mere transient delight stirred by external circumstance; it is a conscious, deliberate choice born from a heart attuned to the Spirit's song, a sacramental reservoir of grace that fortifies believers even in the shadows of sorrow, pain, and uncertainty.

The pilgrimage of faith is often marked by moments when the soul is tempest-tossed and the spirit faint within us; yet it is precisely in these seasons of trial that the grace of joy manifests as an iron pillar within the soul, enabling perseverance beyond the limits of human endurance. The apostle Paul, who bore his own afflictions with unwavering cheerfulness, proclaims amidst affliction, "Rejoice in the Lord alway: and again I say, Rejoice" (Philippians 4:4). This liturgical cadence of rejoicing is not naïve optimism, nor is it a denial of hardship; rather it is a profound testament to faith's power to transfigure suffering, refining the soul as gold through the furnace's fire. Joy, as a fruit of the Spirit, is imbued with the sustaining ability to uplift the heart above earthly trials into the loftier realms of divine perspective. When faith seizes hold of the eternal verities, the immutable love of God, the certainty of salvation, the promise of resurrection, joy blossoms even amidst desolation, becoming a well of strength from which believers draw courage and hope. It teaches us to step beyond the immediate and visible, anchoring our spirits in the unseen glories of God's kingdom.

To cultivate such joy is to embark upon a sacred discipline of the heart, one that requires intentionality and spiritual vigilance. The Scriptures provide a rich soil in which the seed of joy takes root, nourished by prayer, praise, and meditation upon the manifold blessings wrought by a faithful God. The Psalmist exhorts us to "Make a joyful noise unto the Lord" (Psalm 100:1), reinforcing that joy is not a passive state but an active engagement of the soul, an offering of thanksgiving and worship that transforms our very being. The rhythm of rejoicing draws the believer into a deeper communion with God, reshaping perception and rekindling the flame of hope. Joy becomes a posture of resistance against despair, a sanctuary where trust in divine providence overcomes the tumult of anxious thoughts. It calls us to measure our hearts not by the caprices of circumstance but by the enduring truth of the Savior's promise: "In the world ye shall have tribulation: but be of good cheer; I have overcome the world" (John 16:33). Thus, joy is enlightenment in darkness, a torchbearer's light illuminating the path through valleys shadowed by doubt.

Moreover, joy in faith must be understood as a communal treasure, woven within the body of Christ and reflecting the unity of the Spirit. It is bolstered through fellowship and mutual encouragement, as believers share testimonies of God's faithfulness, lifting one another in times of discouragement. The apostolic letters repeatedly highlight rejoicing as a collective exercise, noting that "the kingdom of God is not meat and drink; but righteousness, and peace, and joy in the Holy Ghost" (Romans 14:17). This rejoicing is both individual and corporate; it binds hearts together with the cords of love and shared hope, making the community a fortress against despair. In congregational worship and brotherly communion, joy becomes a tangible force that animates and enlivens spiritual growth, reminding us that our strength is multiplied when we bear one another's burdens with gladness. It manifests in the laughter shared, the prayers lifted, and the sacramental moments where grace is palpably felt, orchestrating a symphony of praise that resounds in the heavens.

Yet, the sustaining of joy amid shifting seasons of life, when losses claw at our peace and the night seems unending, is no small endeavor. It requires deliberate daily surrender and a recalibration of the heart's eyes to behold the subtle emanations of God's goodness. Such cultivation beckons us to embrace a theology of gratitude that refuses to let the soul grow weary or despondent. The psalmist's song, "Bless the Lord, O my soul: and all that is within me, bless his holy name" (Psalm 103:1), becomes a balm in bleak moments, urging the believer to recount the manifold mercies and tender kindnesses that never fail. This act of remembrance assures that joy does not slip away unnoticed, that it is not surrendered to the tyrannies of circumstance but grasped as a gift renewed each morning. Faith becomes a garden where joy is watered continually by the dew of heavenly grace, flourishing even when earthly trials threaten to cast shadows. This perseverance in joy amidst adversity is itself a testimony to the invincible nature of God's sustaining love, an emblem of spiritual victory.

Within this tapestry, prayer plays a pivotal role in birthing and nurturing joy. It serves as the sacred conduit through which the soul pours out its burdens and receives the assurance of divine peace. In prayer, the believer entwines rejoicing with petition, interweaving praise with supplication, creating a dialogue where joy is both expressed and fortified. The Psalms offer a profound example of this spiritual synthesis; they are replete with declarations of joy amidst lamentation, bearing witness that true rejoicing is not the absence of suffering but the presence of God in suffering. "Thou hast put gladness in my heart, more than in the time that their corn and their wine increased" (Psalm 4:7) reflects an experience where joy surpasses material abundance, affirming that spiritual wealth eclipses earthly gain. Prayer thus becomes the sanctuary where joy is replenished, a celestial wellspring insulating believers from the depletion wrought by life's upheavals.

Steeped in this understanding, one comes to recognize joy as a profound act of trust, a spiritual surrender that transfigures the weary heart. It is an intentional casting of cares upon the Lord, confident that He who began a good work within us will perform it unto completion (Philippians 1:6). This trust is not passive acquiescence but a vibrant, living faith that chooses joy as a means of resistance and renewal. In this choice, joy functions as armor against the corrosive effects of fear and doubt, strengthening the believer to stand firm amidst spiritual battles and temporal afflictions. The writings of the prophets and apostles alike resonate with this truth, encouraging the faithful to rejoice in hope, be patient in tribulation, and continue instant in prayer (Romans 12:12). Each act of rejoicing is a small victory, a spiritual declaration that God's grace suffices and that no darkness can obliterate the light kindled within.

Indeed, to be anchored in joy is to be anchored in God Himself, for He is the source from which joy perpetually flows, the wellspring of an immortal gladness that death cannot claim nor sorrow overwhelm. This joy transcends human understanding, surpassing the confines of circumstance, and reveals itself in the daily patterns of grace that crown the believer's life. It is found in the quiet mornings of prayer, the steadfastness amid trials, the moments of fellowship and worship, and the serene assurance of God's abiding presence. Like a mighty oak rooted deeply in fertile ground, joy endures the storms and flourishes, offering shelter and strength to the weary soul. It is the music of the heavens echoing on Earth, the unyielding song of faith that sustains and uplifts. To cultivate and sustain joy is thus to walk in the diligent footsteps of Christ Himself, who, for the joy set before Him, endured the cross, despising the shame, and is now seated at the right hand of the throne of God (Hebrews 12:2). It is a holy fortitude, a grace that transforms sorrow, and the dynamism of faith in daily practice.

As the believer navigates the changing seasons of existence, joy remains an unwavering companion, a divine inheritance secured by covenant and sealed by the Spirit. It calls the soul to rise above despair, to greet each new dawn with the gladness of a heart assured in God's unchanging love. This joy, both gift and discipline, reminds the faithful that they are not alone, that even as the storms rage without, the calm assurance of God's presence within provides an invincible strength. Culminating in the serenity of an anchored spirit, joy thus becomes not only a fruit of the Spirit but a throne upon which the soul rests securely, a fortress amid the battles of life, and a perpetual wellspring of strength that persuades the believer to continually declare, "My soul shall make her boast in the Lord: the humble shall hear thereof, and be glad" (Psalm 34:2). It is here, in the sacred embrace of joy, that faith finds its sweetest and most enduring expression, the triumphant song of a soul that knows the Lord and delights in Him forevermore.

Living by the Spirit

Guided by the Spirit

In the stillness of our innermost being, where the clamor of the world fades and the soul awakens to divine whisperings, there dwelleth a presence far more powerful than mortal understanding, the Holy Spirit. To be guided by the Spirit is to open oneself to a celestial melody that sings beyond the noise of earthly distractions, a sacred call to transformation, empowerment, and the unfolding of spiritual gifts. The King James Bible, with its majestic cadence and profound simplicity, beckons us into this intimate dance with the Divine Counselor, encouraging a listening heart and a responsive soul. "But the Comforter, which is the Holy Ghost, whom the Father will send in my name, he shall teach you all things," saith our Lord (John 14:26), inviting us to trust wholly in the Spirit's gentlest touch as both guide and teacher through the tides of life.

This divine companionship is not merely a theological concept reserved for the learned or the devout; it is the lifeblood of true spiritual renewal, accessible and vital for all who seek to be more than conquerors. The Spirit's guidance begins with a soft awakening within, the subtle stirring that enlighteneth the heart, revealing God's purpose and direction in moments both quiet and urgent. How often do we miss these heavenly promptings, drowned by the urgency of our own ambitions or silenced by doubt and fear? Yet, the Scripture assures us that the Spirit "will guide you into all truth: for he shall not speak of himself; but whatsoever he shall hear, that shall he speak," (John 16:13). Herein lies a sacred promise: the Spirit is not an enigma but a divine voice speaking our deepest truths, illuminating our path with purity and love. To cultivate this sensitivity is to cultivate patience, stillness, and a willingness to be led, and therein lies the paradox of power, for it is in surrender that strength is born.

Transformation under the Spirit's guidance is a quiet revolution within the soul. It is the shedding of old thoughts, hardened fears, and worldly shackles that bind us to lesser selves, ushering in new creation and holy renewal. "Be not conformed to this world: but be ye transformed by the renewing of your mind," exhorts the Apostle Paul (Romans 12:2), reminding believers that the Spirit's work is not external alone but a thorough alchemy of the heart and mind. This process is rarely abrupt or loud but rather a continual, gentle reshaping that carves us into vessels worthy of divine purposes. As the Spirit breathes life anew into weary places, there arises a sweet empowerment that fortifies our resolve and emboldens our witness. No longer are we left to stumble in darkness or navigate life's perils with timidity; instead, we are anointed with wisdom, courage, and gifts woven from heaven's own tapestry. The world sees not the hands of the Spirit at first, but they witness the fruit, love, joy, peace, longsuffering, gentleness, goodness, faith, meekness, temperance (Galatians 5:22-23), a testimony more potent than any loud proclamation.

Yet, to be truly guided by the Spirit requires a heart attuned through prayerful communion. The sacred dialogues of the soul make room for divine revelation. When we seek not only to speak but to listen, the Spirit's whispers become clearer, guiding us past the briars of confusion into the green pastures of purpose. This sacred conversation is no mere ritual; it is the lifeline that connects mortal to eternal, the human to the divine. "If any man have an ear, let him hear what the Spirit saith unto the churches," (Revelation 2:7) is both a gentle command and an invitation to heightened awareness. It challenges us to shed complacency and to nurture an ear that discerns not only the words of scripture but the living word spoken in the trembling depths of our hearts. As we sit before God's throne in humble reverence, the Spirit renews our senses, enabling us to detect the fragrance of truth and the direction of grace hidden within daily moments.

Spiritual gifts, bestowed by the Spirit, are the evidence of this divine guidance made manifest. Each believer receives according to the Spirit's will, the gift of healing, prophecy, wisdom, or tongues, each a tool fashioned to build up the Body of Christ and to carry forward God's redeeming mission. These gifts, however, are not trophies for self-glorification but sacred trusts to be wielded in service and love. "Now there are diversities of gifts, but the same Spirit," reminds Paul in his letter to the Corinthians (1 Corinthians 12:4), underscoring the unity that underpins our diversity. To be led by the Spirit is to recognize these gifts not as marks of superiority but as signs of shared responsibility, a call to minister to others with humility and zeal. This divine empowerment ushers the believer beyond solitary faith into active witness, where the Spirit's prompting lights the way to acts of mercy, bold proclamation, and sacrificial love. In these moments, we find our truest expression, not as isolated believers, but as branches of a living vine, sustained and energized by the Spirit's very lifeblood.

The journey upon which the Spirit leads is often unpredictable, challenging the very foundations of our understanding and habits. Yet the Spirit's guidance is ever faithful, like a wise shepherd who knows the terrain of the soul and leads us beside still waters. The promises of Scripture encourage perseverance in this walk: "For as many as are led by the Spirit of God, they are the sons of God," (Romans 8:14) a declaration of both identity and belonging. To be led by the Spirit is to step into the inheritance of God's children, marked not by the flesh but by the spirit, clothed with power to overcome trials and to radiate divine light. This path may compel us to relinquish control, to swim against prevailing currents, or to embrace unknown horizons. Yet it is here, in the yielding, that the Spirit's mighty work unfolds fully, crafting beauty from sacrifice and strength from surrender.

In prayerful response to the Spirit's leadings, a heart finds rest and renewed purpose. Prayer becomes both the conduit for divine guidance and the fertile soil in which spiritual seeds take root.

Through meditative reflection on Scripture, we discern the Spirit's voice, aligning our desires with divine will and sharpening our resolve to act in faith. It is a sacred dance of listening and responding, of waiting and moving forth, where each breath is a prayer and each step an act of worship. "Quench not the Spirit," cautions the Apostle Paul (1 Thessalonians 5:19), urging openness to the Spirit's continual movement within and without. To quench is to close the heart, hardening ourselves against promptings, while to yield is to unwrap the gift of daily renewal, of grace sufficient for every trial, and of joy unshaken by circumstance.

Thus, to be guided by the Spirit is to embark on a transformational pilgrimage where the heart is softened, the mind renewed, and the soul emboldened. It is to trust in a divine companionship that leads beyond sight into faith, beyond human wisdom into heavenly insight, and beyond fear into perfect love. The Spirit's guidance invites us to lay down our burdens and to rise on wings as eagles, soaring above the tumult of this world into the radiant peace of God's presence. As we cultivate sensitivity to the Spirit, may our lives become a living testament to the power of divine leading, marked by humility, grace, and an unwavering commitment to walk in the path of holiness. In that sacred guidance, we find neither confusion nor loneliness, but the settled assurance that in every step, the Spirit calleth and we, like ready children, answer with hearts wide open, "Here am I, Lord; send me."

Transformation Through the Spirit

In the quiet sanctuary of the soul, where the tumult of the world recedes into a whisper, there lies the profound invitation to transformation , a divine artistry wrought not by human hands, but by the gentle yet mighty breath of the Holy Spirit. The Spirit, as the eternal Comforter and sanctifier, moves with a grace unperceived by the hurried mind, yet felt by the heart attuned to the whisperings of heaven. Thus, to embark upon the sacred path of spiritual growth and renewal is to cultivate a sensitivity, a sacred listening, to the Spirit's leading, a soft call that beckons the believer beyond the shallow confines of mere religiosity into the vast expanse of intimate communion with God. It is within this divine fellowship that transformation unfolds, a metamorphosis so profound that the form and essence of the believer's life come to reflect the very nature of Christ.

Scripture teaches us, "And be not conformed to this world: but be ye transformed by the renewing of your mind, that ye may prove what is that good, and acceptable, and perfect, will of God" (Romans 12:2). Herein lies the heart of spiritual renewal, the mind's persistent surrender to the Spirit's sanctifying work, a daily crucifixion of selfish patterns and worldly conformities that bar the soul from the richness of God's perfect will. To be transformed is not a mere alteration on the surface, but an inward re-creation, a sanctum of holiness deep within, wherein the Spirit fashions a new nature, erecting within us the temple of divine love and wisdom. This renewal beckons the believer to shed the old vestments of fear, pride, and doubt, and to clothe oneself anew in garments of faith, humility, and hope, a transformation both subtle and majestic, wrought moment by moment in the quiet hours of faithfulness.

The Spirit's work is an ever-unfolding mystery, a tapestry of grace that empowers the believer to rise beyond weakness and limitation. Paul reminds us in 2 Corinthians 3:18, "But we all, with open face beholding as in a glass the glory of the Lord, are changed into the same image from glory to glory, even as by the Spirit of the Lord." This process, reminiscent of the gentle polishing of a precious gem, takes place as we fix our gaze on the glorious Christ, allowing the Spirit to illuminate our hearts and cleanse our motives. The phrase "from glory to glory" captures the progressive nature of this sanctification; it is not a single, static event but a steady journey of spiritual ascent. The Spirit imbues the believer with strength to resist temptation, courage to embrace obedience, and wisdom to discern God's voice among the many clamoring sounds of the world. In this way, transformation is both a gift conferred and a labor embraced, a sacred dance of surrender and empowerment.

Central to this transformation is the outpouring of spiritual gifts, which the apostle Paul describes with reverence and awe throughout his epistles. These gifts, manifestations of the Spirit's power, are bestowed upon believers not for self-glorification, but for the edification of the church and the extension of God's kingdom. Whether gifts of prophecy, healing, knowledge, or tongues, each serves to reveal the manifold wisdom of God and to enable believers to function as vital organs within the body of Christ. Yet these gifts require nurture, discipline, and a heart attuned to humility and love to flourish rightly. The Spirit's transformative work thus encompasses both the inward renewal of character and the outward empowerment for ministry, weaving together the private and communal dimensions of spiritual life.

In this sacred process, spiritual growth becomes a journey marked by both light and shadow. The Spirit may at times lead the believer through trials that refine faith as gold is tried in the fire. These seasons of testing are not signs of abandonment but tokens of divine discipline aimed at deepening dependence on God and purifying the soul's affections. Like the potter's hand shaping the clay, the Spirit molds us through adversity, teaching patience, endurance, and trust. As Isaiah proclaims, "But they that wait upon the LORD shall renew their strength; they shall mount up with wings as eagles; they shall run, and not be weary; and they shall walk, and not faint" (Isaiah 40:31). This promise enshrines the hope that even amid dryness and difficulty, the Spirit sustains and revitalizes, granting renewed vigor and vision.

Moreover, renewal through the Spirit calls for a posture of continual repentance and openness to divine correction. The believer is invited to examine the heart with discerning eyes, confessing sin and embracing forgiveness through Christ's blood, which alone purifies and reconciles. This humility fosters a receptive spirit, one that is quick to obey and slow to resist, that embraces the Spirit's convictions not as burdens but as blessings. In this sacred humility, the believer finds balance: neither relying on sheer willpower nor passive resignation, but actively cooperating with the Spirit's refining fire. Such cooperation nurtures spiritual fruit, love, joy, peace, longsuffering, gentleness, goodness, faith, meekness, temperance, which the Spirit produces naturally as the believer yields fully to divine influence.

The intertwining of prayer and meditation deepens this sensitivity to the Spirit, creating a sacred rhythm of communion that nourishes spiritual growth. As the Psalmist declares, "My meditation of him shall be sweet: I will be glad in the LORD" (Psalm 104:34). To meditate upon the Word inspired by the Spirit is to drink deeply from the wellsprings of life, anchoring the soul in eternal truth. Prayer becomes the breath of the spiritual journey, a dialogue where the believer pours forth petitions, thanksgiving, and adoration, while also listening in silence for the Spirit's guidance. This vibrant interplay is the fertile soil wherein transformation flourishes. The Spirit speaks through the Word, through prayer, through the stirrings of the heart, forming a holy triad that leads the believer into ever-deeper nearness with God.

Thus, transformation through the Spirit is at once a profound mystery and a tangible reality accessible to all who seek with sincerity. It requires patience, faith, and an abiding trust that God's promises are sure and His work perfect. The Spirit, who descended like a dove upon Christ at His baptism and empowered the apostles at Pentecost, continues to be the living presence within the believer, a divine source of renewal and power. This transformative grace does not merely change lives superficially but restores the soul, renews the mind, and rekindles the spirit. In its wake, the believer emerges not as one overcome by the world's trials but as a radiant vessel filled with the light of Christ's love, equipped with gifts for service, and anchored in unshakeable hope.

It is a transformation that calls the believer to rise each day with renewed purpose, to seek the Spirit's guidance with humble expectation, and to embrace the sacred task of spiritual growth as a lifelong pilgrimage. This pilgrimage, marked by seasons of victory and struggle alike, is a testament to the Spirit's unfailing presence and power, an ongoing miracle that draws the believer ever closer to the heart of God. May the reader be encouraged, therefore, to open the heart's chambers wide, to welcome the Spirit's gentle yet powerful touch, and to journey joyfully in this blessed transformation, knowing that the fruit of the Spirit is the very essence of life renewed and hope eternal. Amen.

Empowerment for Service

In the sacred dance of the believer's walk, there lies a divine promise whispered through the ages: that the Spirit of the Lord shall descend upon those who seek Him with an eager heart, breathing life into dry bones and setting aflame the embers of a humble soul. The empowering of the believer is no mere metaphor; it is a profound transformation wrought by the Heavenly Advocate, the Spirit who procedeth from the Father and the Son, manifesting not only as a balm to the weary but as a mighty power to fulfill the divine commission. When Christ ascended, He did not leave His followers orphaned but sent forth this Comforter, the Holy Ghost, to abide with them forever, to be their guide, their teacher, and their strength. This Spirit does not merely hover without effect, but seeks to penetrate the depths of the interior man, sanctifying, refining, and equipping, so that the follower of Christ may walk not in their own feeble strength but in the fullness of divine enablement.

To ponder this holy empowerment is to consider the manifold ways wherein the Spirit moves upon the heart, granting gifts and manifesting fruits according to the sovereign will of God. It is recorded in the Apostle's epistles, especially the epistle unto the Corinthians, that the Spirit divides to every man severally as He will: gifts of wisdom, knowledge, faith, healing, prophecy, and discernment – all fashioned to build up the body of Christ. But more than the gifts is the transformative presence of the Spirit, which renews the inner man, bends the will towards holiness, and ignites a passion for service that transcends mere duty or religious ritual. This empowerment is not for self-exaltation but for the edification of others, for the advancement of the gospel, and for the manifestation of Christ's love in broken hearts and weary lives. It is a flame to illumine darkness and a river to nurture parched souls.

As the believer yields to the Spirit's leading, there is a subtle yet profound attunement that arises, a sensitivity that discerns the gentle prompting toward service, the silent call to sacrifice, and the quiet empowerment to act in love and courage. This attunement does not arise from human striving or intellect, but through prayerful surrender and continual communion with the Lord. By cultivating an ear to listen and a heart to obey, the believer enters into a sacred partnership with the Spirit, whereby the supernatural becomes natural, and divine power flows through frail vessels to accomplish God's eternal purposes. It is in such moments that the ordinary is transfigured; a meek hand becomes a healing touch, a timid voice a prophetic thunder, a solitary act of kindness an enduring testimony of grace. The Spirit's empowerment does not demand perfection but perfects the willing heart, molding it into an instrument fit for His use.

The scriptures call us to consider the example of the early church, empowered by the Holy Spirit to bear witness unto the uttermost parts of the earth. The fearful disciples in the upper room were transformed into bold heralds of truth, not by their own bravery, but through the anointing of the Spirit. This ancient narrative echoes through time, inviting the modern believer to a similar experience of empowerment – one that equips for service in homes, workplaces, and communities. The Spirit gifts are not relics of a bygone age but living realities, ever-present to equip those who open their hearts to divine influence. Let us remember the words of the psalmist, "Thy spirit is good; lead me into the land of uprightness," acknowledging our dependence upon the Spirit's guidance and strength in every endeavor undertaken for the kingdom.

Yet, the journey of empowerment is marked by the ongoing exercise of faith and obedience. It may not always be a tumultuous fire; oftentimes, the Spirit's work is gentle, persistent, and patient, growing the believer's character, sharpening discernment, and fostering humility even amid powerful manifestations. The Spirit invites each soul into a lifelong process of sanctification and empowerment, not an instantaneous transformation, but a progressive unfolding of grace. In this way, the believer is cultivated into a fruitful servant who embodies the virtues of love, joy, peace, longsuffering, gentleness, goodness, faith, meekness, and temperance – the fruits that testify to the Spirit's abiding presence. Such a life, anchored in the Word and alive with the Spirit, becomes a beacon of hope and strength amid the trials of life, a testimony that power to serve comes from recognition of one's own weakness and dependence on God's almighty Spirit.

Prayer becomes the gateway to such empowerment, a sacred dialogue that harmonizes the believer's will with the Spirit's promptings. In earnest supplication, the heart is laid bare, and the Spirit moves freely to impart gifts, wisdom, and the grace necessary for faithful service. It is in these moments of intimate communion that one may hear the still small voice urging forth a word of encouragement, a timely act of mercy, or a bold proclamation of truth. To neglect this divine interaction is to forfeit the abundant grace offered, for the Spirit honors those who seek diligently and are quick to obey. Therefore, the believer is encouraged to cultivate a life of continual prayer, fasting, and meditation upon the Word, ever inviting the Spirit to fill and empower anew, so that every act of service flows not from human effort, but from the living power of God Himself.

In contemplating these truths, the reader is beckoned to ponder the mystery of the Spirit's work within – how an unseen presence can so profoundly alter the course of a life, equipping the humble for heights of service unimagined by natural understanding. This empowerment is not a fleeting emotional sensation but a steadfast disposition, a settled confidence rooted not in self but in the Spirit who sanctifies and strengthens. Such power carries with it the responsibility to wield gifts with wisdom and love, to build up, not to tear down, to heal, not to harm. It is a grace that compels the believer toward consecration, toward a selfless love that mirrors the heart of Christ, flowing outward in acts of kindness, justice, and proclamation.

Thus, the role of the Holy Spirit in equipping the believer is both profound and practical. It begins with an inward transformation, a renewal of mind and heart, and extends outward to the tangible expression of gifts for the common good. The Spirit empowers not only to endure trials with steadfastness but to actively engage in the ministry of reconciliation, extending grace and hope in the power of Christ's name. The reader is invited to embrace this empowering work, to seek with fervency the Spirit's guidance, and to allow divine enablement to permeate every thought, word, and deed. In doing so, one becomes a vessel through which God's kingdom advances, a servant made strong by the Spirit to carry forth the very life and light of Jesus into a world desperately needing His touch.

May this meditation stir within the soul a holy desire to be ever sensitive to the Spirit's leading, to lean not on one's own understanding, but to trust fully in the divine equipping promised by our Savior. The path of true service, marked by sacrifice and love, is made fruitful only by the Spirit of truth who dwells within us, guiding each step, igniting each gift, and sustaining each weary heart. Let us therefore be vigilant in prayer, humble in submission, and zealous in action, knowing that the empowerment for service is a sacred gift given not for our glory but for the eternal praise of God's holy name. In this sacred partnership with the Spirit, the believer finds a strength beyond measure, a courage unshaken, and a joy unexplainable, anchoring the soul firmly in the unshakable foundation of divine grace and power.

Fruitfulness in Spirit-Led Living

To be fruitful in spirit-led living is to embark upon a divine journey wherein the soul is continually cultivated by the breath of the Living God, that Holy Spirit who dwelleth within the believer, guiding, transforming, and empowering from within. It is a call far beyond mere outward observance or dutiful attendance; it is the heartbeat of a life yielded wholly to God's influence, an existence shaped and marked unmistakably by the fruit it bears, as the Apostle Paul so eloquently expoundeth in his letter to the Galatians. "But the fruit of the Spirit is love, joy, peace, longsuffering, gentleness, goodness, faith, Meekness, temperance: against such there is no law." (Galatians 5:22-23) These virtues are not to be stumbled upon by chance or human striving alone but are wrought within the depths of our being by the Spirit's tender and mighty hand. They sprout forth as living testimony that the Spirit of God taketh residence in the heart, producing godly character that enriches the soul and illumines the path of righteousness before us.

Such transformation begins when we surrender our own will, desires, and understanding, laying down the sword of self-reliance to take up the quiet yoke of the Spirit's guidance. To live spirit-led is to acknowledge that the flesh and the spirit are at enmity; that our natural inclinations often lead us away from holiness and righteousness. Yet, through the Spirit, which maketh alive and reneweth, we are given power to overcome the bondage of sin and to walk in newness of life. The renewal is not instantaneous nor superficial; it is a profound, sanctifying process fraught with seasons of pruning and growth, reflecting the tender care of the Divine Gardener who knoweth precisely what to cut away and what to nourish. The yielding heart, poised attentively to the Spirit's voice, reaps in due season the fruits that are not merely ornamental but vital, evidence of a soul alive to God's presence and purpose.

Moreover, the fruitfulness of spirit-led living extends beyond personal character into the realm of good works, those visible acts of love and service which flow naturally from a heart enlivened by grace. "For we are his workmanship, created in Christ Jesus unto good works, which God hath before ordained that we should walk in them." (Ephesians 2:10) These works are not conceived of as burdensome duties or means to earn favor, but are the natural outpouring of a soul transformed. When the Spirit leads, actions reflect God's goodness and mercy, touching the lives of others with healing, encouragement, and tangible expressions of divine love. The believer becomes in effect a vessel, emptied of self-will and filled afresh by the Spirit, carrying forth the light of Christ into a world hungering for truth and kindness. Spirit-led works have eternal significance, for they are sealed by the hand of God and echo in the chambers of heaven.

Yet, fruitfulness is not produced by human might or wisdom, but by dependence upon the Spirit's empowering presence. Like the branches abiding in the true vine, Christ Jesus, so the believer must learn the art of abiding in the Spirit's fellowship, drawing strength and nourishment from Him continually. "Without me ye can do nothing." (John 15:5) This dependency is a sacred acknowledgment that apart from God, all human striving is vain, but through Him, all things are made possible. Therein lies the quiet power of spirit-led living, not in noisy displays or the clamor of many works, but in the still, small voice of the Spirit guiding each step, breathing holy courage into worn hearts, and endowing the believer with gifts fashioned for the upbuilding of the church and the spread of the gospel.

Speaking of gifts, the Spirit's role in fruitfulness is also made manifest in the varied spiritual endowments bestowed upon believers for the common good. These are not arbitrary or prideful distinctions, but sacred trusts given with divine purpose. As Paul declareth to the Corinthians, "There are diversities of gifts, but the same Spirit. There are differences of administrations, but the same Lord. And there are diversities of operations, but it is the same God which worketh all in all." (1 Corinthians 12:4-6) To walk in spirit-led living is to recognize one's own gifts, however modest or grand, and to employ them in harmony with the body of Christ. When the gifts are exercised in humility and love, they bear fruit that edifies the church, brings healing to the broken, and stands as witness to the world of God's life-giving power. This collaboration of spiritual gifts under the Spirit's sovereign guidance ensures that fruitfulness is not a solitary endeavor, but a communal flourishing that glorifies God beyond measure.

The daily practice of tuning one's heart to the Spirit's whisper requires intentionality and discipline. It demands moments of stillness amid the tempest of life's cares, a willingness to listen and obey, even when the path seems steep and uncertain. The Spirit often leadeth not only in grand gestures but in subtle promptings to kindness, patience, or forgiveness. Such small steps build up the fruit of the Spirit within, shaping a character increasingly aligned with God's holiness. The journey is marked by continual self-examination, prayerful seeking, and joyful surrender, a spiritual interplay between divine initiative and human response. Those who persevere find their lives increasingly marked by peace that passeth understanding, a joy untethered from circumstance, and a love that mirrors heaven itself.

In meditating on the sacred scriptures, we behold many exemplars of spirit-led fruitfulness, from the servant heart of David to the apostolic fervor of Paul. Each story reveals not human perfection but a surrendered spirit, one that drank deeply of God's grace and bore forth harvests of righteousness. The Psalmist often pleas, "Create in me a clean heart, O God; and renew a right spirit within me." (Psalm 51:10) Herein lies the very essence of fruitfulness, to be continually renewed, fashioned anew day by day by the Spirit's sanctifying fire. It is a sacred alchemy whereby human frailty is transformed into vessels of honor, equipped for every good work. As we meditate upon these truths, we are invited to reflect not only on the fruit evident in our lives but also on the root from which it must spring, the intimate fellowship with the Spirit that animates every motion of grace.

Therefore, let us seek to cultivate a soul garden that is sensitive to the Spirit's leading, aware that Christ's promise endures: "If ye abide in me, and my words abide in you, ye shall ask what ye will, and it shall be done unto you." (John 15:7) To abide is to dwell in constant communion, allowing God's Word to take root and blossom from within. As the Spirit meditates Christ in our hearts, so our lives become living epistles known and read of all men, shining forth the glory of a God who maketh us fruitful for His kingdom. This fruitfulness is the joy of the believer, a divine melody composed in the hidden chambers of the soul and shared freely with the world, pointing all to the Author of life and love.

In conclusion, the spirit-led life is marked not by the seeking of reward or human acclaim but by the steady growth of godly character and the unfolding of good works done in the Spirit's power. It is a life where love reigns supreme, kindness flows freely, and faith is steadfast amid every storm. Let this be our prayer: that the Holy Spirit would so fill and guide us, that the fruit of righteousness might abound, and our lives be a fragrant offering, pleasing in the sight of God. May we continually surrender afresh, girded in humility and clothed in the fruits of the Spirit, walking boldly in the path He hath ordained, until the fullness of His glory be revealed in us. Amen.

Eternal Perspective

Hope of Resurrection

Amidst the ebb and flow of mortal existence, when shadows lengthen, and the heavy weight of temporal sorrows presses upon the heart, the soul finds its surest solace in the blessed hope of resurrection. This hope is not a mere wishful fancy or a pale consolation; it is the radiant beacon that pierces the darkest of nights and whispers with certainty that death shall not have the final dominion. Rooted deeply in the sacred words of the King James Bible, the promise of resurrection stands as the fulcrum upon which eternal life pivots, inviting believers to anchor their faith firmly beyond this fleeting world and to fix their gaze upon the glory that awaits beyond the veil. The Apostle Paul, writing with the fervor of a heart anchored in truth, declares, "If in this life only we have hope in Christ, we are of all men most miserable. But now is Christ risen from the dead, and become the firstfruits of them that slept" (1 Corinthians 15:19-20). This declaration is not merely a theological assertion; it is a clarion call to live each day clothed in the assurance that through Christ's victory over death, our own resurrection is secured. The "firstfruits" metaphor breathes vivid life into the promise, for just as the first harvest is a guarantee of the fullness to come, so Christ's rising is a pledge of the resurrection awaiting each believer.

To dwell upon the hope of resurrection is to orient one's entire perspective away from the temporal's transient and toward the eternal's unshakable reality. Life's myriad trials, the gnawing questions of suffering, loss, and the inevitable closure of death, find reconciliation only when viewed through the lens of this divine truth. The Psalmist, in his soulful lament and trust, captures the essence of this hope when he declares, "Thou wilt not leave my soul in hell;

neither wilt thou suffer thine Holy One to see corruption" (Psalm 16:10). This assurance does not promise ease in the present, nor deliverance from the valley of tears, but it assures that beyond this veil of flesh and frailty lies a realm where corruption and decay hold no dominion. To know this is to be reminded that the faithful journey is not an endless descent into obscurity but a pilgrimage toward a new dawning, a resurrection morning that conquers death and restores all that was lost.

Indeed, the Christian hope of resurrection speaks of a profound and glorious transformation, for it is not the mere restoration of flesh, but its glorious renewal. The apostle's words echo through the corridors of time: "It is sown a natural body; it is raised a spiritual body" (1 Corinthians 15:44). This passage lifts the veil on the mystery of resurrection, revealing it as both continuity and glorious change. The body that returns from the tomb shall be fashioned anew, imperishable, radiant, and free from the bondage of decay. This transformation is the crowning hope that preserves the integrity of our being while elevating it to a celestial splendor, fulfilling God's original design for humanity. It is here, in this hope, that believers find the courage to lay down their earthly expectations, knowing that the final word is not the silence of the grave but the triumphant song of eternal life.

Such hope is not an abstract doctrine confined to theological debate but a living, breathing reality that shapes daily existence with an unyielding strength. When the heart is anchored in the hope of resurrection, grief finds its voice not only in lamentation but also in confident expectation. The tear-streaked face looks beyond the tomb, beholding the promise of reunion where sorrow shall be no more, where the family of God shall be gathered in a holy embrace unbroken by the divisions of mortal life. This hope softens the sting of death and transforms the pain of loss into a sacred anticipation that wounds, though grievous, are but temporary shadows retreating before the everlasting light. The writer of Hebrews exhorts the faithful to consider "that ye sorrow not, even as others which have no hope" (1 Thessalonians 4:13), thereby reminding us that the hope of resurrection is the balm which soothes the soul and the fortress against despair.

Furthermore, the resurrection hope extends beyond personal assurance to a cosmic restoration. The breath that once quickened dust is destined, through the grace of God, to awaken in a world redeemed and renewed. The vision of New Heaven and New Earth described in the book of Revelation offers a breathtaking panorama of eternity where righteousness dwells and God's face shines upon His people with unending favor. This renewed creation signals the consummation of God's redemptive work, in which death itself is swallowed up in victory (1 Corinthians 15:54). Here, resurrection hope entwines with the promise of divine justice and peace, where tears are wiped away, and the former things pass away. To hold fast to this hope is to be drawn into the divine narrative of restoration, recognizing that our lives are threads within the grand tapestry of God's eternal kingdom. This eternal perspective imbues even the humblest acts of faith with eternal significance and transforms the believer into a pilgrim journeying steadfastly toward the divine horizon.

Yet, this blessed hope also calls forth a response, a life shaped by the anticipation of resurrection glory. The apostle Peter exhorts the believers to "gird up the loins of your mind" and to live soberly, righteously, and godly in this present world, knowing that the heavens and earth shall pass away but God's promises stand forever (2 Peter 3:11-13). The hope of resurrection engenders holy living, not out of fear or mere duty, but from the joyous expectation of standing faultless and radiant before the Lord. It breathes a divine urgency into the soul, compelling a life of faithfulness, generosity, and love that mirrors the eternal kingdom. This hope reshapes motives and actions, causing the believer to treasure the unseen rather than the seen, to labor not in vain, and to invest eternally in that which endures beyond the fleeting shadows of time.

The prayerful heart, meditating upon this hope, finds solace in lifting its voice heavenward, seeking strength for the journey and grace to persevere amid trials. To pray in the hope of resurrection is to commune with God in a language of expectation and trust, rejoicing in the surety of the promise even when the present is fraught with uncertainty. These prayers are threaded with both trembling humility and buoyant faith, acknowledging human weakness while extolling the power of Christ's resurrection. They beseech God to root the soul firmly in His word, to kindle the flame of hope, and to grant the patience to wait for the fullness of revelation. Such prayers echo the longing of the Psalmist who cried, "My soul cleaveth unto the dust: quicken thou me according to thy word" (Psalm 119:25), a yearning for renewal that only the resurrection can fulfill.

Therefore, to be anchored in the hope of resurrection is to stand upon a radiant rock that no tempest can move, to possess a treasure that fades not with time nor dims with tribulation. It is to enter each day with the assurance that our lives are not confined to momentary breath, but encompass eternity's vast expanse. In a world beset with uncertainty and shadows, this hope becomes a piercing light that guides, a gentle hand that sustains, and a song that emboldens the spirit to press onward. The path may be strewn with trials and the night may seem long and weary, yet the dawn of resurrection beckons with a glory beyond all telling. As the Apostle Paul beautifully intones, "For if we be dead with him, we shall also live with him: Knowing that Christ being raised from the dead dieth no more; death hath no more dominion over him" (Romans 6:8-9). This living hope, born of Christ's triumph, anchors the soul immovable, offering peace that surpasses understanding and joy unspeakable in the anticipation of life eternal.

May this blessed hope, then, become the heart's anchor, holding fast in every storm, illuminating every dark valley, and pouring forth a river of peace that refreshes weary spirits. Let every breath, every prayer, every act of faith be suffused with the radiant anticipation of resurrection, that we might live not as those without hope but as children of the eternal kingdom, heirs of that incorruptible inheritance reserved in heaven for us. Thus, may the last words of this spiritual journey be a hymn of courage, a declaration of faith, and a sacred promise fulfilled, that death is but a door, and beyond it lies the everlasting life secured by Him who rose again, the First and the Last, the Resurrection and the Life. Amen.

The New Heaven and Earth

As we stand upon the threshold of our earthly pilgrimage, our hearts naturally turn toward the promise of a New Heaven and a New Earth, visions that blaze with holy fire, casting luminous hope beyond the dim veil of time. The sacred scripture unfolds before our inward eye a panorama not merely of finality, but of glorious transformation; it reveals a reality where sorrow dissolves and the very fabric of creation is renewed by the Almighty's hand. In the inspired utterance of the Apostle John, the veil is lifted to disclose holy mysteries: "And I saw a new heaven and a new earth: for the first heaven and the first earth were passed away; and there was no more sea" (Revelation 21:1). With these words, the Spirit beckons our souls to fix their steadfast gaze upon Eternity's dawn, where all that is fractured is made whole, and all that is weary finds celestial rest.

In this eternal realm, the trials and tribulations that so often eclipse our present joy are rendered but shadows fleeing before the dawning light of God's unending kingdom. The text proclaims with sublime certainty that the former things have ceased, that death, mourning, crying, and pain will be no more, for the Lord God shall wipe away all tears from the eyes of His people. This sacred vision is not a mere abstraction or fanciful hope, it is the very heartbeat of Christian faith, the wellspring that nurtures perseverance amid the temporal storms of life. To dwell on the promise of the New Heaven and New Earth is to anchor our spirits in a reality transcending the fleeting satisfactions and sufferings of mortal existence. It offers a sanctuary of hope, a firm foundation upon which to stand when the ground beneath us seems perilous and insecure.

The resurrection, the cornerstone event through which this eternal hope is anchored, affirms the doctrine that life triumphs over death, that the perishable shall put on the imperishable. Christ's own resurrection is the pledge and prototype of our destiny, the firstfruits of them that sleep, assuring us that corruption shall not claim us, nor the grave's cold embrace subdue us in the end. This glorious truth, revealed with majestic clarity, invites the believer into a transformative vision where the promise of restored bodies and revived spirits stirs within, emboldening faith and rekindling an ardent longing for the consummation of redemption. It encourages us to envision a state where our union with God is total, unmarred by sin or separation, a communion enriched by eternal light and unceasing praise.

More than a distant hope, the foretold New Heaven and New Earth propose a radical reordering of reality itself. The vision encompasses not only the individual's renewal but the healing of all creation, a restoration where justice flows like a mighty river and mercy like an unending fountain. The prophetic whispers that once stirred the hearts of venerable saints now resound with greater clarity: the wolf shall dwell with the lamb, and the lion shall eat straw like the ox. The ancient enmity between God's creatures and creation is dissolved in the waters of divine grace. The heavens clap their hands, and the earth rejoices as the glory of the Lord reigns supreme. It calls us to live in consonance with this cosmic hope, imbued with justice, kindness, and humility, as preparatory steps toward our eternal abode.

To meditate on this heavenly vision is to invite a holy reconfiguration of present priorities, for when the eternal perspective takes root within the soul, the mundane anxieties that so often beset us lose their tyrannical bite. The Apostle Paul, from his place of imprisonment, exhorts believers to "set their affection on things above, not on things on the earth" (Colossians 3:2). This command is no mere spiritual platitude, but a profound call to orient every moment, every choice, toward the radiant horizon of eternal life. The texture of daily living, once dominated by transient gains and losses, is thereby sanctified and infused with lasting meaning, as each act of faith becomes a brick in the celestial city whose builder and maker is God. Our footsteps on earth are thereby directed by the footprints of the incarnate Savior, pointing us steadfastly to the land where sorrow is vanquished and joy is unending.

The weight of this hope carries deep consolation when the shadows of grief or uncertainty fall heavy. The vision of the New Heaven and New Earth pierces through despair like the morning star's light, offering assurance that our loved ones who have fallen asleep in Christ shall be raised incorruptible and reunited in an eternal embrace where parting is no more. It assures us that God's redemptive work remains unwavering, eternal, and all-embracing, knitting together the very fabric of existence in perfect harmony. This eternal portrait serves as balm to the afflicted spirit, a celestial song that plays softly even in the most profound darkness, calling forth faith that does not waver and hope that does not disappoint.

Yet this vision is both a gift and a summons, a summons to live each day with hearts attuned to the glad news of restoration. To anticipate the New Heaven and New Earth is to cultivate a life of holiness, of sincere repentance, and of ardent love for God and neighbor, that we might be found worthy inhabitants of that celestial domain. The Scripture reveals that in this eternal city, there shall be no temple, for the Lord God Almighty and the Lamb are the temple thereof

(Revelation 21:22). The presence of God, immediate and unmediated, suffuses that holy place with light and life, dispelling every shadow of doubt, fear, and death. Knowing this summons us to a spiritual readiness, a life abounding in the fruit of the Spirit, so that when the heavenly trumpet sounds, we are as watchful servants awaiting the return of their Master.

Thus, the vision of the New Heaven and New Earth does not depreciate the value of our earthly sojourn; rather, it dignifies it with eternal significance. It lifts the veil on the grand design that threads each moment, each trial, and each blessing into the tapestry of redemption. The veil between temporal and eternal becomes permeable, inviting the soul to taste now a foretaste of heaven's glory here below. This spiritual perspective invites a serene courage in the face of adversity, for the believer walks with an eye fixed upon the "city which hath foundations, whose builder and maker is God" (Hebrews 11:10). It is a city whose streets gleam with translucent gold, whose gates open to receive the redeemed, and whose peace surpasses all understanding.

In conclusion, the vision of the New Heaven and New Earth beckons us to dwell in the eternal promise that lies beyond the realm of our present afflictions and limitations. It calls us to anchor our faith in the immutable word of God, to stand firm upon His sure promises, and to live lives marked by the beauty and love that reflect His kingdom. May this sacred hope be the lamp to our feet and the light to our path, guiding us through the shadows of this world into the radiant dawn of divine glory, where we shall forever rejoice in the unending presence of our Lord and Savior. Amen.

Living with Eternal Purpose

In the stillness of the morning, when the world lies hushed beneath the gentle breath of dawn, there arises within the faithful heart a stirring, a solemn resolve to live not by fleeting shadows, but by the radiant light of eternity. To live with eternal purpose is to fix one's gaze beyond the transient measures of time, beyond the ceaseless cares and clamors that so often ensnare the soul, and to anchor every thought, word, and deed in the unchanging promise of the life to come. The sacred word of God beckons us to a higher calling, to orient our daily steps not toward vanities that perish, but toward the transcendent realm where glorified spirits rejoice in the presence of the Almighty. It is here, in the grand perspective of eternity, that the weary pilgrim finds unfathomable hope and unshakable resolve, a wellspring of peace that defies the tempests of earthly existence.

The Apostle Paul, in his epistles, exhorts the believer to fashion their life "not after the flesh, but after the Spirit," mindful always that our citizenship is in heaven (Philippians 3:20). This divine citizenship demands a holy allegiance, a life lived in conscious homage to the eternal King. It is a call to live as sojourners, rooted deeply yet briefly in the soil of this temporal world, eyes lifted heavenward where the inheritance of glory awaits the faithful. Each act of love, each sacrifice of self, each moment surrendered in prayer and worship becomes a precious offering laid upon the altar of eternity. In this sacred economy, seemingly small deeds swell with infinite worth, and daily labors, though oft unheralded, cultivate treasures that neither moth nor rust can corrupt, nor thieves steal away (Matthew 6:20).

Contemplating the resurrection, the foundational hope of our faith, imbues this earthly sojourn with profound meaning. The resurrection is not merely a distant event clothed in mystery but a living reality that transforms how we approach the mundane and the miraculous alike. The King James Scriptures declare with majestic clarity, "For if we be dead with Christ, we believe that we shall also live with him" (Romans 6:8). This victorious truth infuses the present moment with eternal significance, assuring the believer that death is neither defeat nor finality but a passage into everlasting life. Such confidence births courage; it steadies the heart when sorrow threatens to overwhelm and lights the dark valleys where doubt might seek to dwell. To live with eternal purpose, therefore, is to walk with hope-born eyes, seeing through the veil of earthly pain toward the dawning day of resurrection and everlasting joy.

Moreover, the grand narrative of Scripture reveals that the eternal God, who sits upon the throne of heaven, calls His people into a divine partnership, inviting them to partake in His redemptive work here on earth as a foretaste of the celestial kingdom. This calls for an intentional alignment of priorities: not the accumulation of wealth, the pursuit of honor, or the fleeting thrills of sin, but the diligent cultivation of Christlike character, the sowing of grace, and the manifestation of divine love. Such a life demands sacrifice and often worldly incomprehension, yet it offers incomparable riches imperishable. Through the lens of eternity, the trials and sufferings of this life assume a new posture, not as meaningless afflictions but as refining fires, shaping the soul into a vessel fit for the splendor of glory. The patient endurance of hardship becomes a testimony to unwavering faith, a beacon to the lost and a fragrant offering to the Lord.

In every season, from the exuberance of youth to the twilight of years, this eternal perspective calls forth a sacred urgency paired with serene assurance. It compels the believer to weigh decisions by the scales of heaven, to measure success and failure through the light of divine approval rather than human applause. One's vocation, relationships, ambitions, no facet of life escapes the gentle scrutiny of this spiritual paradigm. Therein lies a freedom profound and yet humbling: to embrace life fully, yet lightly; to engage with the world wholeheartedly, yet undetached; to invest in others generously, yet with the wisdom of knowing all earthly gains are but fleeting shadows. This tension, held in the embrace of faith, cultivates a life of balanced devotion, where the joys of creation are treasured not as ultimate ends but as graces that anticipate the eternal consummation of God's kingdom.

And what sustains this perspective but the continual and fervent communion with God, a seeking after His face that renews the soul day by day? Prayer, meditation upon Scripture, and worship are not mere duties but vital lifelines connecting the believer to the unfathomable heart of the Creator. As the Psalmist proclaims, "In thy presence is fulness of joy; at thy right hand there are pleasures for evermore" (Psalm 16:11). To dwell habitually in the presence of God is to awaken from the slumber of worldly distraction into a vibrant reality where the eternal becomes tangible and the promises of grace are felt deeply within the spirit. Such sacred encounter rekindles the flame of purpose, sharpens the vision, and strengthens the resolve to run the race not as those who are aimless, but as those who have eternal prize set before them.

Finally, to embrace an eternal purpose is to live as a herald of hope amid a world marred by despair and uncertainty. The believer becomes a lighthouse amid stormy seas, shining forth the glorious gospel that proclaims victory over sin, death, and the grave. This sacred trust compels a life of witness and compassion, an outpouring of the divine love that has so lavishly been received. Every act of forgiveness, every gesture of mercy, every proclamation of the truth is imbued with eternal consequence, instrumental in drawing souls into the fold of everlasting light. Thus, living with eternal purpose is not a solitary journey but a communal pilgrimage, a shared voyage toward the heavenly city where God Himself shall wipe away all tears, and where the redeemed shall sit eternally at His throne, basking in the unending radiance of His glory.

May this sacred truth anchor your soul: that to live with eternal purpose is to live fully alive, tethered to the hope that transcends time, and sustained by the love that never fails. May each day find you renewed in this divine calling, ever mindful that your life's moments are threads in the glorious tapestry of eternity, woven by the hand of God, fashioned for His praise and for the everlasting joy that awaits those who abide in Him. In this sacred orientation, may your faith deepen, your hope flourish, and your spirit find rest secure, anchored in the Word, steadfast in the promise of eternal life.

The Crown of Life

The radiant hope of the believer finds its consummation in the promise of the crown of life, a divine reward bestowed upon those who have faithfully persevered amid the trials and temptations of this fleeting world. This celestial diadem, incorruptible and sovereign above all earthly honors, is proclaimed in the sacred texts as the blessed recompense for steadfast souls who have loved God, embraced His commandments, and refused to shrink when faced with suffering for righteousness' sake. "Blessed is the man that endureth temptation: for when he is tried, he shall receive the crown of life, which the Lord hath promised to them that love him" (James 1:12). What a profound encouragement to the weary spirit, a clarion call to fix the eyes upon eternal realities rather than the transient shadows of present affliction. The crown of life is more than mere imagery; it is the glorious assurance that the path of faith diligently trod shall bring lasting honor and joy that neither moth nor rust can corrupt, nor thieves can steal.

In the quiet moments of reflection, when the world's clamor fades, and the soul is left to contemplate the unfathomable vastness of God's kingdom, one is drawn irresistibly toward the vision of heaven. This sacred realm, wrought by divine hands and shimmering with eternal light, stands as the final rest and reward for the faithful pilgrim. It is a place where sorrow is no more, and where every tear is wiped away by the tender hand of the Almighty. The richness of this promise breathes life into the deepest chambers of the heart, rekindling hope even when earthly circumstances seem dire. The King James Bible, with its venerable cadence, paints this portrait of glory with phrases that echo through the corridors of time: "Eye hath not seen, nor ear heard, neither have entered into the heart of man, the things which God hath prepared for them that love him" (1 Corinthians 2:9). This mystery surpasses human understanding and invites us into a boundless expectation that elevates the soul beyond despair. To be anchored in the Word in these final reflections is to grasp firmly this eternal sanctuary as the quintessence of spiritual renewal.

Resurrection forms the heartbeat of this hope, a testimony to the triumph of life over death, assuring us that death's sting is but a gateway to a new and incorruptible existence. The solemn assurance that "the dead shall be raised incorruptible, and we shall be changed" (1 Corinthians 15:52) lifts the believer's gaze beyond the grave. It proclaims that the story of each faithful servant does not end in darkness but dawns in the brightness of Christ's victory over the grave. The resurrection is not solely an event in the future and distant, but a present reality that sustains the believer's faith through every season of trial and loss. To know that our mortal frame shall be transformed into a glorious body, fashioned after the pattern of the risen Christ, is to embrace a promise that fills the soul with unshakable peace. This hope, rooted deeply in the Word, is a spiritual anchor that steadies the heart amid the anguishes and uncertainties of earthly sojourn.

The crown of life, therefore, embodies the culmination of a journey marked not by ease but by faithful endurance, a testimony to the power of divine grace sustaining those who walk humbly before God. It calls forth a life wholly consecrated to obedience and love, challenging the believer to persevere in faith even when the path is rugged and companionship scarce. The struggle is real; the adversary relentless; the temptations numerous. Yet the promise of this eternal reward enkindles a resolve that transcends human frailty. It bids us to remember the exhortation found in the Scripture: "Be thou faithful unto death, and I will give thee a crown of life" (Revelation 2:10). This sacred vow ignites hope and fortitude, assuring every wearied pilgrim that the investments of love, sacrifice, and patience shall not be in vain but shall be crowned with glory from on high.

To meditate upon the crown of life is to enter into an intimate dialogue with the eternal, where time's chains fall away, and the soul is uplifted in holy expectancy. It is to stand at the threshold of glory, glimpsing the splendor of rewards beyond earthly comprehension. Yet, these promises do not detach the believer from the present but rather infuse the present with meaning and purpose. Each act of kindness, each moment of prayer, each decision to trust in God's promise becomes a sacred thread woven into the fabric of eternity. This realization transforms the mundane into the magnificent, the ordinary into the sacred. Living with the crown of life in sight nurtures a daily resilience, an unyielding spirit anchored in the sure and certain hope of eternal life.

The prayerful heart, therefore, is drawn into this celestial anticipation, lifting supplications that mirror the language of Scripture, words that intertwine faith's confident hope with humble dependence on God's mercy. "O Lord, Almighty and Everlasting, who hast promised life everlasting unto them that love Thee, grant that we may cleave unto Thee with a steadfast heart, enduring all trials and temptations that assail us. Strengthen our souls to run the race that is set before us, looking not unto the things that are seen but unto the things which are unseen and eternal. Let the crown of life be our portion, that we may rejoice before Thee in the day of Thy appearing, and with all the saints sing praises unto Thy name forevermore." Such prayers echo the yearning of the spirit to dwell in the eternal presence of God, awaiting that great and glorious day when the veil shall be lifted, and we shall behold Him face to face.

As the soul contemplates the crown of life, it is also moved to gratitude and praise for the manifold mercies that sustain the journey.

The promise of eternal reward is intimately tied to the boundless grace of God, who calls sinners into fellowship and strengthens the weak. This grace empowers believers to overcome the world, to lay down their lives in service, and to keep the faith amid adversity. Recognizing this, the reflection becomes a hymn of thanksgiving for divine patience and unmerited favor. The crown of life is thus not an achievement born of human merit but a gift bestowed by a loving Creator whose promises never fail. To hold fast to this truth is to find rest in the assurance that by God's grace, we are preserved to receive this glorious reward.

Moreover, the anticipation of the crown of life gently reshapes the believer's perspective on suffering, transforming trials from burdens into opportunities for spiritual growth. The Word testifies that affliction refines the soul as gold is refined by fire (Job 23:10), and with each test endured, faith is proven genuine and precious. Thus, the crown is not merely a final prize but a symbol of the transformative journey itself, a journey where love, patience, and steadfastness are forged through adversity, making the believer more like Christ. This sacred perspective embraces suffering with hope, recognizing it as a divine instrument that prepares the soul for its ultimate reward.

In the culmination of this devotional journey, the crown of life stands as a powerful spiritual anchor, a serene yet potent reminder that our faith is not in vain and that God's promises endure through all generations. It summons the believer to live with an eternal horizon, to navigate life's tempests with courage and joy, knowing that a glorious inheritance awaits. Herein lies the peaceful assurance that through faith, prayer, and divine grace, the soul is firmly anchored in the Word, steadfast against every storm of life, and lifted toward the eternal light of God's kingdom. This is the divine promise that completes the spiritual voyage, a crown of life, pure, unfading, and glorious, reserved for those who love Him and hold fast unto the end.

Peace in Everlasting Presence

As we draw near to the culmination of our sacred journey through these pages, we stand at the precipice of an eternal promise, a boundless wellspring of peace that transcends the temporal confines of mortal strife and the fleeting shadows of earthly sorrow. This peace, dear reader, is not a fragile truce nor a passing respite but an ever-constant covenant held firm in the everlasting presence of our Almighty God. In the quiet embrace of this divine promise, the soul finds ultimate rest, a fulfillment so profound that it eclipses all previous longings and trials. The King James Bible, with its majestic cadence and timeless truth, beckons us to cast our gaze beyond the veil of this present life, inviting us to fix our hearts upon the glorious hope of heaven, the dawn of resurrection, and the unshakable joy that awaits the faithful beyond all measure of time.

Consider, beloved, the beautiful certainty declared in the sacred text: "In thy presence is fulness of joy; at thy right hand there are pleasures for evermore" (Psalm 16:11). These words, penned ages ago yet vibrant with enduring power, paint a portrait of a reality where pain, weariness, and the burdens of earth dissolve into a radiant light of divine fellowship. To be in God's presence is to know peace not as man giveth, which is often transient and frail, but a peace that surpasseth all understanding, a peace that guards the heart and mind in Christ Jesus. Here lies the ultimate sanctuary, the final refuge, where the restless spirit is finally stilled. The restless heart, wearied by life's storms, finds its anchor in the eternal now, resting assured in the unending arms of a God who is the Alpha and Omega, the beginning and the end.

It is within the profound mystery of resurrection that this peace takes on its fullest dimension. The words of our Savior echo with incomparable assurance: "I am the resurrection, and the life: he that believeth in me, though he were dead, yet shall he live" (John 11:25).

What staggering hope is wrapped in this promise! Death, that formidable enemy who stalks the living, is rendered powerless in the face of resurrection life. This is not merely a return to existence, but a transformation that transcends the limits of time and frailty. The body, once subject to decay, shall be clothed with incorruption, and the soul, once wearied and burdened, shall awake in a newness of life, bright with the glory of God's eternal kingdom. Such hope, tenderly woven through the fabric of Scripture, encourages the believer to rise above despair and despairing winds, to look faithfully beyond the horizon, and to place unwavering trust in the promise of eternal communion with the Divine.

As we meditate upon these sacred assurances, we come to see that the peace spoken of is inseparably tied to holiness and complete surrender. The soul finds its ultimate fulfillment not in transient pleasures or fleeting triumphs but in a profound connection to the living God, whose presence saturates every moment with unapproachable light. The ancient psalmist's cry, "Create in me a clean heart, O God; and renew a right spirit within me" (Psalm 51:10), remains the melody of the faithful who long to be wholly united with God's will. This intimate renewal is the heartbeat of peace itself, a peace that is not simply an absence of conflict but a rich, abundant life flowing from the depths of divine grace and love. It invites the believer into a divine dance, where surrender births strength, and trust cultivates serenity, building a soul foundation that no tempest can overturn.

The everlasting presence of God is, therefore, the wellspring from which all true peace flows. It is the eternal sanctuary where the weary find rest, the broken find healing, and the lost find their way home. In this sacred place, we are invited to enter stillness beyond the frenzy of worldly clamor, to hear the "still small voice" that whispers hope and renewal to the heart. This presence does not abandon, nor does it wane with the changing tides of circumstance; it remains steadfast, encompassing us with unending compassion and mercy. Such peace renders fear silent and anxiety powerless, reminding us that our lives are not adrift but deeply anchored in the unchanging promises of a God who neither sleeps nor slumbers over His beloved.

Moreover, this eternal peace calls us to a holy endurance, a perseverance that refines faith like gold tried in the fire. The trials of this mortal life, while harsh and often bewildering, are but momentary afflictions preparing us for a weight of glory beyond any earthly comparison (2 Corinthians 4:17). This perspective transforms suffering from a place of despair into a pathway of sanctification, encouraging a steadfast hope that is unshaken by the vicissitudes of worldly existence. The apostle Paul, in his magnificent confidence, exhorts us to "stand fast, and hold the traditions which ye have been taught" (2 Thessalonians 2:15), reminding us that the anchor of our souls is firmly fixed in the unyielding foundation of God's eternal love and promises.

In the considerate silence of reflection, we might ask ourselves: how does this peace manifest in our daily walk? How does the certainty of everlasting presence shape the choices of each moment and the trembling steps along the narrow path? The answer unfolds through a spiritual disposition marked by trust, surrender, and grateful acceptance. We learn to lay aside anxieties as one casts off garments from a weary frame and to embrace life's challenges with the quiet confidence that our times are in God's hand. The inner dialogue of the believer is then transformed from fretful questionings to joyful declarations, from despair to hope, and from frantic striving to rested obedience. Through this ongoing posture of faith, the peace of God becomes a living reality, permeating the soul's every fiber and coloring even the darkest days with the golden hues of divine assurance.

This divine peace also transcends individual restoration, extending itself into the communal life of believers. In the fellowship of saints, the promise of eternal unity in God's presence serves as a powerful bond, knitting hearts together in love and mutual encouragement. The King James Bible, with its majestic phrasing, offers this reminder: "Behold, how good and how pleasant it is for brethren to dwell together in unity!" (Psalm 133:1). Such unity is but a foretaste of the heavenly communion that awaits, where tears are wiped away, and joy is unending. As we participate in this earthly fellowship, strengthened by the Word and prayer, we draw nearer to the fulfillment of the eternal community God has prepared, a community anchored in peace, hope, and love, unshaken by the storms of time.

Finally, let us rest in the assurance that this everlasting peace is gifted freely by the grace of God through Christ Jesus, the Prince of Peace. It is the fruit of a reconciled relationship, wrought at the cross and sealed by the resurrection. In Jesus Christ alone, the veil is parted, the barriers of sin and death are broken, and the glorious pathway into God's eternal presence is opened wide. As the beloved hymn declares, "O for a thousand tongues to sing my great Redeemer's praise!", so may our hearts swell with gratitude for this immeasurable gift. The restful assurance of God's eternal presence is not a distant dream but a present reality, to be embraced daily with faith and hope, shaping every breath until, at last, we behold Him face to face.

May this reflection inspire within you a serene heart, dear reader, one that rests fully anchored upon the unshakable rock of God's Word and promises. May you carry this peace as a lamp unto your path, a shield amidst trials, and the sweetest song in moments of solitude. So let us journey forward, our eyes fixed on the eternal horizon, our souls buoyed by the everlasting presence that awakens joy, dispels fear, and fulfills every longing of the heart with the rich and unending peace of God. Amen.